Memoir
Of A
Moron

Memoir
Of A
Moron

by

Coleman Porter Hood

Bilbo Books Publishing
www.BilboBooks.com
bilbobookspublishing@gmail.com
(706)-549-1597

ISBN 979-8-9867043-5-7

Printed in the United States of America

All rights reserved. Published in the United States of America by Bilbo Books Publishing.
Athens, Georgia

....

The man who doesn't read good books has no advantage over the man who cannot read good books.

Mark Twain

....

"Most Southerners are good storytellers. Coleman is a great Southerner and a captivating storyteller."

– Ronda Rich
  Best-selling Southern Author of *St. Simons Island: A Stella Bankwell Mystery*

"Coleman Hood is a classic storyteller whose sage view of the world and its inhabitants is stimulated by a wealth of life experiences, which he has embellished with keen observations. Wry and irreverent, he will entertain you with his musings about the colorful characters and scenes he has known. Coleman Hood is a damn fine Double Dawg."

– Loran Smith
  Author of *Return to Glory: A History of the Georgia Bulldogs*

"When I first read one of Coleman's yearly newsletters, I said, 'Coleman Hood, you are either insane or a genius.' His wit is something so spontaneous that you shake your head and laugh, and then wonder how in the world did he ever think of that!!!! He's unique, funny, and someone you would want to go to dinner with. He's interesting and amusing and one heck of a writer."

– Barbara Dooley

"I met Coleman Hood when we sat next to one another in an Organic Chemistry class. We have been friends ever since – over forty-five years. Coleman is a gifted writer. For decades I have looked forward to receiving his annual tome, *The Newsletter*. I relish carving out a special time to read it with glee. Coleman is politically incorrect, humorous, and an astute observer of people. He is a kind man, but does not suffer fools gladly – his wit can be biting, but he calls it like he sees it.

"I am beyond delighted that he has pulled together a collection of his writings. We are in for a real treat. Be ready to laugh out loud and often, but also to shed a tear or two as you read his poignant musings on life."

– Garth Boyd, Ph. D.
Partner, The Context Network

"Coleman Hood is one of the brightest minds aboard this planet that wobbles on its axis. He is not a moron, although his book may cause readers to regard themselves as morons for failing to see and say the wickedly funny things he sees and says. These hilarious pieces will cause readers to bust guts in laughter."

– Ralph Wood, Ph. D.
Professor of Theology and Literature
Wake Forest University and Baylor University
Author of *the Comedy of Redemption: Christian Faith and Comic Vision in Four American Novelists*

A triumph of the human spirit. Destined to become a classic.
– Coleman Porter Hood
Best-selling author of *Memoir Of A Moron*

Preface

Thirty years ago, I began writing an annual family newsletter (*The Newsletter*). Let me assure you that this newsletter was nothing like what just went through your mind. I would write this newsletter each year around December, as a satire of everyone else's family Christmas letters, where little Susie was the head cheerleader and little Johnny was the star quarterback. My daughters' greatest accomplishment was that typically they had had no cavities any given year. *Memoir Of A Moron* is an anthology of all those issues of *The Newsletter*. While it was written very much tongue-in-cheek, it is nevertheless quite honest and compelling.

The stories span family events, of course, but also include published editorials, pets and wildlife, poems, eulogies, church service, and occasional skewers of politics and The Media. I've also sprinkled in a collection of the cosmic truths that I have shared with readers through the years – quotations and aphorisms that are life-guiding principles. I'll strike this bargain with you: give me an honest reading of two dozen pages, and I think you'll be hooked. If not, I'll ask Mike Lindell to refund your money. I sincerely hope that you will enjoy this book, especially those of you who have hounded me over the past thirty years to write it.

Dedication

This book is dedicated to my paternal Grandfather,
Cyrus Lee Hood, the wisest Moron I have ever known.

When I was growing up at his elbow, on his heels, and in his
shadow, he was always scribbling notes to himself on anything
he could find to write on – paper, gum wrappers, and matchbook
covers. He kept these notes in a collection of Maxwell House coffee
cans. When I asked him what he was saving them for, he told me
that someday he intended to write a book, and that its title would be
Memoir Of A Moron. He never got around to it. Cy, this is for you.

and to

The journey. That death is our earthly life's final destination is a
certainty. The mystery is in the journey, and what we make of it.

Happy Trails (until we meet again).

. . . .

*I think the concept of transcendence is based on
a misreading of creation. With all respect to heaven,
the scene of the miracle is here, among us, now.*
Marilynne Robinson

. . . .

....

On the outskirts of every agony
sits some observant fellow who points.

Virginia Woolf

....

1998

————————

Some of you who receive *The Newsletter* have presumptuously and politically incorrectly referred to it as a "Christmas" letter, as I am sure my many friends who are Jews and Muslims and Agnostics and Blacks (oops, sorry, wrong minority!) would be glad to point out to you (And yes, I know that *Christians* are actually the minority when compared to two of the above.). This is a "Seasonal" letter, not a Christmas letter. We wish people "Season's Greetings!" and "Joy of the Season," but we're not allowed to say what the Season is. Is it "Hunting Season"? Are we supposed to "Season" (as in lightly with salt and pepper)? Are we "In Season" (My dogs can't do that anymore, thank goodness!). And speaking of Christmas, or almost mentioning it obliquely, it's just not the same without Tennessee Ernie Ford. It's not just that he's no longer with us this Christmas. That was bound to come to pass. No, the problem is compact discs. No one but me still has vinyl, long-playing records in stereophonic sound. Now my record player has died, and just try getting one of those babies fixed if you really want to give someone a laugh. That means no Ernie Ford Christmas carols... no *Star Carol*, no *Some Children See Him*, none of the wonderful Alfred Burt carols that I grew up listening to while peeking in closets and under beds.

1

Anyway, what all of this has to do with Christmas begins with ice skating. For those of you who are still reading this, I hope you're sitting down, because this isn't going to be as obvious as it sounds. As I write this, on Christmas Eve, I remember a time – actually it was last night – when I was watching ice skating on TV. Really, I wasn't watching ice skating, but it was on one of the channels as I surfed by at Warp Speed in my daily ten minutes of quality time with myself whether I need it or not. This is normally the sort of programming I blow by faster than fruit-juicers or miracle healers (How come none of those TV healers ever heals a double amputee? Shoot, I'd settle for replacing a missing tooth if it were *real*!!). Anyway, the ice skating was featuring this Oriental gal, who was fourteen going on forty, and she was doing all these complex ice gymnastics and before I knew it I had stopped... not just channel surfing, but maybe even breathing. It wasn't until this gal, right in the middle of a double milk cow or a triple ax handle or some such skating thing, did what we in the unrefined wilderness of Georgia refer to as "busted her butt."

It hit me right about the same time she hit the ice that I was really watching a train wreck, or a stock car race, take your pick. In the thirty seconds that I caught of her routine, I realized that my stomach was in knots, my fists were clenched, my jaws were set, and *none of my three teenage daughters was even in the room!!* It was then that I realized that I dreaded this girl's eventual butt-busting almost as much as she did. If she had made it through her routine without doing so, it was more a delay of the inevitable than a vanquishing of the indomitable. That's when it dawned on me... people didn't feel this way when they watched Sonja Henie. If you go back and watch the film on Peggy Fleming's gold medal performance, it looks like a junior varsity tryout in Minnesota, or Michigan, or one of those flat, frozen states where people don't see their shadow between Labor Day and Easter, which explains so much about them, but not nearly as much as the fact that they continue to live there *in the complete absence of a gun to their heads!!* Anyway (again), what hit me was that

2

Times were simpler then. Not "time," which is always pretty simple, unless Einstein is trying to explain it in relative terms, or unless your father is whipping you with a belt 'til you bleed for not understanding the difference between "forty after" and "twenty before," but now we've got Freud in this too, and times aren't simpler at all, but they are more lucrative at $150 per hour. Anyway (finally) what was simpler then was that we watched ice skating for the beauty of the accomplishment rather than the spectacle of the failure. We knew that Sonja and Peggy could do a single-anything without any likelihood of failure, and most likely even a double-something. But then someone pushed the envelope and did a *triple*-this-or-that successfully, at least five out of ten times, and began practicing on a quadruple-anything. Pushing the envelope has its place, but sometimes simple is simply better. And I think that's the way it is with true people and true families and true Christmas. And I don't think that's something that Hollywood or Madison Avenue can compromise. Only we can do that by the way we handle families and self and Christmas.

Well now, Christmas Eve has passed to Christmas Morning. The living room floor is littered with boxes and paper from presents that were whipped through faster than my changing the channel. Carol Jeanne has fulfilled our parental duty yet another year, and our children are sated with gift receiving, at least until after lunch. Which has got me to thinking about my childhood and my Christmases, and my boxes and papers. And Lord knows I got 'em. The Hood children did quite well at Christmas time. I know, 'cause we have the 16mm home movies to prove it. But the only time I remember those bikes and balls and coon skin caps is when I watch those movies.

The thing I *really* remember about Christmas, the truly special gift the Hood children received, was family. Of course, we didn't realize it at the time, but now when we think back, it's family stuff we remember most about Christmas. I remember my Grandmother Porter's three-story house where all branches of the family came for Christmas, because *all* the branches on either side, up and down, and several layers deep, lived in Charlotte. In addition to a three-story house, my Grandmother had a basement (with a coal chute!), plus even a rental house in the backyard, plus it was downtown so there were always lots of sirens and strangers standing on the corner waiting for the bus. I remember sliding down two flights of banisters, clanging the chimes (real ones, solid brass) in her front hallway, and playing with the phone switchboard down in the foyer (When we weren't there, Granny's house doubled as a boarding house for nursing school students.).

And I remember family. There'd be Hoods and Porters and Darnells in various shades and varieties. The Hood parents were always imploring of the Hood children why couldn't they "be more like the Darnells... why don't you get along like the Darnells... why can't you share like the Darnells?!" A kid could begin to resent the Darnells if pushed too far (It wasn't until after we were grown and married that a Darnell confessed they sometimes resented the Hood children because their parents were always lamenting, "Why can't you be more like the Hood children?!"). The Darnells were the highlight of any family gathering. They were fun, good looking, and they would poot if you pulled their finger. Steve could play the trumpet and David could put five golf balls or two light bulbs in his mouth (Go ahead and try it!). I can still remember the night I was coming from the third floor and hit the landing just in time to see Steve turning the corner outside in a Santa Claus suit, only to reappear a minute later at the front door.

The Darnells ate pickled peaches and celery stuffed with pimentos, olives, and cream cheese. The Darnells also vomited a lot. I don't know why it was, but for all their vivaciousness and performing talents, the Darnells had tender stomachs. Throw 'em in a crowded house with a bunch of Hoods, and it was just a matter of time until a Darnell upchucked. I can still hear Aunt Carolyn, "Somebody bring a towel – Debbie's upchucked on the sofa!!" Or, "Somebody grab a rag, Stuart upchucked in the hallway!!" When the Darnells were in an uproar, you watched where you stepped and sat. The worst thing about a Darnell throwing up

4

was that when one of 'em went, they all went. Dominoes didn't have anything on Darnells when it came to chain reactions. I was glad to see them all get a pot in hand, but I have to admit it made me kind of queasy when I saw creamed corn being cooked in that same pot just a few hours later.

Anyway, Christmas was always a spend-the-night affair, extending over several days. Actually, the season officially began on Thanksgiving Day, when we all gathered to eat, and watch the Thanksgiving Parade which started in front of my Grandmother's house, and which always ended with the Santa Claus float. At Christmas, all the boys slept on the third floor, where fire had once broken out, and every Christmas we would venture through the attics and eaves, flushing the pigeons out as we went, looking at the charred rafters and beams. Also, on the third floor, we learned about women's underwear. As I said, the other fifty-one weeks of the year, this was a boarding house for nursing students. But on that fifty-second week, we took over, and there wasn't a dresser or closet that was safe. On Christmas Eve, we'd stay up late talking and lying, waiting to hear reindeer hooves on the roof. Eventually everyone would become exhausted and start to drift off to sleep, and then it would happen... a Darnell would vomit!!

. . . .

If you would rule the world quietly,
you must first keep it amused.

Ralph Waldo Emerson

. . . .

To The Editor
Athens Banner-Herald

In recent weeks, there have been numerous articles in your paper regarding bicycling, to wit, the need for more "bicycle friendliness" and more bicycle infrastructure. Before we work on these concepts, perhaps we need to work on the bike itself. Take the seat, for example. Generally speaking, there is only one. This cuts way down on the potential to increase rider density, and pretty much dictates that every bike rider will have their own bike, which is the situation we already find ourselves in with cars. Since I am a real estate agent, I need more than one seat. If I am showing property to a married woman, right away, I'm going to need a second seat, probably a third as well, since her husband will feel obligated to come along, even though he doesn't have any say-so in the matter of selecting a home. If there's a kid or a mother-in-law involved, well we're up to four seats at a minimum.

You start lining up four seats one after another, and before you know it, you have yourself a pretty long bicycle. It's hard to turn a corner, and parking becomes a major issue. No, it would be better if you could put the seats side-by-side, maybe two in the front, and two in the back. The problem with that design is that balancing the load on just two tires can be tricky. The obvious solution would be to increase the stability of the bicycle by doubling the number of tires. Now we're making progress, although we probably ought to call our bicycle a quadracycle at this point.

Real estate these days is a pretty fast-paced affair, and even though Clarke County is geographically the smallest of our 159 counties, it can still feel pretty spread out when you have to pedal it. What our bicycle – quadracycle – really needs is something to boost its speed in going from Winterville to Bogart. I've seen a lot of students with these little scooters putting their lives at risk in places like Broad Street and the Atlanta Highway, and I think they may be on to something (other than suicide). We need to do like they've done, and put an engine on our quadracycle.

Of course, real estate clients can be pretty demanding, almost down-right unreasonable, really. They want to be warm in the winter, cool in the summer, dry when it rains, and some of them can be pretty picky about getting their hair blown out of place. I think a heating and cooling system, along with some windshields and doors might do the trick. Once you've come this far, it wouldn't be a moment's thought to trim that bad boy out with a stereo system, maybe even some GPS guidance, and throw in some headlights in case we aren't back before dark.

I really think I'm on to something here, and not just for real estate. I bet that soccer moms could put my quadracycle to immediate use, and the whole family could pile in for church on Sunday mornings. I'm thinking I could expand and modify this concept so that companies like FedEx, Coca-Cola, and even ambulances and the like could make major leaps in efficiency and productivity by employing my four-wheeled, engine powered, fully enclosed quadracycle. Yes sir, this bicycle concept has real potential. I predict it will become the wave of the future.

May your chain never break!

. . . .

Praise without end for the go-ahead zeal
of whoever it was invented the wheel,
but never a word for the poor soul's sake
that thought ahead, and invented the brake.
Howard Nemerov

. . . .

2014

This year Carol Jeanne retired after thirty-two years at Athens Regional Medical Center (which doesn't count the time she worked in Virginia when we were first married). The hospital has been very good to her, and she has been great for it – they've gotten the better half of a mutually beneficial bargain. She has four or five different retirement plans with them, more than I can keep track of, but we've always contributed every penny allowed to every one of them. For thirty-two years she has left home in the dark and come home in the dark. For as long as I can remember, certainly ever since her last child left the house, she has come home, eaten her supper (which I prepared, along with her breakfast and lunch!), taken a shower, put on her pajamas, then sat in front of a computer until bedtime, doing hospital business.

She started out in physical therapy, doing home health care in all the outlying counties. She ended up in administration, and her last title was Administrative Director of Clinical Services. Along the way, she took the hospital "paperless," crisscrossing the country to select the software and vendor to take the hospital digital on patient records, doctors' charts, prescriptions – everything in the way of documentation that a hospital does, which is more than you could ever imagine. The last two years, under a new CEO (who is no longer there), she was primarily responsible for medical staff performance, quality of patient care, and institutional improvement. I don't know how closely you keep your finger on the pulse of medical care in America, but the last decade has not been a bed of roses – there has been some stress. When she started working at Athens Regional Medical Center, it was called Athens General Hospital, and it had three doors (front, back, and on one side). Now it covers three city blocks, and is referred to as a "campus." The hospital has two medical towers (North and South), and there are two parking decks. There is always a crane looming in the skyline over some new construction project. I think it safe to say that Carol Jeanne had a career at Athens Regional Medical Center.

I, on the other hand, have had a more checkered employment history, something less than a "career" any way you cut it. The first job that I remember getting paid for – by someone who was not a family member – was in Pageland, South Carolina, "the water-melon capital of the world." You started the day in the dark, on your hands and knees, waiting for it to get light enough to see the ground. Your job was to crawl between two rows of watermelon plants, and thin the mounds of seedlings that had sprouted from four or five down to two, on both the left and right. You did this by pinching the surplus vines between your thumb and forefinger, and pulling them out. The soil was sandy and appropriately full of prickly sand burrs, the air was almost liquid, the mosquitoes were thick but the flies were thicker, and from the time that the sun cleared the horizon, it was hotter than a weasel's ass in a pepper patch! You were paid one dollar an acre. I made eleven dollars in one day, and never went back. Little did I know that the trajectory of my employment history had reached its zenith!

Now stick with me a minute (if you happen to still be reading this), because I'm going somewhere with this. Exactly where, I don't know, but it will definitely be somewhere. When Carol Jeanne and I married, my first job was as a forester for The Chesapeake Corporation Of Virginia. That was when we lived in Bowling Green, between Richmond and Fredericksburg. It was one of the mutually happiest times of our lives. The problem with that job was Jimmy Carter. As long as he was running Georgia, he wasn't too big of a problem. But then the American public decided to send him to Washington DC, and asked him to occupy the White House until they could elect a new President. After his first two years at that address, the percentage of unemployed workers was double digits, as was inflation. Today – this very day, but not for long – gasoline is about two dollars a gallon (Milk is now more expensive than gas.), with the cheapest gas in the country being $1.79 per gallon in Grand Rapids, Michigan, and after paying up to

$4 bucks a gallon in the not too distant past, today's prices are a bargain. But thirty-five years ago, under the Carter expedition, it was $1.55 a gallon, when that was real money! AND that was IF you could get it, after waiting all weekend in a line for it. To top it all off, in 1981, if I had gotten a mortgage to buy a house, the interest rate in Northern Virginia was 21.75 %. That is NOT a typo. Today, a mortgage for a thirty-year, fixed-rate mortgage is about 2.5%. Back then, it was almost NINE TIMES more costly to borrow money. I was going out of the world backwards, so Jimmy Carter and I decided that I would quit my nascent career in forestry, pack up for Georgia, and pursue my Master's degree in engineering. Thus it was, that on January 1, 1982, Carol Jeanne began her career at Athens Regional.

Eventually this led me into one of the oddest jobs I ever had. After completing graduate school, I took a position at our local electric cooperative, and began a run (not quite a career) at utilities and engineering. Now this was not a bad job; I liked the work and most of the people. Carol Jeanne's favorite thing about it was that it allowed her to remain close to her family (No more driving 550 miles, one-way, down I-85/I-95 every blessed holiday and vacation to see her mother. Now she was right next door, and if you've never lived next door to your mother-in-law, well, you just don't know what you're missing!). In time, we sold the little house that I built while I was in school, which was on the right side of her mother's house, and built a much bigger house on the left side of her mother (the house, not the person). This was basically a good idea, as our two-bedroom house, which sheltered the two of us and our two dogs when completed, by then also housed the two daughters that Carol Jeanne conceived while I was unemployed.

Well now, about this job at the electric company. A month after they hired me, they hired a new general manager. Suffice it to say that we did not see eye-to-eye. I remember telling him that it was just a personality conflict – I had one, and he did not, something along those lines. For the next decade, he and I made the entrenched warfare of World War I look like child's play. He would come to learn that the art of management is to keep the five guys that hate you away from the five guys that haven't made up their minds. I would come to learn that a person with a sharp tongue often cuts his own throat!! But leaving was not something I could do. By this time Carol Jeanne was entrenched at the hospital, and she wasn't about to move away from her family again. So, moving for me to pursue a career of my own was never an option.

In fairness to me, since I am the one writing this (*"History shall be kind to me, for I intend to write it."* Winston Churchill), the other guy started it – several times over, if the truth be known, and I do by-God know it. I'm all for turning the other cheek, but I only have four, and when they are all spinning, it's time to take a stand. This guy was the most clueless soul I had ever met – more tone deaf to the subtleties of relationships than Barack Obama. On top of this deficiency, he added several others, all in prodigious quantity. He was a micro-manager. He was paranoid. He was cruel. He was a son-of-a-bitch. With absolutely nothing in common, is it any wonder that we did not get along?

Quite seriously, I acknowledge that I am a control freak, obsessive-compulsive, and a perfectionist. I am fairly tightly strung, oscillate at a relatively high frequency, and, like a shark, if I come to a rest, I will die. I am impatient, and it takes next to nothing for me to become exasperated with an idiot (say, perhaps, a teenage girl, too busy texting while behind the wheel at a very short-cycle, left-turn traffic light to notice that it is, briefly, green). Other than that, I'm basically a teddy bear. It truly (*truly!*) does take an amazing amount of transgression to make me genuinely angry about anything. I will absorb an extraordinary amount of poor behavior, and give you a plethora of warnings about the zone you are about to enter, before I totally lose it. But if pushed hard enough, long enough, when I do lose it, things are not pleasant for anyone, to put it extremely mildly. There is no equivocating, no middle distance, no retreat, and no quarter. I do not suffer fools gladly, which brings us back to the matter of my manager at the electric utility.

Over the years, this manager filled my personnel file with letters of censure. My desk was messy. My company car was unwashed. I fraternized with hourly employees at lunch. One Christmas I rode a donated bike intended to be a gift to an under-privileged youth down the hall to the break room instead of pushing it on foot, and he wrote me up. As you can see, he was a cosmopolitan man of deep thought. When I started fighting back, my enthusiasm knew no bounds.

I started out with simple stuff. Back in those days, you could set a car's controls before you started it. I would turn on his wind-shield wipers, and set the radio volume all the way up. If you knew which window in the building to happen to be standing at when he got in his car, you could watch him jump when he turned the switch, and I am told that it was a heartwarming sight to behold! And, oh, I forgot to mention the transformer grease! As an electric utility, we had a steady supply of transformers, and they came with these packets of grease to lubricate their fittings when they were installed, a one-time application that might well have to last for thirty years or more. I don't know what kind of grease it was, but it was the greasiest grease I've ever encountered, and once it got on your clothing, not even battery acid was going to remove it. I would take a packet of this grease, and as I walked by his car on my way into the building, I would squeeze a big shot of it under the driver's door handle. Once again, I am told that if a group of employees were standing at the right window at just the right time, it was a jolly sight!

His response to this subterfuge was to install closed-circuit security cameras. Since he could hardly have justified it to the board of directors for just his parking spot without going into embarrassing detail, he had the cameras put around the entire building. While this sadly brought about an end to this phase of our relationship, it was not without some measure of satisfaction. He and I both knew exactly who had been doing this stuff, and more importantly, we both knew that we both knew! The only thing he lacked was any evidence. Sweet!

But the time had come for me to move on, and so I did. I took out an employment ad in the local newspaper... for his position! At first, I said that a high school diploma was required, but then I downgraded it to preferred. However, a GED was an absolute minimum! I cannot honestly say that I recall all the other denigrating qualifications for the successful candidate that I penned, but I can hear myself laughing at that ad to this day.

Then there was the time I bought a bumper sticker for his car. I bought it at a store at the mall called Spencer's. It was full of off-the-wall stuff and crude humor. I waited until he had an important meeting in Atlanta on his calendar, then I followed him to it. While he was inside hobnobbing with the big wigs, I put that bumper sticker on his car. It read: *I'm looking for the perfect woman... a nymphomaniac that owns a liquor store!* There were two great things about that bumper sticker. First, when he found it, he had no way of knowing how long it had been there, or how many people had seen it. Second, he and I both knew exactly who had put it there, and more importantly, we both knew that we both knew! The only thing he lacked was any evidence. Sweet!

Then there was the time he made me fulfill one of the requirements of my job description, which I had artfully avoided for years. My job description said that, as a member of management, I was to be involved in the community. I always maintained that I was. I was a member of a church, a member of the PTA, I was in several professional and trade organizations that met regularly, but suddenly that was not good enough. He decreed that I had to join a civic organization. My options were things such as Lions Club, Rotary, and Kiwanis. Apparently, any organization that sold brooms, fruit, raffle tickets – anything other than electricity – would qualify. I thought about applying for membership in one of his clubs, which were the Rotary Club and the Masons, but I decided against it – there would be too many witnesses. Eventually I chose the Athens Kiwanis Club. I did this for two reasons. First, it met at noon, not at 7:00 in the morning, and not at 6:00 in the evening, so I could do it on company time. Second, the

Athens Kiwanis Club met in, of all places, Athens. Since my office was in a wide spot in the road called Monroe, Georgia, this gave me company transportation, on company time, to drive the twenty miles to Athens every week, taking me right past treasured retail places like Sears, Lowes, Walmart – all kinds of incidental destinations that I was allowed to stop at briefly when in need. And oh yeah, it also took me by the mall in Athens, where they had a store called Spencer's that sold bumper stickers.

Let's face it, in the long run, the guy had done me a favor. In the heat of the moment, however, I could not recognize that, because I had my hackles up about the civic club crap. That's why one day I slipped out of the office just behind him when he left to go to his Rotary meeting (Somehow, this guy never got around to applying the Rotarians' Four Way Test to his behavior towards me: Is it the truth? Is it fair? Will it build goodwill and better friendships? Is it beneficial to all parties involved?). I waited across the street at a gas station, and gave the meeting about fifteen minutes to get going. Then I slipped over to the parking lot and took a valve stem remover and slightly loosened up the valve stem on all four tires of his big Ford Crown Victoria. By the time he left his meeting, I was back in my office, and all four tires were flat as a pancake, as witnessed by every member of the Rotary Club. He called a wrecker to tow his car back to the office, no kidding! The best thing about this, of course, was that both he and I both exactly who had done it, and more importantly, we both knew that we both knew! The only thing he lacked was evidence. There were no security cameras in the Rotary parking lot. Sweet!

But the best thing I ever did to this sorry excuse for humanity was to get him fired. Before his lousy ass hit the pavement, he also happened to fire me, but the fact that he had never managed to think of that in the preceding decade was the platinum standard of his lack of grasp of the obvious. This man served at the pleasure of a board of directors. Half of them hated him almost as much as I did, as did 99% of the employees (One of the greatest lessons that I ever learned was that, in any circumstance, there is always that

14

1% of obsequious, unctuous, sycophants who will shake your hand and smile to your face, even as they sell you out to the very gates of Hell if it will so much as get them a simple "atta boy" from management. Just Google "Judas Iscariot."). But the board could never manage to get that one last vote that would allow them to dispatch this miserable wretch.

Well, the board couldn't get that last vote, but I did. The directors serve in staggered terms, with three of them up for re-election in any given year. In both the culture and history of electric cooperatives, the only way to NOT get re-elected is to die. But then this guy jerked my chain, and all of that changed. It just so happened that one year all three of the directors who were up for re-election were supporters of The Idiot. Their nomination for re-election was assured by virtue of a Nominating Committee ("*A committee is a cul-de-sac down which ideas are lured, then quietly strangled.*"). This committee was appointed by that very same board of directors!! How could they lose? Answer: the corporate bylaws. The bylaws, which I just happened to have read, provided for the nomination of candidates for the board by petition of the voters, an option that had never before been exercised. I quietly went about finding three genuinely qualified members of the community who would agree to serve, if elected. I guaranteed them that if they ran, they would be elected. I looked every one of them in the eye, and told them to their faces that there was one string attached. At their first board meeting after being elected, they had to vote to fire the guy. With the balance of the board behind them, they would have an unstoppable majority.

I did not accomplish this by myself, or even mostly by dint of my own efforts. It was the old-timers who did him in, people who had worked there all their lives and had no option to work elsewhere, people who now toiled in dread, fear, and misery. Employees could not serve on the board, but their neighbors did, their cousins did, their bankers and preachers and doctors did. In terms of the voters, it was a very small community indeed when you came right down to it, and all three of those directors were quickly shown the door. There was just one hitch. One of the new directors that I had solicited, that I had helped elect into office, that I had sat across from at his very own kitchen table and told about the one string attached, blinked. At the next board meeting, he said maybe they should give the guy one more chance. This new director was an ex-Marine and had served in combat. I figured if any of them had a pair, it would be him, and he sold me down the river! I followed him home from that meeting, and, once again at his kitchen table, asked him one question. "What are you going to do for my family when this guy fires me?" "Oh, I'm sure he won't do that," he said. He was dead wrong, and when it happened, he left me dangling in the wind. I was fired the next day. Thirty days later, at the next board meeting, they did in fact vote to terminate his sorry ass. Later, they offered me my job back, and I took it.

But not for long. As I said, my employment history has been checkered, and it was time to move on down the road. The new manager wasn't much better than the old one. He immediately set about a campaign to get rid of all the old-timers who had gotten rid of the last guy. He didn't want history to repeat itself. He had more sense than to try to fire them, so he came up with an "early retirement" plan that was an offer too good to refuse, especially when he simultaneously announced significant changes to future personnel policies. In a nutshell, he offered these long-term employees the chance to take early retirement AND be allowed to cash in all of their accumulated personal leave: vacation, holiday – an ambiguous term for an electric utility – and sick leave, which had never before been allowed. If they didn't take it, that leave time would forever be capped at thirty days (Some of them had *hundreds* of days!!). They left in droves. I was one of them. I wasn't an old-timer, but the new manager failed to specify who could "retire" under this program. So, about the age of thirty-eight, after a dozen years without ever taking a day of sick leave or vacation, I walked out of there with $55,000 to invest towards early retirement (which Carol Jeanne has just taken!).

That's probably enough of this for now. Suffice it to say that after that, I became the staff engineer for a municipal utility, then shortly thereafter, I became its general manager. Shortly after that, I left to become an owner/partner in a private engineering firm. That went very well financially, but poorly in just about every other respect, so in 2001 I sold my ownership. I took just enough cash from the sale of my stock to buy a new Toyota Sequoia for Carol Jeanne, the only new car we've ever owned, and which we still drive to this day. The rest of the money we plowed into investments for early retirement (which, again, Carol Jeanne has just taken!). After that, I managed a couple of small businesses for their owners, and when that either played out, or didn't work out, I looked around for the next thing. I told Carol Jeanne that I wanted to do something that did not have a boss, a partner, or an employee – if it weren't for people, I'd be great at business. She added one condition: "When you get up in the morning and complain, do it to the mirror. The rest of us are tired of hearing about it." So, I obtained my real estate license, and for just over a decade, I worked as an associate broker with Coldwell Banker (although I don't have any billboards, not even my picture on the side of my car). After that, I obtained my broker's license, and opened my own firm. And while Carol Jeanne has retired, I can't quite afford to do so just yet, so I am still working, trying to decide what career to pursue, trying to figure out what I want to do for a living when I grow up. If you know anyone looking for a good man, please keep me in mind. Just don't tell me to join a civic club!!

. . . .

You have not converted a man
simply because you have silenced him.

John Morley

. . . .

Here's a poem that I wrote:

Critics

Who is this man
with words so sharp,
who wields a poison pen,
who stands apart
from the fray,
the victory does not win?

In the midst of the toil,
amongst the strain and strife,
he disdains to join in,
to contribute to the life.

Who is this soul
who no one loves,
this awful, evil witch,
with acid words
to destroy,
to whine and moan and bitch?

No contribution can she make,
save only to complain.
No effort ever good enough,
no praise can one attain.

How easy it is
to tear things down,
never building up.

Any wonder
no monument stands
to this half-empty cup?

An honest thought has merit,
encouraging or less,
but only if I first have strived,
and tried to pass the test.

What benefit in casting stones,
our neighbor to decry?
People can change the course they chart,
but only those that try.

. . . .

I couldn't wait on success, so I went ahead without it.
Johnathan Winters

*The great source of pleasure is variety. Uniformity must tire
at last, though it be uniformity of excellence. We love to expect,
and when expectation is disappointed or gratified,
we want to be again expecting.*
Samuel Johnson

. . . .

2015

Carol Jeanne's first year of retirement has been a learning experience for both of us. One of the first things we learned is that it's much more rewarding if only one of us is home at a time. It has been hard for her to learn that I should not be thought of as a moving part in her daily experiment. When she takes two chairs in the living room and switches their assigned places, it really is not critical that I immediately drop what I am doing, and go sit in them (*both* of them) to see if I like the difference. For my part, I am learning not to say that I don't give a @!%*. I might still think it, but I am verbalizing it less often.

There have been other sources of friction. For example, for some unfathomable reason, now that she is home all day, she has decided that she wants a light on in every room of the house (including the front and back porch!), from the time she gets up to the time she goes to bed, even if she is not in that room, even if she will only go into that room (or that entire floor of the house!) all day, except to turn the light on and then off. This drives me crazy. I tell her it makes no sense; she says she likes it that way. I tell her it's a waste of energy; she says she likes it that way. Now that she is living on an essentially fixed income, I tell her that it's a waste of money. She says it doesn't cost much. I tell her that whatever it costs, it's money down a rat hole, might as well wad up the cash and flush it down a toilet. It is, of course, pointless to employ rational thought in an irrational argument, much less with an irrational woman.

Before she retired, our mornings were an exquisitely engineered ballet. There was not a wasted moment, not a wasted movement. Every motion was a study in efficiency. She would rise, and prepare for the day (and possibly the evening) at the hospital. In the interest of getting her on her way with the minimum of distractions, I would fix her breakfast and her lunch. Her coffee – with mug preheated in the microwave – would be waiting for her at the precise moment she was scheduled to walk out the door. None of this required communication or conversation beyond "Good morning" and "Good bye." There was no time for pleasantries.

This will come as a shock to some of you, but since I don't know which ones of you that will be, perhaps you all better sit down. Here it is. I am a man of habit and routine. One of my great life ambitions is "the rut" (not the kind that deer go through – I left that behind long ago!). No, I mean the predictable, the mundane, the quotidian. I have established a pretty good rut, and I manage it quite well. It's the unpredictable, the unexpected, the surprises in life on which I stump my proverbial toe. The point is this: I have a morning routine. Part of it is feeding myself, part of it is feeding the critter population, both furred and feathered. I do stretches, isometrics, and core exercises – same order, same number – right after breakfast. Then the dogs and I walk down to get the paper, a trek of about a quarter of a mile. Before we grab the paper, we feed Babes, the horse across the street, two carrots. Then we head back towards the house, but now we walk faster, because by this time it's passing 7:00 AM, and there's something else that I'm really regular about – my nickname is 7:11.

Later in the morning, the dogs and I walk a different route, about eight-tenths of a mile, around the lake (Our evening walk, just before supper, is yet another route of about a half mile.). This gives the dogs some respectable exercise, but it's mostly for their mental health and stimulation. They do a lot of sniffing, seeing who's come through in the past twenty-four hours (other dogs, cats, squirrels, rabbits, deer, foxes, coyotes, raccoons, 'possums, and bobcats), and of course they mark their territory as needed... I can't do it all by myself. After she retired, Carol Jeanne decided that she would begin going on this morning walk with us. That lasted less than a week. She wanted it to be a power walk, a cardio workout, and the dogs and I wanted something more reflective – transcendental even – more of a stroll, and all of us would become stressed (After walking the dogs, I would take them back to the

21

house, then head out for a three-mile run, so I did not need a power walk.). I went so far as to point out that if she would walk a step or two behind me, she would be certain to not walk too fast for the intended purpose. That suggestion was not received as gratefully as you probably thought it would have been.

Anyway, reading the paper each morning is the official start of my business day, and afterwards two of the dogs and I head downstairs to my office, where I do a second round of stretches. Then I check my email, check voice mail, and check the previous day's market activity in real estate. Finally, I read the day's edition of *The Writer's Almanac* by Garrison Keillor – including the poem for the day – which often passes very productively as my daily meditation. It has taken the better part of a year, but Carol Jeanne is finally learning that when I am in my office, when I am at my desk, I am at *work*!! It might not look like much, and more often than not, it isn't. But it's my routine, and I am pretty focused on it – and I don't like it interrupted!! When I am at my desk, I am not "available" to visit, or to discuss whether it's cold enough outside to build a fire in the basement stove (Carol Jeanne's rule of thumb is that if the air conditioning is not running, you need a fire. And for the record, there's no such thing as building "just a little fire." It's like trying to dig half a hole!).

For my part, I am learning not to ask too many questions early in the morning, because asking questions has taught me two things. First, ten minutes after I ask a question (about some fairly insignificant or very straightforward matter), the answer is still being delivered, but I quit paying attention at about nine minutes and forty-five seconds earlier. Second, that really irritates Carol Jeanne, so much so that she will frequently rewind the tape and begin her answer anew! So there have been some adjustments, there has been some give and take, and just who did the giving and who did the taking isn't really the point. The point is that *living* with your wife is much different than just being married to her, and everyone has to work together to adjust. Just remember this, "*It is easier to be a saint than it is to live with one.*"

....

I'm a lousy writer. Fortunately, most people have lousy taste.

...

Why do men write? Because it isn't there.

Anonymous

*Writing is easy. All you do is stare at a blank sheet of paper
until drops of blood form on your forehead.*

Gene Fowler

*Writing is not like dancing or modeling; it's not something where
— if you missed it by age 19 — you're finished. It's never too late.
Your writing will only get better as you get older and wiser.
If you write something beautiful and important, and the right
person somehow discovers it, they will clear room for you on the
bookshelves of the world — at any age. At least try.*

Elizabeth Gilbert

*Compulsion and money... the only two reasons I can think of to
go through the hell of trying to fill 500 blank sheets of paper.*

Fredrick Forsyth

Easy reading is damn hard writing.

Nathaniel Hawthorne

*Reading makes a man well rounded.
Writing makes a man exact.*

Francis Bacon

Writing is for those small hours of the night when you can't remember how you got from where you were to where you are.

Tim O'Brien

Sit down and put down everything that comes into your head, and then you're a writer. But an author is one who can judge his own stuff's worth, without pity, and destroy most of it.

Sidonie Gabrielle

When I am, as it were, completely myself, entirely alone, and of good cheer – it is on such occasions that my ideas flow best and most abundantly. Whence and how they come, I know not, nor can I force them.

Mozart

I don't write stories. I write stories down.
Anonymous

An author is someone who writes books.
A writer is an author whose books sell.

Mickey Spillane

To the man with an ear for verbal delicacies – the man who searches painfully for the perfect word, and puts the way of saying a thing above the thing said – there is in writing the constant joy of sudden discovery, of happy accident.

H.L. Mencken

. . . .

2014

I can recall two instances in my life where my father told me that he was proud of me. One time was in a letter he wrote to me after completing my Master's degree – leaving a job, going to graduate school, being a husband, building a house, having two children along the way, becoming an engineer – he said that he could not imagine doing that, and that he was proud of me for having done so.

The other time was perhaps a year or so before he died. We had gone to Charlotte for a quick visit, and in the driveway, as I was loading the car to head back to Georgia, from out of the blue he shared with me the second time that he was proud of me. He pointed to a spot in the driveway just a few feet from where I stood, the spot where his father had died on a Friday night, November 10, 1972. My grandfather had stopped by the house that night to confirm that he would collect my younger brother and me the next morning to head to the family farm to work on a chimney that he was building. This was the only grandfather I had ever known, and in whose shadow I had been reared. After supper, I headed upstairs, and he and my father headed out to the car for him to drive around the corner to his house. In only a moment, my mother was shrieking from the bottom of the stairs to come to the driveway.

"Coleman, get down here. Cy has collapsed!" Cy had already gotten into his 1963 Plymouth Valiant – the car that my father would drive the rest of his life. He was telling my dad about a black snake that he had caught earlier in the day and put in a croaker sack (a burlap bag), but that the snake had somehow escaped while in the car. He was in the process of buckling his seat belt (which he insisted on calling a "lap belt") when his head slumped forward. For a moment, my father thought that he might have been glancing down for the snake. The merciful truth of the matter is that he was dead in less than an instant, but of course no one could have known it, thus the scream from my mother to get downstairs.

I pulled my grandfather out of that car, and laid him on the pavement between my father and younger brother. My father was a physician, but he and my brother were frozen (Ironically, in years to come, my father would save the lives of two neighbors by doing CPR on them. One guy, arrested in ventricular fibrillation, my father pounded so hard that he broke the man's sternum... but he came back to life!). I started to perform CPR. My grandfather had vomited (a pretty good sign of death), and I had to swipe that out of his airway before trying to breathe for him. I pounded and puffed until the ambulance arrived, which seemed like forever but was only a few minutes. A large, black EMT gently pulled me out of his way, and took over the CPR all the way to the hospital. My father rode in the ambulance. I was sixteen, and drove behind them right up to the emergency room doors. There, the first doctor on the scene was my father's uncle, my grandfather's brother-in-law, Leon Kennedy. It was Leon that told us what we already knew, that Cy was gone. Leon's signature is on Cy's death certificate. Now, forty years later, some synapse in my father's Parkinson's plagued brain fired, and he was pointing to that spot in the driveway, and telling me that he was proud of me that night, proud of what I had tried to do for his own father when he could not do it himself. He was so sincere, his mind so present in that long-ago moment. I found some excuse for readjusting some suitcases in the back of the car while I wiped the tears from my eyes.

. . . .

Too many of us are trying to tiptoe through life
so that we can reach the grave safely.
Earl Nightingale

. . . .

2013

I lost my father on March 14, 2013. Chris Hood was a couple of weeks shy of his 84th birthday when his physical ailments overtook him. As a physician, he understood that his Parkinson's disease and his prostate cancer could never have gotten better. But they could have gotten much worse. Certainly he knew that, and I imagine he was grateful to have passed on when he did. As I said in his eulogy, the last years were cruel to him, but they were only a small part of his life and they do not ultimately define him. I have not a doubt that if Chris' Creator, at any point in his life, had laid his life out before him, from the cradle to the grave, Chris would have gladly taken it – twice if given the chance. In my estimation, that's a pretty good life.

Ten days after I lost my father, I lost my best friend. Mike Guilbeau was a tennis pro, a fitness freak, and his word was his bond. Mike and I were runners. I was never in the same league as Mike, because he was truly gifted, plus I was seven years older than he and had had surgery on both knees. But I have this one claim to fame. Mike and I once ran a 5K together over one of his favorite courses. He knew exactly where he was going, and what was coming next (uphill, downhill, intersections). I didn't have a clue, so my only hope was to keep him in sight. Because of where we started, I knew that the last part of the course would be uphill. I was a little better than Mike at running uphill (He would absolutely blister me running downhill.), and I hoped that I might be able to catch up to him in the homestretch. I didn't. Mike beat me that day, as he always did, and he set his personal best time ever on that course. I finished seven seconds behind him. That's my claim to running fame, and I am damn proud of it – I finished seven seconds behind Mike Guilbeau on his best day. Mike was only fifty when he lost his life to cancer.

Eulogy for Christopher Kennedy Hood
March 17, 2013

In a moment, Reverend Jane Fobel is going to indulge me in reading two letters to you as a eulogy to Chris. I say that she is going to "indulge" me because it's going to take her about twelve and a half minutes to do that, which exceeds the proscribed Presbyterian limit for such affairs. I have asked her to read these letters because she will emotionally be able to handle it, whereas I would not.

These two letters were written upon the occasion of Chris' retirement. The first is a letter I wrote at the request of his office staff. The second letter was written by my father, and it summarizes what we seek here to accomplish today better than anything we might say. I have resisted the urge to edit either of these letters in a revisionist manner, and so they will be read today just as they were written, almost sixteen years ago.

My father was a man of medicine and science. My father understood that he was mortal, that he suffered from three terminal afflictions: he had Parkinson's disease, he had prostate cancer... and he was human. He understood that neither medicine nor science could reverse his destiny. I do not think that he believed in an interventionist God who would promote a cure for his infirmities above the greater suffering of the rest of this world. He accepted that.

But there were two things that he refused. He refused to live out his life in any place other than his own home, which he did, and which is a testament to his tenacity, and to the sacrificial support of my mother and sister.

Second, he wished to die with his dignity intact. The final

years were hard on him – cruel – but as in the poem *Invictus*:

> In the fell clutch of circumstance,
> I have not winced, nor cried aloud.
> Under the bludgeonings of chance,
> My head is bloodied, but unbowed.

His final days were an answer to prayer. The good saints at Levine-Dickson Hospice Care allowed him to die with dignity, painlessly, surrounded in love by the family he lived for.

Let me share with you a brief passage from William Alexander Percy's *Lanterns On The Levee* that was a favorite of Chris':

> Of all the hours of happiness granted me, none has been so keen and holy as a few unpredictable moments alone. I have never walked with God, but I had rather walk with Him through hell than with my heart's elect through heaven. Of the good life, I have learned what it is not. I have loved a few who lived it end to end. I have seen the goodness of men, and the beauty of things. I have no regrets. I am not contrite. I am grateful.
>
> Here among the graves, in the twilight, I see one thing only, but I see that thing clear. I see the long wall of a rampart somber with sunset, a dusty road at its base. On the tower of the rampart stand the glorious high gods, Death and the rest, watching. Below on the road stream the tribes of men, tired, bent, hurt, and stumbling, and each man alone. As one comes beneath the tower, the High God descends and faces the wayfarer. He speaks three slow words, "Who... are... you?" The pilgrim I know should be able to straighten his shoulders, to stand his tallest, and to answer, "I am your son."

Chris faced stern trials at the end of his life, but they were only a very small part of his life, and they do not, ultimately, define him. And so I invite Jane to share a broader perspective of happier times, and a life well lived. And as for Chris, he "...*now walks unafraid back to Eden, where the foliage is always green, where joy and peace abide, where life and death are one in our Creator.*"

My Letter To Commemorate My Father's Retirement
May 29, 1997
—————————————————————————

Dear Friends and Staff of Tower OB/GYN:

It is my understanding that several among you have asked members of Chris Hood's family to write a few lines to assist you in commemorating his retirement. If that is indeed the case, I would first reiterate the words of Voltaire, "If you would converse with me, define your terms." Specifically, there are three terms that we must agree upon. First is *vocation*, which is a call to the priesthood of a religious order. Second is *avocation*, a subordinate occupation pursued in addition to one's vocation, for enjoyment. All of which brings us to the final term, *family*, which is essential to a corrected understanding of your request.

I would have thought it apparent to anyone who had spent any part of their career associated with Chris Hood in his forty-six years in Obstetrics and Gynecology that YOU are his family!! We are merely those who were fortunate enough to be the ones you shared him with when he was not with you. Ob/Gyn is my father's vocation, his spiritual calling, which he has always pursued in a priestly fashion. It has also been his avocation, his hobby, which is a great blessing for any man to experience. My father has often come home late and exhausted, but almost always contented and

30

fulfilled. What time and energy he had left, after ministering to his beloved mistress – no, not Ruth – his 1963 Plymouth Valiant, he would spend curled up in his favorite chair with his favorite distraction – no, not Ruth – his latest issue of *The New England Journal of Medicine*.

I remember his first office well. It was across the street from Park Road Shopping Center when it was the only shopping center in Charlotte. Oh sure, there was the Charlotte Town Mall, but it was downtown, way past the Center Theater and almost to the Thompson Orphanage. Park Road Drugs was a few blocks down the street from Chris' office, where he sent a lot of prescription business. The pharmacist, Bob Lewis, would treat us to fountain sodas and hand-dipped ice cream. In the office building next to Chris was our dentist, Bob Watson, whose practice benefited from all the cokes and ice cream. Down the street in the other direction was our pediatrician, Blair Bryan. I remember the names of physicians from my childhood such as M.D. Childers, Bryant Galusha, Bud Bishop, Don Kellam, and Julian Albergotti.

I hope and trust that someone among your gathering today will take time to remember two ladies who meant so much to my father's career – Lila and Frances – whom I know will one day receive the very special benediction, "Well done, thou good and faithful servant." Then there was Vicki, and later Blanche, my first unrequited love. And of course there are the two who have actually maintained the practice on Fourth Street, Ann and Cheryl.

These two ladies have been burdened with shot-giving, blood-drawing, and birth-control pill dispensing (even after we were married!). These rigors pale in contrast, however, to the mountains of Xeroxing and mailing over the last twenty-five years that these ladies have had to do to four children whose four addresses were as shifting as the sands. If anything in a Xerox is ever found to be a carcinogen, these ladies will be as dead as the people in the articles they were copying. Ladies, I once cut out the Sunday obituaries from the *Atlanta Journal-Constitution*, and mailed them to Chris so that he could fabricate whatever bizarre cause of death he wished, rather than having to wait on nature to provide the necessary freak accidents. I even pointed out that he could pencil in that each of them was the child of a physician, for in all of God's creation there is no curse of morbidity more damning than to be born the child of a physician!

We grew up in a Charlotte where Mayberry was a reality, during a time when Ward and June Cleaver were a way of life. Ruth stayed home and reared the children (Being good Presbyterians, we were not *raised*, as was a crop of corn or a prize hog. We were *reared*). While Ruth reared, Chris worked. And worked. And worked. Consequently, many of our worldly indoctrinations and rites-of-passage were delegated to Chris' father, Cy, much to my eternal blessing. I cannot remember my father ever throwing me a ball of any sort, nor attending one of the rare school events in which I participated. But every summer without fail, Chris would load up the family, and head off for Litchfield Beach. At night, we'd eat out at the best restaurants, and then head to the pavilion at Myrtle Beach, where we'd ride all the rides, especially the Wild Mouse. We'd spend the days at the beach, of which I was mortally afraid. I remember being out in the waves, scared to death, when Chris would sweep me up in his arms, and declare, "Stick with me kid, and you'll never get wet!" And I would believe him. Chris' kids didn't do much in the way of Little League, Pop Warner football, or Cub Scouts. But he did produce four independent – albeit slightly skewed – thinkers and self-confident individuals. Whatever our shortcomings, time has proven us to be reasonably happy, moderately successful, and socially responsible. We have supported and celebrated our father's calling, and in so doing we have participated in it as well.

Which is not to imply that it has all been a bed of roses. OB/GYNs can frequently arrive home short on patience for teenagers who have engaged their mother in mortal combat for the preceding fifteen hours of the day. Chris adopted with vigor the philosophy of Bill Cosby's father, "I brought you into this world, I can take you out. Make another one just like you." The truth is, the man could beat the hell out of anything or anyone when he was ill. He once "disciplined" one of us half to death before he realized that in his rush to dispense justice and/or the wrath of God – whichever came first – he had seized upon one of the neighbor's offspring, rather than one of his own. But we all learned valuable lessons from this – accepting the consequences of our actions, as well as how to duck quick!

I have intimated that my father's practice has had a strong spiritual influence. I can recall an incident from my teens – a time of acute spiritual enlightenment for me, which I was only too glad to share with those of lesser insight – which taught me something about my father's spiritual state. Being an OB/GYN is not particularly conducive to regular church attendance. After having myself maintained perfect attendance over a period of weeks, I pointed out to my father (with the self-righteous fervor that only a latent Baptist or a Porter – and I was both – could manage), that he never attended Sunday School, and frequently missed church. Chris quietly replied, with an edge to his voice which I had never before heard, that he had "spent more hours on his knees with Jesus in the middle of the night than I would in my lifetime." I was immediately convinced of two things. First, that he was earnest in his assertion. Second, that his intercessions were doubtless for the benefit of the patient, and not the practitioner.

Finally, and it is intentionally so, I must mention my father's life-long partner – no, not Ruth – Bill Eubanks. If there is any man who has integrity, quiet assurance, honor, and discipline in measure equal to that of my father, it is Bill Eubanks. If there is anyone who could stomach those traits in someone else for over forty years, it is Bill Eubanks. My father and Bill have always separated their business and social lives. I believe this to have been a wise decision, since as near as I can tell, neither one of them has a social life. Bill is the man whom my father has trusted completely with all that was his to entrust. Bill has never, ever, disappointed him. Between the combined integrity possessed by

Bill Eubanks and my father, one of them should surely be able to walk on water. Thankfully, Bill would have the sense to wait until it was frozen before he tried. Thank you, Dr. Eubanks, for all you have done for *both* of Chris' families through the decades.

Thank you Daddy, for all your hard work, for your integrity, for all the comforts you provided to your family, for all of our educations. Enjoy what you've earned. I love you.

Your middle son.

My Father's Letter To His Patients Upon His Retirement, May 1997

———————————————————————

Dear friend and patient,

In 1951, as a medical student in Philadelphia, I was allowed to conduct my first obstetrical delivery. It was an event in my life that so impressed me that I knew immediately and exactly what my lifelong profession would be. I've loved every day of it.

That seems so long ago now. But those 46 years have gone so quickly by! During those years I've been blessed by friendships with each of you that are genuine. Your trust in me has been so flattering, whether it was deserved or not.

Together, some of us have also gone through some dark and frightening times, of course, as well as sadness.

I've seen the children I've delivered grow up, marry, and have their own children and even an occasional grandchild (Remember that first little boy I delivered is now 46 years old!).

But it is time for me to gather up those warm memories and move on to the next arena of life while I have my health and hope to enjoy retirement. So I shall be retiring as of 31 May 1997.

Your health will always be my first priority. I hope you will continue your care here with Drs. Little and Schoen, whom I recommend to you without reservation. I also leave you with Ann and Cheryl who've been with me and you so, so long.

Thanks again. You have made my life gratifying. Your children have made it satisfying. I've been most fortunate to have had the sheer joy of sharing your concerns as well as successes.

Thanks for giving me a great and happy life.

C. K. Hood, MD

....

I long to accomplish a great and noble task, but it is my chief duty to accomplish small tasks as if they were great and noble.

Helen Keller

....

Eulogy for Mike Guilbeau
March 24, 2013

I like this quote from Garrison Keillor, "They say such nice things about you at your funeral, it makes me sad that I'm going to miss mine by just a few days." I'm sure that Mike would have been delighted to hear all of the wonderful thoughts and stories that we are about to share. My comments today will obviously be about

Mike; they will be drawn from my relationship with him, which I considered to be special. I hope that you will be able to hear my thoughts in that context.

I remember quite vividly the first time I ever laid eyes on Mike Guilbeau. Patti, I don't know if you'll remember this, but I believe that it was a Sunday afternoon. Mike had just pulled up at Jennings Mill in a Ryder rental van, and he had an entire tennis pro shop loaded in it. He had massive stacks of peg board in the van, plus all the mounting hardware, and about a thousand pounds of red laminate counter tops. He had pulled up in the cul-de-sac below the playground area (This was back when the pro shop was in a cinder-block building, as an afterthought to the golf pro shop, and was next door to what I affectionately called the Redneck Lounge, otherwise known as the Mill Room.). Anyway, I was headed home when this van pulled up, with Mike and this blonde woman in it, and he's trying to wrestle all this stuff out by himself. How he planned to get it up the hill, up the steps, and into the shop by himself, I'll never know. But I'm certain of this – he would have done it! Well long story short, about three hours later, in the dark, we had it all set up. I was the first member of Jennings Mill Country Club that Mike met.

Perhaps I flatter myself, but in my opinion, Mike Guilbeau and I are so much alike that I should be worried about myself. From my perspective, Mike was a little bit on the opinionated side. He tended to be a somewhat impatient. Mike leaned slightly towards the obsessive-compulsive end of the spectrum. I played a good bit of golf with Mike, as did many of you. I think it took at least five years to get it through Mike's head that, in a game among friends, it was okay to "give" someone a twelve-inch putt. The world wasn't going to end if you did that, and you could still turn your score in for your official handicap. It wasn't cheating, even though, yes, Mike, it was conceivably possible to miss a twelve-inch putt, which I often did! If he had lived longer, I suspect that Mike might have become a control freak. Am I looking at my brother, or in a mirror?

36

At one time, Mike and I were both good runners. At that time, Mike was also an exceptional runner, but we were both good. We both played tennis, but again, Mike was exceptional. We both played golf, although I don't know that I ever beat him.

But we weren't alike in everything. I can't imagine two people who would call themselves brothers – and we did – that were more UNalike than Mike and I when it came to religion and matters of faith. Nor can I imagine any other two people in this gathering having deeper, more earnest, more sincere, discussions about their faith than Mike and I had. We weren't the best golfers in the world, but we were the fastest. When we played eighteen holes (not counting the ones where we leap-frogged players in front of us that did not possess the necessary golf etiquette to invite us to play through... we called them "IDIOTS!"), just about every minute of those rounds of golf were spent discussing God, both before and after Mike's diagnosis. In the last few years, we occasionally discussed Obama. But we had to discuss God first, because if we started with Obama, we could not proceed to God.

I cannot imagine two people disagreeing more over just about every aspect of their perception of God than Mike and I did. And in our disagreement, we were vocal, vehement, and sometimes almost violent. But we were never disrespectful, we were never angry, we were just sharing, just being honest, just searching. Mike and I believe in the same God, but we express our beliefs quite differently.

Honesty compels me to share with you today what I shared with Mike many, many times.

I do not believe in an interventionist God. I do not believe in the theistic God of supernaturalism, a God that indeed created everything, but that somehow exists as a discrete entity outside of that creation, and must re-enter it – however infrequently – in order to interact with it in some miraculous way. Mike and I very strongly disagreed about that.

Modern science, modern medicine, can cure cancer – sometimes – but God does not.

Not because a God capable of all creation could not also be capable of curing cancer, but because that type of God is too problematic to reconcile and sustain. How could such a God cure one cancer while tens of thousands of cancers go uncured each day, or while tens of thousands of babies starve to death each day? That type of list is endless. Why would such a God cure one cancer, when such a God could just as easily cure EVERY cancer? Why allow cancer at all? Why wouldn't such a God simply banish cancer, banish all suffering and anguish? That, too, would be problematic, of course; your cancer is cured, but you will still die of something. This old earth would be a crowded place indeed if there were no such thing as death. No, death – whether by disease, or accident, or old age, or whatever – is a completely natural part of life.

Mike and I both believe in the Kingdom of God. Mike is in it now. Mike entered into that Kingdom, not at his death, but at that moment that he turned his heart and his mind towards it. If the Kingdom of God proclaimed by Mike's Jesus is not a part of *this* world, not part of the here and now, then I don't believe I care to have anything to do with it. The essence of Christianity is not a set of beliefs; the essence of Christianity is a way of life. We might not have seen eye to eye on Jesus, but like everything Mike gave himself to, he gave himself totally and without reservation to his God, and he was fiercely loyal to his God. He trusted his God; he trusted his God to death. Eleven days before Mike died, my father, who also had cancer, died. Mike texted me his condolences. He ended his text by saying, "... now your father knows what I so long to know." That was the last thing he ever said to me.

Whatever Mike did, he did the best he knew how. He set the performance bar for everyone quite high, but for no one did he set that bar higher than for himself. He was his own harshest critic. While he was not perfect, his integrity was absolute. Whether for tennis, for friends, for family, or for his God, Mike Guilbeau's integrity was absolute. I cannot think of a higher compliment to pay him. It was just one more arena of life in which he managed to out perform me – if I do the right thing, it is because I know it is the right thing to do, but Mike did the right thing because he did not know how to do otherwise. Being around Mike Guilbeau made me want to be a better person.

There is much about theology that Mike and I did not agree on. That's okay. Our differences are inconsequential in the context of eternity. Nonetheless, I have searched to find some common ground to stand on in these comments today, some thought that I might leave Patti, MacKenzie, and Adam with that would honor Mike's faith, while respecting the integrity of our differences. I prayerfully give you these thoughts of the poet Richard Baxter (1681):

> Lord, it belongs not to my care
> whether I die or live;
> to love and serve thee is my share,
> and this Thy grace must give.
>
> If life be long, O make me glad
> the longer to obey;
> if short, no laborer is sad
> to end his toilsome day.
>
> Christ leads me through no darker rooms
> than he went through before;
> he that unto God's kingdom comes
> must enter by this door.
>
> Come, Lord, when grace hath made me meet
> thy blessèd face to see:

for if thy work on earth be sweet,
what will thy glory be!

Then I shall end my sad complaints
and weary, sinful days,
and join with the triumphant saints
that sing my Savior's praise.

My knowledge of that life is small,
the eye of faith is dim;
but 'tis enough that Christ knows all,
and I shall be with him.

And so he is.

Amen.

. . . .

Essential wisdom accumulates in the community much as fertility builds in the land. The past is our definition. We may strive, with good reason, to escape it, or to escape what is bad in it, but we will escape it only by adding something better to it.

Wendell Berry

. . . .

2020

———————

This year, China gave us the wonderful world of Covid, the Kung Fu Flu. THE VERY FIRST DAY that this was mentioned in the media, I told Carol Jeanne that this was going to be a big deal. I told her THE VERY FIRST DAY that the truth about this virus was not yet known, but that, eventually, it would be. That truth has not yet come out, but again, it will. I am concerned that there has been no announcement of a formal investigation into the origins of the virus. There should be, and it should be international in scope; there is so much data to be mined in so many nations (e.g., timelines, cases, mortality rates, genetic variants), that the investigation will have to be coordinated throughout the world. Typically, the World Health Organization would be the ideal party to spearhead such a project, but this time, maybe not.

Let me adjust my tin foil hat, and tell you that I think that the Chinese government intentionally developed this virus. Their reason for developing it was to advance their nation and its interests over those of every other nation on earth – primarily economically, but also politically and militarily (get ahold of the money, and the policies and power will follow). And here's where my tin foil hat gets even shinier. BEFORE they infected their unsuspecting citizens and put them on planes to travel around the globe, spreading Christmas cheer (Antibody analysis of Red Cross blood donations indicate that the virus was spreading throughout the world in September of 2019, but no one knew then what it was.) – BEFORE any of this happened, China developed a vaccine. China's population is about 1.4 BILLION (At 331 million people, the US population is a midget by comparison, about one-fourth the size of China.). China constitutes almost twenty percent of the world's population.

This Coronavirus came from China, but how many deaths from the virus do you hear about in China? Granted, there may be many deaths in China that no one knows about... no one knows much of anything that goes on inside of China, and it's not as if their rulers particularly care about their peasants. But if the virus affected unvaccinated Chinese in anything approximating global infection and fatality rates, there would be over 1.2 MILLION dead in China alone (to date, the world-wide total is 1.8 million), and even if you're China, that's a lot of bodies to dispose of without attracting any attention. Of course, the Chinese rulers don't care if the Chinese peasants die of cancer, starvation, execution, or Covid-19.

The point, however, is that in the world's most populous nation, the nation in which this wretched plague originated, no one seems to die of it, certainly not the ruling elites. I believe that they created the virus, they created the vaccine for it, THEN they unleashed the hounds. I'll go one step further (and at this point, you really do have to have a tin foil hat). I would not put it past the Chinese to have studied the nature of the vaccine for the virus that they developed – probably several variants of it – and to have come up with a second virus, which, if you have been vaccinated for Covid, would zero in on that, and make you even more susceptible to the second infection, with a much higher mortality rate than the current 1% for the infected population. So, the answer to the question that you are by now asking, is "No." No, I would not be vaccinated today, if given the opportunity. I am not an "anti-vaxxer." I take a flu shot every year, I have been vaccinated against Shingles, and against pneumonia. My children received the MMR vaccine. But I will not be at the front of the line to be vaccinated against China's Covid. I'll let the rest of you establish herd immunity, and I'll send you a thank-you-note in a couple of years, if it all works out.

The pandemic, oddly enough, has not had much effect on my routine. I discovered that I was a natural at social distancing – I never wanted to be around most of you anyway. As it happens, Carol Jeanne and I began pioneering research into social distancing a number of years ago, about the time that she went through menopause, perhaps even before then. Additionally, I have conducted independent research into prevention of Covid through internal sterilization utilizing Scotch. Results thus far exceed the efficacy of Pfizer and Moderna, maybe even the Chinese vaccine. In an effort to assure the accuracy of my trials, I have been administering a placebo of green tea to other volunteers. Whether this constitutes a double-blind study depends on whether you are receiving green tea or Scotch, and how much of it. The results, of course, are preliminary, and will require much more field testing. This will be a very thorough study, conducted over an extended period of time. And, of course, once my study is complete, I will have to begin immediately to see if the results can be replicated, but it is the type of sacrifice that one makes in the face of a pandemic.

In the meantime, with the outbreak of the pandemic, I have played tennis once a week without fail (except for being on the Injured Reserve list for four weeks following hernia surgery in November). I have gone grocery shopping at Kroger once a week – Mike, Louis, Frank, and Sandra in produce, Sara and Carol in the deli, JR (Carol's son) in the meat department, Howard in health foods, Bryant in stocking, Miss Stephanie at checkout, Nancy, DeRita, and Tim in customer service – without incident. I used to go to Kroger on Sunday, right after church. Now we don't go to church. We sit in front of a computer, and listen to "church." So I go to Kroger on Sunday morning, but not to church. That makes sense, doesn't it? I go to Walmart on Friday mornings, after tennis, and then to the recycling center, and the Scotch store. But I do not go to church, because that wouldn't be safe. People wanted mail-in ballots and absentee ballots in record numbers for the election, because it wasn't safe to enter a polling place (I did it, in person, three times.). But I see all those same people, most of them not wearing a mask, in Kroger, Walmart, and the Scotch store (Those particular people seem not to recycle, because I don't see them there.).

There are narcissistic hypocrites in government (i.e., idiots) that tell you that you can't go to a gym or a restaurant or a church, not a wedding or a funeral, not a beach or a national park, but you CAN go to Walmart and the liquor store – even to a strip club, for the love of God. They are sworn to uphold our Constitution, but they trample it, due in large part to the fact that most of them have never read it. You have no God-given, inalienable rights. You merely have, from moment to moment, the privileges that they allow you. They draw a steady government paycheck, and a generous one at that, at your expense, and they haven't missed collecting a single one. Then they tell you that you can't go to work, you can't earn a living, you can't run your business or feed your family or pay your bills. They argue endlessly about affordable housing, while you are losing yours. They debate the merits of universal health coverage while you lose whatever you might have had, because you can't pay the premium while being unemployed for a year. And guess what else you can't pay in these circumstances? Taxes!! No sales tax on stuff that you can't afford to buy, no gasoline tax for places you aren't driving to, no income tax on money that you're not earning. I wonder what effect that might have on governmental budgets and deficits down the road.

Do these sanctimonious idiots (I'm thinking specifically of people such as Pelosi, Newsom, Cuomo, Lightfoot, and De Blasio.) give a rat's ass about your family and your misery? No, no they do not. You are a pawn in their self-important, self-righteous, condescending pissing contest (I apologize to every reader for having used that imagery, but what other way is there of seeing it? I realize that the expression is vulgar, but not nearly as offensive as the behavior of those in question.). They vote on a 6,000-page bill that NONE of them have read, send BILLIONS of dollars to foreign governments, including ten million dollars for "gender studies" in Pakistan, then they tip some of you with $600 to pay the last six months' bills, AND the next six months' as well (Any of you out there getting by on $600 a year?). I don't qualify for ANY of this because I am self-employed. I cannot be laid off. I cannot collect unemployment. These Congressional bastards do not care about me, do not care about you, and do not practice what they preach ("Rules for thee, but not for me."), but you better listen to them when they tell you to get vaccinated against Covid. You can trust them – they are from the government, and they are here to help.

Breaking news, this just in!!! Carol Jeanne has been diagnosed with Covid. The Tuesday before Christmas, she thought she had a sinus headache, and with children and grandchildren arriving, she decided to be tested. The result was negative, but after working thirty-five years in a hospital environment, Carol Jeanne is a little paranoid about this virus, and extremely cautious about all the protocols for prevention. She is the last person in the world that I would have thought would get this virus. But to be on the safe side, for the time that the kids were here, she kept her distance, wore her mask at all times, indoors and out, and did not handle food prep. The weather was mostly pleasant, so we held a lot of our family time outdoors during the day, and we even had bonfires a couple nights. The last of the kids left on Christmas Day. The next morning, Carol Jeanne realized that she had no sense of smell or taste, so she took a second test, and this time the result was positive. She had some vertigo, and a low-grade fever for a couple of days, nothing major, and her temperature is normal now. I guess that either I have it, or will have it, before it's all over, but at the moment (New Year's Day) I am fine, so far as I know. Thank goodness I started in early on the Scotch!!

. . . .

A government that robs Peter to pay Paul
can always count on the support of Paul.
George Bernard Shaw

The American republic shall endure until the day that Congress discovers it can bribe the public with the public's money.
Alexis de Tocqueville (1850)

*There is only one government institution that
needs enlarging, and that's the insane asylum.
Put all of us in there until we know enough to vote
to cut at least fifty-percent of our governing expenses.*
Will Rogers

. . . .

1999

————————

By far the biggest personal event in my life in 1999 was in having two of my cousins come to dinner at our house. Charlie and Eddie Porter attended a dental convention in Athens on September 24th, so they called and said they'd like to come to dinner. When they were growing up, everyone always called them the "little boys" (along with littlest brother Chris), only now they are grown up, and I have to use a stepladder to look them in the eye.

Over the years, I had convinced myself that I was the dominant male in our generation of the family (physically, not mentally). This was a title which I actually won in mortal combat from my senior cousin, David Darnell, in a fierce wrestling match in my driveway one summer afternoon after a hard day of cleaning houses under construction for the John Thomason Company, eating apple strudel pastries, drinking Sealtest Lemonade, and smoking Salem cigarettes, and the outcome of which David conveniently forgot about after a decade or two. He even forgot why we were fighting, which was because I said that you could bag cut grass, spread it on bare dirt, water it, and it would take root. He disagreed. He was right, but I really liked to argue back then, and the fact that I was blatantly wrong only improved the odds that we would end up fighting about it, and I liked fighting even more than arguing. Before that clash of the titans, it appeared the title of Alpha male would pass to my older brother, Rennie (who didn't even own an earth-toned suit), especially after a 7th grade growth spurt earned him the nickname "Lard." But when the growth spurt sputtered and the lard remained, he was re-christened the Alpo male instead.

Anyway, the last time I had seen the "little boys" was the preceding winter at our grandmother's funeral. At the funeral, I was secretly relieved to see that the little boys were getting a little large, mostly around the waist, thereby assuring my continued reign as King of the (Yard) Apes, despite their being half a foot taller and ten years younger. But when they cruised in for dinner in September, they had both lost so much weight that I was genuinely worried about them. After a couple of beers, I asked them if they were HIV positive. After a couple of more beers, they said no, they had just started running. After a couple of more beers, I told them I ran every day (I didn't tell them it was just to the refrigerator and back so that I wouldn't miss any of *Married, With Children*). After a couple of more beers, they said they were running fifteen miles at nine minutes a mile. Without even thinking about it (which I couldn't have anyway after so many beers), I said something to the effect that if nine-minute miles was all I had to do, then I could run from sunup to sundown. (Which wasn't a complete lie, because there was a time long, long ago, in a galaxy far, far away, when that was true.) With their trap so carefully laid, and with me walking into it so obligingly, they pounced. "Well in December," they cried, "we are going to run in a marathon (26.2 miles) on Kiawah Island!!" At the mention of Kiawah, Carol Jeanne exclaimed, "Kiawah?! That's where we went on our honeymoon! We'd love to go back to Kiawah!"

And there I was. Once again, my five-dollar mouth had overloaded my fifty-cent ass, and I had no way to duck this marathon thing and keep my self-respect. Of course, I would have gladly abandoned my self-respect – it's not like I have that much of it – if I could have thought of any excuse, but there had simply been too much beer! Curse you, beer!! Out, damned beer!! I banish you from my kingdom forever!!! The following morning, severely hung-over, I rode out a training course in the car, came back to the house, selected a pair of swimming trunks (I didn't own any running shorts.), and ran four miles. I started out thinking I was going to die and ended up hoping I would. I was ready to junk the whole notion and have a cold one, but then I had a stroke, which was quickly followed by a stroke of inspiration. Back at the house, after stripping off my soaking wet clothes, I held my swim trunks to the sky – much like Scarlett O'Hara clutching the Georgia clay – and vowed, "As God is my witness, I will never be this clean again!" And so was born the germ of an idea, along with many germs. I would train for this marathon, I would pound the pavement, I would log my mindless miles. *But!* I would *not*, under any circumstance, wash these swim trunks-cum-marathon-shorts until *after* the race was over, a scant but humid eleven weeks away!

And so it was. On December 10th I arrived on Kiawah Island, which is Indian... oops, I meant to say Native American. I don't want to offend any Native Americans because I am one, too. Anyway, Kiawah is Engine for "shorts that stand in the corner on their own." I was slathered in sun screen and Bengay ointment, but it was not enough. Even encased in a zip-lock baggie, the shorts lived and breathed (or gagged) a life of their own.

December 11th dawned warm and breezy, perfect weather for The Shorts. With 1,500 runners registered for the marathon, the starting line was a log jam. Miraculously, I was able to find a spot right at the front where no one else wanted to stand, so I got off to a very good start. I quickly fell into position behind an Oriental gal named Sonja, who offered to pace me for the first twenty miles, before she "kicked the last 6.2 miles." I didn't know what any of that meant, because Sonja had a ponytail and the other kind of tail that moved like metronomes, and I was hypnotized. Sonja proceeded to click off eight-minute miles like a machine, and I proceeded to study her form. But alas, when she finally began her kick, not even lust could keep me a-breast of her. With six miles of the unknown before me, I felt completely abandoned.

Then, from behind me, I heard the heavy footfall of One Who Is Large. Gradually she pulled along side of me, and then proceeded to pass me... and pass me... and pass me. Have you ever seen the Saturday Night Live skit about the family with the big butts, really huge butts that you could put a serving tray on and it wouldn't fall off? This girl was one of them, and she was passing me! She had two runner's numbers, one for her and one for her butt. That's when my male pride (I know, it's an oxymoron.) kicked in. No way was this girl (She looked to be about eighteen years old, and I'm assuming her butt was roughly the same age, depending on which part was born first.) going to beat me. So I began to de-vise a plan. Being both an engineer and a redneck, I understood the principle of slipstreams. "I'll fall in behind Chunky Cheeks," I thought, "like Bill Elliott behind Darrell Jarrett, and I'll coast right behind her until the finish line, then blow her away." I then proceeded to enact my great strategy, and that's when it all fell apart. There was no slipstream, only severe wake turbulence!! It was like trying to take off in a single-engine Cessna behind a departing C-140 transport. I was blown to the curb and through a dense hedge, and even though I managed to return to the race, I knew that all hopes of beating Big Buns were gone. The best I could do was a 3:33 (8 minutes, 8 seconds per mile for 26.2 miles) finish, which placed me in 242nd place out of 1,499 runners and the Human Hippo. For my age group, that qualified me for the Boston Marathon. And it was good enough to allow me to whip my cousins and retain the family crown. So, Charlie and Eddie, when you read this, "Merry Christmas, Little Boys!"

Marathon Epilogue

———————————

Dear Charlie and Eddie,

I'm taking a minute to write you guys because I'm too sore to do anything else! What a great weekend!! I don't think the two of you realize how much you accomplished, and how much you have to be proud of. First of all, thanks so much for having taken the time to call me and let me know you were going to be in Athens for your dental convention back in September. If you hadn't made that one, simple gesture, none of the rest of this would have happened for me. Second, thanks for inviting my family to join all of you in Kiawah. I'm so glad that all of our kids got the chance to meet one another. I can't wait to see the pictures. Send us copies of any good ones, and we'll do the same.

I really, really, *really* want the two of you to appreciate a simple truth. In all of life's great adventures, the treasure is in the *journey*, not the destination. You put together a great group of guys, quality people and quality friends, and formed the 4 AM Club. You trained and shared and hurt and hoped together, and that is what you'll remember the most. I can't imagine finding the time and energy to have done that when I was your age and at that point in family and career.

This marathon business was a great adventure for the two of you to undertake as brothers, and you have added a special bond to that relationship that I cannot imagine sharing with my own brothers, and I envy you for that. *That really is special*, so tuck those memories away for safe keeping. One day, when you're old and gray like me, you'll want to drag those memories out to keep you warm.

Thanks for including me in your adventure. My journey to

get there was a little different, but I enjoyed the training and learning some things about myself (You get a lot of time to think when you do twenty-milers solo!). I really enjoyed hearing from the two of you along the way and swapping stories, progress reports, and aches (and alcoholism). For all of us to make it to the big day in one piece and to finish the damn thing is amazing and humbling at the same time. I spent the last two weeks paranoid of hangnails and coughs, and went through enough ice and aspirin to sink a battleship. Carol Jeanne told me that as part of my post-training taper that we could have sex again after the first of the year!

I am proud of you both. You are fine young men, good husbands, and devoted fathers. You have married ladies of great substance. You are making so many good choices and doing so many of the right things in life. Your lives are so full and hectic right now... remember to take the time to step back and be aware of how good life is and what joyous times you're experiencing, especially with your children. And remember to be *grateful* for every single, precious moment. Thanks again for everything. I love you guys, but the next time I run anywhere, there's gonna be a large man with a weapon right behind me!!!

....

Life is what happens while you're making other plans.
John Lennon

If you want to make God laugh, tell him your plans.
Yiddish Proverb

....

This year's entry from the pet department comes courtesy of our dogs. It was a Sunday afternoon, and I was out working on a stone wall. The dogs were in the woods barking and growling, which was nothing remarkable. We live in the sticks, and there's always something for the dogs to bark at: a squirrel, a lizard, or the UPS lady. Most anything will do. This time, however, there was a distinctly different pitch to the frenzy, and after a couple of hours, I decided to check it out. Whatever it was, it was down in the creek below the house.

When I came up on them, McKenzie, my Jack Russell Terrorist, was in full cry, but nowhere to be seen. I could hear her up under the creek bank, barking, growling, whining, and yipping all at once. Just about then, she exploded backwards from a small hole in the bank as if shot from a cannon. She was Georgia-clay red over her entire body and dripping wet. The only thing that wasn't red was her eyes. Since they were in the creek, I figured it was a coon or a 'possum, but it just as easily could've been a snake or a crawdad. I was wrong. Whatever it was they had cornered, it picked that moment to announce its extreme displeasure. From deep within the creek bank came an even deeper growl, and I mean it was mad. Zoe, our border collie, heard that growl, looked up at me, and quoted Mohammed Ali, saying, "I ain't got nothing against no Viet Cong." With that, she departed for the sanctuary of the carport. The three terriers and the hound, Ginny, went berserk.

They dove into that bank, digging for all they were worth. They had mud flying between their legs, roots ripping between their jaws, and water going everywhere. The focus of their attentions was an old stump in the bank. Whatever it was they were after – and it was becoming increasingly ill – was clearly in the void behind that stump. That's when I got the bright idea to fetch a shovel. I figured I could dig downward from the top of the bank and expose whatever it was that was in there. For the record, my bet had switched from raccoon to Linda Blair. I don't know if it was throwing up pea-green soup, but it was making the same guttural groanings as in *The Exorcist*. Well, just about the time I got the hole to that stump opened up, McKenzie flashed by, and down the hole she went. All hell broke loose. She popped back out, momentarily, and was covered with blood, but whose I couldn't tell. Down below, the other dogs broke through on the backside of the stump and the race was on.

There came a roar from under that creek bank that convinced me those dogs had cornered a bobcat. What erupted from that hole was a twelve-inch high, three-foot long, gunmetal-gray otter that was seriously mad. The dogs were in this for high drama and entertainment. The otter was in it for survival. The dogs were about to learn the difference.

Down the creek the otter went, with four dogs hot on her trail. Just about the time the dogs would catch up to the otter, it would come to a pool in the creek, and dive into it. It would swirl around and muddy up the water, and I swear it knew what it was doing. While the dogs plumbed the depths of the pool, over to one side or the other, you'd see these nostrils poke up out of the water like a submarine periscope. Sooner or later, one dog or another would probe in just the wrong spot, and that otter would latch onto its snout with jaws like vise grips. There'd be a murderous yelp and whipping of the head, and the race would be on again. That otter's teeth were sharper than a knife, and it was quickly apparent that the dogs were outmatched.

Envisioning the vet bill to get them all sewed up, I was running down the creek snapping up dogs as fast as I could, and soon was covered in muck and blood. Three of the four dogs were grateful for the excuse to retire from the field of battle, but not McKenzie. It took several more efforts to corral her, and by then she was hardly recognizable. She was missing parts of ears, was bleeding like a butchered hog, and had several flaps of skin dangling from her snout that I later clipped off with a pair of kitchen shears. She looked like she had come out on the short end of a straight-razor fight in the wrong part of town on a Saturday night. It took about three tubes of Neosporin ointment to get her healed up, and her snout still bears the scars. As I dragged her up the hill in retreat, that otter looked at me, rolled its eyes, and I swear the look on its face said, "Dumbass." I could hardly have argued the point.

....

The difference between genius and stupidity
is that genius has its limits.
Albert Einstein

....

2003

‒ ‒ ‒ ‒ ‒ ‒ ‒ ‒

This year marked the 100th anniversary of my grandfather Cy's birthday, January 26th, 1903. I have now lived twice as many years without him as I did in his shadow. I once determined to extract from Cy an admission as to the most shameful thing he had ever done. Just why I took on this crusade, I do not recall. Probably it was a plot to later extort chewing tobacco from him. I had tried that once before. On our way out to his brother Dan's farm for Sunday dinner, I had asked him what we would be eating. "Knowing Avery (Dan's wife), we'll probably be eating mustard greens and chittlins," he replied. When I asked him what that meant, he obfuscated. Sensing I was onto something, I pressed him. "Never mind," he said. I told him that if he didn't give me a chew of tobacco when we got there, I would ask Avery if we were having chittlins. He gave me a cold stare and said, "That would not be a very gentlemanly thing to do." That was the last of that.

At any rate, Cy Hood wasn't about to confess any act of shame that would have truly appeared on his Top 100 countdown. What he did confess to me was that his father had once bought him a pair of shoes, which were pretty much optional equipment in those days, and new ones were unheard of and no doubt a source of great envy to his six brothers and maybe even to his sister, Martha. The problem was, Cy didn't like the shoes. Out near the barn there was a tool shed. In the tool shed was a foot-cranked whetstone for sharpening farm implements – plows, scythes, knives, and such. Cy snuck out there with that pair of shoes, and by suppertime those shoes were shot. A few weeks later he presented them to his father and reckoned as how they must've been pretty cheap shoes. He honestly bore that shame sixty years later.

It reminded me of the time I had the mumps. My little brother and I rode with my father up to Dr. Lewis' drug store. I don't know why we called him "Dr." Lewis, as he was a pharmacist, but we did. I can remember as a little kid – I couldn't have been five years old – being in Dr. Lewis's with my Father and Mother, when Dr. Lewis proudly displayed a bottle of Johnson's Shampoo in a *plastic* bottle! It was one of the first ever made. Can you believe that before that, shampoo bottles were made out of glass? Think about that: kids, water, shampoo, cast-iron tubs, and glass bottles! Dr. Lewis commented on how much lighter and safer the plastic bottles were than the glass ones. To prove his point, he handed me the glass-bottle version. "Now be careful with that; it's glass, not plastic, and if you drop it, it will break." Is there anyone who doesn't know what happened next? While Dr. Lewis went for the mop and bucket, my father rolled his eyes at me and said, "Dumbass." I could hardly have argued the point.

Anyway, when we pulled up in front of the drugstore, Chris told me I couldn't go inside the drugstore since I had the mumps. This is my first recollection of the worldwide conspiracy to treat me unfairly, which prompted me to whine, "That's not fair!" Chris said, "Fair is where you go to get cotton candy. Stay in the car. We'll be back in a minute, and I'll bring you a special treat."

A minute later, out came my brother, who, incidentally, didn't realize that the reason he had been sent along on this trip was so that he would catch the mumps, and Ruth could cut the convalescence time in half. This is the way it was back then. If a Darnell cousin came down with the measles, all the Hoods got loaded into the car to go "visit" them. Ruth would admonish, "Y'all go outside and play, and don't come back 'til you're covered with red, viral blotches." I never heard June Cleaver say anything like that! Anyway, my brother came walking out carrying two ice cream cones. His cone was one scoop of chocolate, our standard fare. Mine, however, was a scoop of chocolate topped with a scoop of fudge-ripple! I had never had fudge-ripple before, but that didn't stop me from making up my mind before it ever made it to the car that I didn't like fudge-ripple. I had been transgressed, and I wasn't about to be bought off with some sorry-ass ice cream cone. I was descended of Scots, by thunder, and I learned early and deep the meaning of our national motto, "*Nemo Me Impune Laecessit*" – No One Attacks Me With Impunity!

My brother got in the car, handed me my cone and said, "Here. Daddy said you get two scoops since you're sick." I hand-cranked the window of that old, black Plymouth down and fired that ice cream cone straight into the parking lot. I never so much as licked it. When Chris walked out, he saw his ice cream cone standing headfirst on the asphalt. Instead of beating the hell out of me like I deserved – and like he did on most every other occasion – he never said a word. Got in the car and drove us home. Cy, I learned the hard way the shame of behaving in an ungentlemanly fashion. I sure hope your Daddy understood about them shoes.

. . . .

Ships in harbor are safe, but that's not what ships are for.
John A. Shedd

Smooth sailing never made a skilled sailor.
Franklin D. Roosevelt

. . . .

Here's a poem that I wrote:

Valentine

Come and sit beside me.
Tell me that you love me.
Talk to me for hours.
Show me all your dreams.

You're my solid anchor.
You're my voice of reason.
You hold my world together
when it's tearing at the seams.

With your arms around me,
I'm as good as others.
They're my mighty fortress.
They hold out all my fears.

I know I don't deserve you,
but oh how much I need you.
If I were to lose you,
I'd give my life away.

So say you'll never leave me;
you always will receive me.

Each night you will restore me
to face another day.

With your arms around me,
with your love inside me,
knowing that you trust me,
how could I ever fail?

. . . .

Charm is a way of getting the answer 'Yes,'
without asking a clear question.
Albert Camus

. . . .

2021
———————————

Over the past four years in North Georgia, we have been
invaded by a non-native species of spider. The Joro spider arrived
from Japan. It spins webs unlike anything you have seen before.
For one thing, their silk is the stickiest spider silk you will ever
touch. And it is strong! You can get wrapped up in it, and it's almost impossible to break. Also, their silk is bright gold; it's really
quite beautiful in the sunlight. They spin their webs a little higher
than most spiders do, but if you walk into one at head level, you'll
find yourself in a mess. Finally, their webs are three-dimensional,
not two, like most spiders. Their webs are giant jungle-gyms of
bright gold stickiness, and they are often communal. The female is
much larger than the male, and very colorful. A fully developed
female Joro will cover the palm of your hand.

A female Joro spider. Coming soon to a theater near you!

. . . .

What are the odds of seeing a pair of snails mating?
Forget that. What are the odds of seeing two pairs of snails
mating at the same time? You gotta pay attention in this old
world, or you're gonna miss out on a lot of stuff!

. . . .

In the spirit of *Napoleon Dynamite* (José for President!), here, totally disconnected from any vein of continuity or pretense of segue, is a list of things I have NEVER done or seen. I have never been to Disney Land or Disney World. I have never seen a single episode of any show about any Apprentice, Survivor, or Idol. Nor any show where celebrities dance or try to lose weight, or where common people eat worm turds. The only Desperate Housewife I know is my own. The only Sopranos with which I am familiar are in our church choir. I have never seen *Sex and the City*, although Carol Jeanne and I spent a night in Atlanta once. My version of a palm pilot is writing notes in the palm of my hand. A Blackberry is something you pick in July, and when you're done you want to check for ticks and chiggers (Putting some sulfur in your socks before you go will help.). I've never touched an iPod, play station, game boy, or choir boy... whatever they are. I have never accessed an ATM (When I was an engineer, ATM stood for Asynchronous Transfer Mode, but somehow I don't think that's what the rest of you are talking about). I have never been on Facebook. I have never Tweeted. I have never programmed a telephone number into my cell phone. I do not understand when people ask about your PIN Number. As I understand it, PIN is an acronym for Personal Identification Number, so asking for your PIN number means asking what is your Personal Identification Number number? If someone asked you for your social security number number, your zip code code, or for your email address address, you'd put a little extra space between the two of you, but nobody except me is paying attention to details anymore.

And while we're at it, here is a list of things that I have never paid for: someone to haul my trash, someone to change the oil in my vehicles, someone to cut my hair, anyone to cut my grass or clean my gutters, someone to wash my vehicles (I am probably the last person you know that still waxes his vehicles [every three months!]), someone to rotate my tires, paint anything. I have never paid interest on a monthly credit card bill.

....

We are all lying in the gutter,
but some of us are gazing at the stars.
Oscar Wilde

....

February 26, 1993

To The Editor
The Oconee Enterprise
Watkinsville, Georgia

Does the state flag of Georgia symbolize our state's history, my heritage, and patriotism? For a majority of our citizens, the answer is yes. Is this the only flag design that can accomplish that goal? The answer is no. Does our flag symbolize bigotry, segregation, prejudice, repression, and suffering? For a significant segment of citizens, the answer is yes.

Regardless of whether you agree with these people, how could any rational person not understand why the Confederate battle-emblem flag is hurtful to them? Does not even the most fleeting acquaintance with history reasonably require one to understand why some citizens feel that our flag symbolizes negative values? Doesn't historic fact justify their feelings, even if my experience has been different? If so, then the issue of the current flag should be a moot point. This is precisely why this issue should NOT be resolved by a majority vote. To attempt to do so would be akin to a referendum on whether blacks could hold elective office. In this theoretical referendum, a theoretical majority might vote in favor of the ban, but that would not make it right.

The flag is significant, and the notion of changing it is volatile, because it is a symbol. It would be a mistake to underestimate the value people place in their symbols. Symbolically, we wish to be what we stand for, not what we actually are. Ideologically, we are not what we have become, but what we aspire to be. This is precisely why our flag will eventually be changed... it falls short of our aspirations, our potential.

Although the current flag does not threaten me, the reasons for many citizens' opposition to it are both obvious and understand-able. I should, therefore, be not only willing, but also insistent, that a non-hurtful, non-divisive, alternative be established. Although no new design will be all things to all people, it should be a simple endeavor to find one that is acceptable to most without being demeaning to any. If there is any challenge in such an endeavor, it is the challenge of opportunity. For example, have a contest in the schools throughout the state to design a new flag. Perhaps you could appoint an advisory board of veterans, university history professors, and artists to create a new symbol, a new image. The possibilities are limited only by the extent of our collective imagination. And remember, "None of us is as smart as all of us."

The Civil War is over. It should no more *directly* impact our lives tomorrow than the Revolutionary War or the First World War. The Confederacy fought for some valid and valiant principals, states' rights being foremost among them. The Confederacy fared no better than did Thomas Jefferson against John Marshall on that point, yet no one is obsessed with carrying Jefferson's torch today. The Confederate States of America were defeated by the United States of America. Would any rational adult hope for less? Who among us would seek to hold title to another human? Why do we struggle to honor our forbearers by deluding ourselves that we can hold onto a society and culture that they themselves abandoned?

Perhaps the patriotic Southerner, seeking to honor his Confederate ancestors, would do well to recall the words of Lieutenant-General Nathan Bedford Forrest as he addressed his troops in surrender:

> That we are beaten is a self-evident fact. The government which we sought to establish and perpetuate is at an end. Reason dictates, and humanity demands, that no more blood be shed. I have never on the field of battle sent you where I was unwilling to go myself, nor would I now advise you to a course which I am unwilling to pursue. You have been good soldiers, you can be good citizens. Obey the laws, preserve your honor, and the government to which you have surrendered can afford to be, and will be, magnanimous.

The ultimate responsibility of that magnanimous government is the preservation and perpetuation of the constitutional and civil rights of its citizens. Can we begrudge a fellow citizen's skepticism of his government's ability to perform its duties, to protect his rights, when that government presents itself to its citizens, *symbolically*, as separate and unequal?

. . . .

If, in the past few years, you have not discarded a major opinion or acquired a new one, check your pulse. You may be dead.
Gelett Burgess

. . . .

September 10, 2005

To The Editor
Athens Banner-Herald

Election Day was a big shocker this year. Homosexual marriage was voted down – in California of all places. [Editor's Note: I am a grown man, comfortable with my own sexual identity (even if that identity is that of a "missing person"), not threatened by your sexual identity, and not afraid to discuss this matter. If you feel otherwise, please skip ahead to the next story.] I suppose you could attempt to argue this subject – either way – on the basis of personal preference, morality, or what you consider to be "normal" (for you), but I cannot for the life of me honestly say, or see, how anyone could deny that this, under the rule of law, is anything other than blatant prejudice against homosexuals. You might not practice it, you might not agree with it, you might have perceived religious reasons for being opposed to it, but none of that has anything to do with the matter at hand, which is, in fact, a question of constitutionality.

But that makes little difference in our culture. It is much too terribly difficult for us to separate the remote threat of a latent homosexual tendency – lurking in the deep, dark recesses of our own subconscious – from someone else's actual practice of it, to let us contemplate the subject rationally. And so, rather than merely disagreeing with it, or more conveniently, simply ignoring it, we strike out against it, often vehemently.

Our social persecution against those who are different from us, and who seek equal protection under the law for their version of a legal union, begs our remembrance of the good old days, when life was simpler, and all we had to hate were Jews and niggers. Give us a sheet and a torch, and we were good to go. By sunup, with virtue intact and values preserved, we could turn our attention, and our angst, towards Catholics. Thank God our forefathers were so quick to hunt witches – today they have been almost completely eradicated.

The Bible clearly states, or at least vaguely infers, that homosexuality is an abomination – at least twice – along with other deviant behavior such as wearing cloth woven of two different fibers, or plowing with an ox and an ass yoked together. I don't know about you, but in the 21st century, I am not convinced of the need to base my worldview of someone else's sexuality upon a five-thousand-year-old transcription of a no-longer-extant document from a society/culture/civilization that thought the world was flat and that the sun orbited the earth. God gave David numerous wives and concubines (yet David still had to murder Uriah in order to get a shot a Bathsheba, who later bore him a son named Solomon), so those polygamist unions were holy and blessed, ordained by no less than God. The Silent Majority is really silent about God's implementation of the institution of polygamy. For that matter, they are pretty silent about the Biblical institution of slavery, as well.

The question of homosexual marriage cannot be determined by ballot – it is not an issue to be resolved by proposition of the electorate. Would a majority vote banning miscegenation legitimate the prejudice of two consenting adults finding love in an interracial marriage? What if a majority voted to require Jews to wear a yellow Star Of David? If only men could vote, and they voted to deny female suffrage, would that be constitutional? Or has most of society already lived through – and past – that mentality? Ella Wheeler Wilcox said, "To sin by silence, when they should protest, makes cowards of men." I must, therefore, publicly protest this injustice.

I once heard a preacher (This one was of a Presbyterian persuasion.) say, "The only orgasm in the world that is any business of yours is your own. Do not concern yourself with anyone else's. It is none of your business." Well that, of course, is simply brilliant. Not only is it short, sweet, and simple, it is absolutely true. If you grab onto that thought, you can let go of a bunch of other crap that wasn't anything more than dead weight in your brain, and move on to something that might actually be productive (The problem with the preacher's statement, of course, is that most folks who would disagree with it are not having orgasms of their own with which they might occupy their attention, and thus feel the compulsion to interfere with those of others.). I absolutely hate being put in a position of defending Rosie O'Donnell, but the simple fact of the matter is that she is right (but *only* on this one point). If women want to marry women, I say let them. Why should only men have to suffer that torment?

Now if a church doesn't want to condone such behavior, that is perfectly alright. Actually, it's more than alright... it is *a right* (the real, God-given, unalienable type). Everyone go to a neutral corner, and at the next meeting (deacons, elders, board, trustees, missions, whatever), come out fighting like a man (or a sissy, as the case may be). If a church wants to ban homosexual marriage, that is perfectly okay, because marriage is essentially a church institution (albeit licensed by the State), and churches are private entities, entitled to endorse, or ban, whatever member behavior they wish, just like the Boy Scouts. Please note, however, that the ice begins to crack when churches wish to extend their prohibitions and control of individual behavior beyond their membership rolls and onto the general public.

But it ain't okay for the government to deny the right to government-recognized partnership, or civil union. Homosexual unions, among other things, are like television: if you don't like what's playing, turn the channel, no one is holding a gun to your head. But for the State to deny equal access – under the law – to a civil union between two consenting adults is oppression and prejudice and discrimination. It is an intrusion into the private lives of its citizens that denies their liberty and pursuit of happiness. It's also naïve at best, and hypocritical at worst. Just what, other than a civil union, does anyone think they have prevented in California? Not relationships, not affection and caring, not bumping uglies! That's all still out there, still going on. Only now it's not a problem, if you can just remember one simple thing: it's none of your business!

. . . .

People change, and forget to tell each other.
Lillian Hellman

. . . .

September 9, 2015

To the Editor
Athens Banner-Herald
A Bridge Too Far

I disagree with Joshua Eaton's assertion that all vestiges of the Confederacy be eliminated from public discourse ("Athens should turn away from its Confederate past," September 3rd). My support for eliminating governmental use of the Confederate flag is well documented ("Confederate flag should come down from public places," July 7th). However, what Eaton proposes is nothing short of radical, historical revisionism on a scale not seen since post World War II Japan.

Eaton suggests that we rename public streets and parks that bear the names of those linked to the Confederacy. What crimes did these people commit in the cultural-historical-legal context of their times? I wonder how his notions would be received in Fitzgerald, Georgia, where all of the streets that run North-South are named after generals and leaders of the Civil War (both Confederate and Union, and that includes Sherman!).

Presumably Eaton would deem it acceptable for a public street or building to be named for Abraham Lincoln, but not for Robert E. Lee. If Confederates are less than perfect in the lens of retrospection, where shall we draw the line? Shall we eliminate the name of George Washington from the American tableau? After all, he was a Southerner, and he owned slaves. How about Thomas Jefferson? Not only was he a Southern slave owner, he also impregnated at least one of them, and as we all know, by today's standards that is not acceptable workplace behavior.

It follows logically that no public facility can be named after anything having to do with Christianity, as historical events such as the Crusades and the Inquisition intruded upon the human rights of countless tens of thousands; so things named "Saint This" or "Saint That" or "Our Lady" or even "Billy Graham" must also go. Possibly readers of this column could think up even more extreme and ridiculous examples of this nonsense. If feet of clay disqualify a person from being memorialized for any compassionate, noble, or honorable deed that they accomplished, then no such practice would exist.

Eaton quotes the apostle Paul, but fails to note that Paul directed slaves to be in submission to their masters. Eaton admonishes "white Athenians to admit that our ancestors were wrong." Is there anyone in Athens today, of any color, claiming that we need to return to slavery (or child labor, or the times of denying women suffrage)? Eaton says that Athens' double-barrel cannon is a legacy of Confederate insurrection that "points defiantly toward Washington, D.C." I would say that's a rather subjective statement, one that lends a connotation to an artifact that has never crossed my mind in the almost forty years that I have lived here. Eaton goes on to state that the cannon is a subversive threat to the federal government, "...as if to say, 'We can take back Lee's surrender any time.'" That is, of course, an anthropomorphic statement, as well as an inane prospect.

Finally, Eaton castigates memorials to those who died in defense of their nation, the Confederate States of America. Those fallen dead were on the wrong side of history and a great moral dilemma, readily observable but of infinitely complex resolution. How unfortunate that Eaton did not live alongside Lincoln, so that he could have magnanimously bestowed his prescient wisdom on the great unwashed. Then the Confederate families of those who also "gave the last full measure of devotion" (to quote Mr. Lincoln, as he applied that phrase to both Union and Confederate casualties at Gettysburg) could have been spared their misguided pride, love, and grief.

Opposition to the governmental use of the Confederate flag is understandable and an egregious affront that demands resolution, but Eaton's complaint is naive and self-absorbed. Eaton has constitutional rights, but the right to never be offended is not among them. This is not a worthy battle – it is a bridge too far.

. . . .

Don't wrestle with a pig. You'll get dirty, and the pig will enjoy it.
George Bernhard Shaw

. . . .

2005

I had an editorial published in the local paper this year. Back in August, around the anniversary of Hiroshima and Nagasaki bombings, the paper ran a number of articles on the event. If they weren't downright apologetic about what happened, they were very sympathetic to anyone who wanted to do so. I thought this to be worth sharing with you:

August 7, 2005
To The Editor
Athens Banner-Herald

I read with interest and empathy the Associated Press article of August 7th by Eric Talmadge ("Atomic Bombing Victims Honored"). It was well reported and well written. Japan's Prime Minister Junichiro Koizumi vows that Japan will be a leader in the international movement against nuclear proliferation. He is quoted saying, "I offer deep prayers from my heart to those who were killed." Hiroshima Mayor Tadatoshi Akiba states that the United States, Russia, and other members of the "nuclear club" are "jeopardizing human survival." He states, "We seek to comfort the souls of all the victims by declaring that we humbly reaffirm our responsibility never to repeat the evil."

By "the evil," I assume he refers to America's use of atomic weapons. Based on that assumption, I also assume that he does NOT refer to the murder by the Japanese government of innocent American citizens while they slept in their ships, soon to become their tombs, on the morning of December 7, 1941. The cowardice and infamy of this act of terrorism far exceeds that of September 11, 2001. I must also assume that Mayor Akiba does not refer to the Bataan Death March, the Palawan Massacre, or the enslavement of American military personnel for forced labor AFTER the surrender of the Japanese Emperor. Prime Minister Koizumi offers prayers, but does not say to whom he prays... is it the Emperor, who was worshipped as God?

I do not find anywhere in this article where the Japanese officials express remorse for the actions of their government in causing the loss of life of hundreds of thousands of Americans. I do not read where they apologize for the actions of their government that brought down upon the people of Hiroshima and Nagasaki the atomic bombs they protest. Nowhere do I read their confession that, as terrible as the war and all its associated death was, they brought it on themselves, and ultimately received their just reward. The article concludes by stating that this year, *sixty years after the fact*, that 5,373 more Japanese were added to the casualty list of Hiroshima as a result of "bomb-related ailments." That's less than American Marine casualties at Iwo Jima. To the Prime Minister of Japan and the Mayor of Hiroshima I offer this Latin phrase, "Nemo me impune lacessit." If they do not read Latin, then share with them this translation - "No one attacks me with impunity."

....

You can blow up a man with gunpowder in half a second,
while it may take twenty years to blow him up with a book.
But the gunpowder destroys itself along with its victim,
while a book can keep on exploding for centuries.
Christopher Morley

....

Here's a poem that I wrote:

Captain John Miller
In honor of the soldier in *Saving Private Ryan*

Had I not died upon that barricade,
did I not lie beneath Spring's shade,
if my time had been fulfilled,
had life not been so suddenly stilled,

had Death crossed alone that battered hill,
postponed its claim on another kill,
left me alive rather than dead,
pillowed in silk upon my bed,

had I awaited that rendezvous in vain,
or deserted the grave in which I was lain,
if I was allowed to finish the game,
would the world have been the same?

I see them now, sifted row by row,
lost opportunities like poppies blow.
Dreams of a generation collect
dust beneath a shroud of neglect.

What might I have done with my life...
fallen in love and taken a wife?
To her and to ours have been true,
to have known hello before adieu?

Perhaps a chance mankind to serve,
to know my duty and never swerve.
Would it matter if I should live,
and to the greater good I give?

Have I not done exactly this?
Can I not also enter Bliss?
Fate alike awaits us all,
each subdued by Death's dark thrall.

Those who hold the torch on high,
keep the faith until you die.
I shall have to be content
with my life as it was spent.

. . . .

*What great cause was ever fought for and won
under the banner of, "I stand for consensus?"*
Margaret Thatcher

. . . .

2003

A study by the Massachusetts Institute of Technology *and* the University of Chicago Graduate School of Business found that "it helps to have a white-sounding first name when looking for work." Can you believe that it took *both* of these stellar academic institutions to investigate this phenomenon? Did you know that names like "Brett, Greg, and Jill" are "white" names? "Black" names, according to the greater intellects at MIT, include "Rasheed, Tyrone, and Tamika." Just out of curiosity, I checked the birth announcements in this morning's newspaper. *This is absolutely the truth.* First of all, 60% of all announced births were to a single parent (i.e., Ms. So-and-So, not Mr. and Mrs.). Second, I found the following names listed. *Do not think that I am making this up.* Pretend that you have a Ph.D. and that you teach at MIT and you are not DUM. Analyze the following names, and categorize them as either "white" or "black":

Freddarius Keontai Woodall
La-Sheena Takisha Wynn
Valdarius T'Montae Cooper
Malachi Tabaious Gordon
Ke'Yantee Kinorrus Thomas
De'Shaun Zy'Quavious Charles
Quartavius Moon

Of these names, my favorite is Quartavius. I guess his dad must've been Pintavius, and someday he will have a son, Gallonius. These are real names of real people in our semi-real newspaper. All of them were born to a single mother. No wonder these kids drop out of school by the ninth grade. I would too if I couldn't pronounce my own name, much less spell it! I'll bet you a thousand bucks that their own mothers could never spell it the same way twice. Makes you long for the good ol' days... Leroy, Roosevelt, Chicken George.

. . . .

The less we are able to laugh at ourselves,
the more it becomes necessary for others to laugh at us.
Reinhold Niebuhr

. . . .

2001

As I sit here writing the Christmas 2001 Newsletter, it's actually January 2, 2002. It is snowing outside, and has been since 10:00 this morning. A big winter storm is sweeping the Southeast.

And the farther south and the farther east you go, the more snow there is, more than in the mountains. (I wonder if my mother, Ruth, will say I should have said "further" rather than "farther. She has a thing about that. Not as big a thing as the proper usage of "lay" and "lie," but bigger than the difference between "well" and "good."). It's coming down (the snow, not Ruth), but it ain't sticking to anything more than a few blades of grass, and yet there is not a loaf of bread nor a gallon of milk left on a store shelf from New Orleans to Richmond. Can you imagine the potential for chaos? What if Scotch drinkers behaved that way, rushing to the package store and forcing some fellow drinker to have to settle for a blend, or even Irish whisky or rye? Totally uncivilized.

At any rate, we are quietly enjoying the first snow of the year and of the millennium (didn't snow at all in 2001, the first year of the millennium). We like a little snow, but not too much. We can't drive (even when there isn't any snow) and if it gets too heavy, we lose our electricity. Now you can live a while without electricity. We have a wood stove in the basement, and it can drive you right out of the house, it gets so hot. Gives you heat and cooking all in one shot, just like the real old days, before men discovered electricity and invented electric ovens, and women discovered carry-out.

Anyway, when the electricity's out, you feel a little foolish walking into a room and hitting the light switch for the tenth time when you know damn well the thing ain't coming on... just force of habit, same thing with the TV clicker. No, when you live in the sticks like we do, the real tragedy of a power failure is water. More precisely, the lack thereof. No electricity, no well, no water, no toilet. If you're a guy, no problem. We live in the middle of fifteen acres, and I keep my territory marked. But when you live in a house with four women, they're gonna avail themselves of the facilities and *then* think about flushing (men, see TV clicker above). That would become problematic except that during one power outage I pointed out to the women that they could easily provide the necessary flushing power by simply dipping a bucket into the creek out back and refilling the tank. Once the women got over the fact that the toilets could be made to flush without electricity (I swear they think it's plugged into a circuit somewhere in the floor), they quickly figured out that rather than visiting the creek a bucket at a time, it would be much more time efficient to have Dad fill up a trash can (a bucket at a time) and dump it into the bathtub (a hernia at a time). Anyway, here's praying that the lights stay lit! Speaking of lit, it's time for a Scotch.

Ok, that's much better. Let's see now, where were we? Oh yes, driving. Speaking of driving, or more precisely, our inability to drive, I would like to point out to the idiots on our local Eyewitness News Team (team motto, "If it bleeds, it leads") that there is only one cause for road rage. It has nothing to do with cell phones, stressful lifestyles, or long commutes. It has to do with idiots (some of whom are *not* on the Eyewitness News Team) who drive in the left lane doing the speed limit. They drive with one eye on the speedometer (their motto, "If they meant 56, they wouldn't have posted 55") and the other eye in their rearview mirror. God bless them, they honestly cannot understand why the person behind them is two inches off their bumper, flashing their bright lights. Nor can they understand why the seventy cars backed up behind the guy behind them are doing the same thing! It used to be called the *passing* lane. Now it's just the outside lane and it's just for passing time and it's full of rage.

It's getting a little late now. I'm going to go bundle up, turn on the floodlights, sit on my back porch, and watch it snow for a while. Then I'm going to bed!

. . . .

Well this beats anything I've ever seen. It has slap snowed steady in Georgia (and I mean all of it, especially Augusta) for over twenty-four hours. It still ain't stuck to the roads or power lines, but it's foot deep on everything else. Quite beautiful. I can sit on my back porch and literally hear the snow coming down...

Whose woods these are I think I know.
His house is in the village though;
He will not see me stopping here
To watch his woods fill up with snow.

My little horse must think it queer
To stop without a farmhouse near
Between the wood and frozen lake
The darkest evening of the year.

He gives his harness bells a shake
To ask if there is some mistake.
The only other sound's the sweep
Of easy wind and downy flake.

The woods are lovely, dark and deep.
But I have promises to keep,
And miles to go before I sleep,
And miles to go before I sleep.

Or how 'bout:

When I see birches bend to left and right
Across the lines of straighter, darker trees
I like to think some boy's been swinging on them
But swinging doesn't bend them down to stay
As ice storms do...

So I was once myself a swinger of birches.
And so I dream of going back to be.

It's when I'm weary of considerations,
And life is too much like a pathless wood...

I'd like to go by climbing a birch tree,
And climb black branches up a snow-white trunk
Towards heaven, till the tree could bear no more,
But dipped its top and set me down again.
That would be good both going and coming back.
One could do worse than be a swinger of birches.

Is it any wonder the man's name was Frost? I can hear him slipping through the snowfall, down near the creek. The only break in the silence comes from over the ridge, out on the state highway... the sliding skid of Georgia drivers on ice!

. . . .

They say such nice things about you at your funeral
that it makes me sad to realize that I'm going to miss my own
by just a few days.
Garrison Keillor

. . . .

2001

This year the Revv-ah-rund Jesse Jackson sired a babe out of wedlock – the babe is out of wedlock, not Jesse. Jesse, gosh darn it all, is quite married, but, gosh darn it all again, not to the baby's mother. Technically speaking, that would make the Revv-ah-rund an adulterer, which is something reverends are required to study, but not generally encouraged to practice (Although practice was just what Jimmy Swaggart needed, he was so incompetent at it!). Note to my mother, Ruth: That parenthetical ended in a preposition. Technically, it was not a sentence. So, Jesse has committed adultery even more technically than Jimmy Carter, and in a way that was a lot more fun than just lusting in your heart.

Now I'm not here to cast stones at Jesse's weakness of the flesh. I am mindful of the admonition, "There is no glory in outstripping donkeys." And there, but for the grace of God, go I. That and the fact that I don't have a charitable foundation to bilk out of millions of dollars so that Carol Jeanne would tend to overlook such indiscretions on her way to shop *for* a mall, as opposed to shopping *in* a mall. At the time Jesse was playing school with a University of Georgia professor from right here in my hometown (I was once propositioned by a professor, but I told him "No."), he was also offering spiritual guidance to Bill Clinton to assist him back to the path of marital fidelity after his "internship." Sorta makes you wonder just who taught what to whom.

The best part of this story is learning just how much Mrs. Jackson and Mrs. Clinton have in common, and boy is "common" the operative word. It's hard to say just what type of women they are, but suffice it to say that both of them are card-carrying members of the oldest profession. (Do you know the difference between a hooker and a lawyer? When you die, a hooker quits.). They prostitute principle for privilege.

Looks like they may have both taken lessons from Coretta Scott King (her motto, "For everything else, there's MasterCard."). You can't even quote from the "I Have A Dream" speech without paying the MLK Foundation a bribe (and no, I ain't paying them for mentioning it here). What I want to know is when they are going to pay me my share of that speech. He gave it while standing on the steps of the Lincoln Memorial on the Mall in Washington, D.C. Clearly, this was public enterprise – spoken on public property, carried on public airways, and subsequently ignored by the general public. As a member of the public who pays for all of that, I want remuneration for my share. And if they raise enough bribes to build a memorial to the man (a worthy project), then I want my share of the family's cut (two unworthy projects). Unfortunately, the comedian Chris Rock had it right. Today, in America, if you're on any street named Martin Luther King Boulevard, you better roll up your windows, lock your doors, and run like hell!

There were two newsworthy issues in this unfortunate mess. First, watching the news media fall all over themselves in seeking to mention the incident without really reporting it... you know, an investigative report with theme music ("In The Heat Of The Night," or, "The Night The Lights Went Out In Georgia") and a catchy marketing slogan ("Double Your Pleasure, Double Your Fun!" or, "Give To The United Negro College Fund."). How do you report that the king (not Martin Luther, and not The King – that would be Elvis [His motto, "I would've been 67 years old on January 8th if I hadn't died on my throne."])... anyway, how do you report that Jesse, as the king spokesman for minorities (When did he ever have time to speak to them all to find out how they feel? Is it just as presumptuous and stereotypical [i.e., biased] to assume that when Jesse speaks, he has the knowledge, insight, and authority to speak for all blacks, all Hispanics, and all left-handed hemophiliacs, as it is to assume that anyone else can make any other stereotypical comment about a class of people? That's dumb. Speaking of dumb, did you hear about the Pollock...) – anyway, how do you allude to the fact that Jesse has no clothes without referring to the fact that he is buck naked? The media need not worry about crossing the boundary on political correct-ness as regards Jesse Jackson... they ain't even gonna approach it!

The second newsworthy issue of this story is much more serious. In light of his contribution to an illegitimate conception, Jessie Jackson announced that he would be stepping down tempo-rarily from his administrative position with the Rainbow Coalition For Idiots. Total length of his sabbatical? Four whole days. For Jesse's part, this is neither surprising nor disappointing. "Will he have the moral credibility to lead?" everyone asked. Of course. Because his moral credibility does not come from him as a leader. Rather, it comes from (actually is bestowed by) those whom he leads. And, as a constituency, they have no morality. Don't look for anyone at *Time* or *Newsweek* to report that. Having the kid is Ok. It is the only acceptable outcome under the circumstances – it beats abortion. Jesse is just a man with feet of clay. But the complete absence of fallout from that pedestal he climbed up on was telling.

After four days of soul searching, The Revv-uh-rund summarily announced that, "The ground is no place for a champion. I'm not going to wallow on the ground." That ain't repentance, it's arrogance, a total lack of shame. And a total lack of consequences from an unprincipled mob whose only social concern is what's in it for them, and for free. Of course, it's not free. You and I had to go out and earn it.

. . . .

Never ruin an apology with an excuse.
Benjamin Franklin

. . . .

2002

In family news, today it fell my lot to take the family cat, Cali, to the Vet to be put to sleep. Cali (which is short for Calico, which is the type of cat she was, which means she was three-colored, which means she was a female since all cats with three colors are female) led a comfortable but tragic life. When we first got her from Carol Jeanne's brother, whom I have yet to repay, Carol Jeanne's mother, who lives next door, had an orange tabby-cat named Sassy. About the second day we had Cali, I went out in the morning to find her. I couldn't. We had put her to bed on the back deck, which was to become her aerie, her sanctuary, and her prison for the next ten years. I looked everywhere. Carol Jeanne looked. The girls looked.

Finally, Carol Jeanne had to leave for work. After she backed out of the carport to leave, I found Cali... and Sassy. They had both been crouched under Carol Jeanne's van (a GMC Safari van which I bought as a surprise for her from Enterprise Rentals when she wanted a van for the kids and which she always hated [the van, not the kids], but which is a story for next year, or the year after, depending on when I select her next vehicle, which she will never have to check the oil in, much less change it, or even wash it, much less wax it). Anyway, Cali and Sassy were locked in a stare-down, to the extent that neither one them noticed the van leaving. Sassy was uttering a low, guttural growl with her orange eyes glowing. Cali was catatonic. Cali was bleeding from her nose and one eye. Her left ear was missing a pie-slice wedge from the center, as it would until this very day.

Sassy never accepted Cali. Cali never overcame her fear of Sassy. Sassy could often be spied in the woods or shrubs around the back deck. Occasionally she would come right onto the deck to attack Cali. Once, when my mother-in-law was out of town, I caught Sassy in the front yard stalking Cali. When I shouted at her, Sassy ran up a tree. Unfortunately for her, it was a short tree. I got out the garden hose and sprayed Sassy for all my well was worth. For the next thirty minutes, I tried my best to blast her out of that tree with the hose, but her survival instincts were too good to come down and eventually the well ran low. I thought about my little Glenfield .22 caliber rifle in the basement, but I just couldn't bring myself to go that far... I hated to lose to a cat in a battle of wits.

Cali remained in solitary confinement in a cell of neurosis the rest of her life. Even after I found Sassy drowned in my mother-in-law's lake (when my mother-in-law was again out of town, but I didn't have anything to do with it, I swear), Cali never left the deck. Her only respite came from scaling down a post on the deck into the yard below to quickly tend to her business in the pine straw around a butterfly bush growing at the base of the deck (After ten years of Cali's ministrations, it is a uniquely large butterfly bush.). Then back up the post she would go, like a lumberjack in a hurry. In addition to the butterfly bush, the deck is collared in jasmine vines. Cali would catch the occasional bird on the deck, and she was death on lizards, but mostly she just perched and observed. Cali was an exceptional observer. Not much on commentary, but keen on detail.

Cali was really Rachel's pet. That's who talked her mother into letting her bring Cali home. But after Rachel left for college, and Cali could no longer sleep in Rachel's room because she had started urinating on the girls' bathroom mat as retaliation against Carol Jeanne in some sort of female turf battle, it was up to me to build her a house on the back deck. It was up to me to wire a heater in it for the winter nights. It was up to me to feed her, water her, brush her, talk to her, and sneak her into the house when it rained too hard. And it was up to me to go to the pet store to buy Nature's Miracle to staunch the stench of cat urine in the girls' bathroom after Cali repaid my kindness and trust by sneaking downstairs when I wasn't looking and firing off a salvo at Carol Jeanne in The War Of The Women. Overall, Cali was a liability and general pain-in-the-butt, so I am totally at a loss to explain why I cried like a baby all the way back from the vet today, her limp body resting on a towel in my lap. I buried her under her deck, between her butterfly bush and her climbing post. She is facing Rachel's bedroom window.

. . . .

Life is not fair, and for most of us, that's a good thing.
Oscar Wilde

. . . .

2005

All my life I've been what you might call frugal. It's also what you might call cheap. I drink wine out of a cardboard box. My beer is Milwaukee's Best – more commonly known as The Beast – which I get for $11 a case at Sam's Club. There are homeless winos who will drink vanilla extract or rubbing alcohol that will not touch The Beast. I buy my Scotch in a plastic bottle for $16 per half-gallon. One time I splurged and treated myself to a very expensive bottle of single-malt Scotch for about $45 for a quart; all I could think about was that I could've had six times as much of my regular Scotch for the same amount of money, and thus I didn't really enjoy any of the expensive stuff. Every Saturday I have oatmeal, raisins, and honey for breakfast (When I say "every Saturday," please understand that what I mean is "every Saturday."). I buy the honey at Kroger's, where I shop every Sunday after church (When I say "every Sunday," what I mean to say is "every Sunday."). I don't buy the Kroger store-brand of honey for my oatmeal, though. For some reason, Kroger carries a brand even cheaper than Kroger's. It's called FMV, which stands for "For Maximum Value." So I buy the FMV brand of honey. One time I looked past the FMV honey, even past the Kroger honey. I figured life is short, a bottle of honey lasts me about a year (Actually, it crystallizes into pure sugar before I ever finish it.). I figured what the heck. I splurged and bought the Sue Bee Clover Honey (How do they train those bees to feed only on clover flowers, and to ignore all the others?) for about three times what the FMV costs. Couldn't tell a damn bit of difference.

I have other penurious, parsimonious, personal (That there's a literary device known as alliteration. Do NOT try this at home!) attributes that drive my wife wild (no, not *that* kind of wild). For example, I have never thrown out a bar of soap. When the current bar dwindles down to the point that you can't get good scrubbing

84

traction with it, I simply get out a new bar, use it once, then press the old one into the back of the new one. It molds into shape beautifully and keeps right on going. I seldom find the first use of a paper towel to be its last. If I use one to dry off a dish, I set it aside and will later use it to dry the countertop. That, too, can be set aside and later be used to dry my hands or wipe off the top of a can before opening it (You should always wipe off the top of a can before opening it. I can remember my father telling me when I was a child that it was important to do so, because while sitting in a warehouse, that can was the place on which a rat would sit and do his business.). Of course, the best way to maximize the economy of a paper towel is to never take a full sheet off the roll. It's much more efficient to assay the task at hand, and then tear off just whatever portion or corner thereof that will suffice. Or how about this... Carol Jeanne has this weird notion that a piece of dental floss can only be used once! Where do women come up with this stuff?!

Well, I could go on and on about this subject, but it's costing me a lot of paper and ink. Where I was headin' with this when I started was that this year, I begged people not to give me anything for Christmas (and most of them listened!). The fact of the matter is that I have reached a point in life where I don't need any more "things." I have every thing I need and a bunch of other things I don't need. I have every thing I want, and some things I don't want. I have things I will never use again and things that I never have used. I have more shirts than any man I know of, and more than most women (although I think they call them blouses). I am fully confident that I could wear a different shirt every day for a year, without ever wearing one twice (even though that sentence was, technically speaking, itself redundant). In the top of my closet, I have two stacks of shirts I have never worn, shirts still in their original packaging. The two stacks of shirts sit next to the two stacks of trousers I have also never worn. I have enough things that they have begun to weigh me down, much like my waistline, and like my unwanted pounds, I now seek to liberate myself from the bondage of excess things. I have reached the point in life where the only thing I want is *time...* time to do things, time to enjoy things, time to think about things, maybe even time to write about things. If any of you can give the gift of time, please give me a call!

....

Two monologues do not make a dialogue.
Jeff Daly

....

2001

___ ___ ___ ___ ___ ___ ___

For Christmas, I got (bad grammar) new underwear. I do this every third Christmas. "Why," you ask? Because that's how long Fruit-of-the-Loom lasts... three Christmases. (Nine-volt batteries in your smoke detectors should be replaced, along with your car windshield wipers, *every* Christmas. Know how long an eight-ounce tube of Crest toothpaste lasts for one person? Six months, two weeks, two days. Know how I know? 'Cause I write the date on the tube when I start using it. My daughter Rachel finds this behavior peculiar... go figure.) Anyway, this past Christmas was underwear Christmas. There's something about new underwear that makes a man feel special. New T-shirts (V-neck, with sleeves) and briefs (100% cotton, boxers for pajamas). But this year something bothered me. Something was different, but I wasn't sure what. Then finally it hit me – the logo. The logo was different. No longer did it say, around the waistband, "Fruit Of The Loom – Fruit Of The Loom – Fruit Of The Loom." Now it's just "FTL – FTL - FTL" interspersed with some kind of racing stripe. What's wrong with this, of course, is that they screwed up the acronym. Correct me if I'm wrong (like that's really going to happen), but the acronym for

"Fruit Of The Loom" is "FOTL," not "FTL." What happened to the "O"? Isn't "of" just as important a preposition as "the"? Doesn't the Declaration of Independence say "... government of the people, by the people, for the people..."? (Well actually, no, it was the Constitution, not the Declaration of Independence, that said that. Oops! Wrong again. That line was penned by Abraham Lincoln in the Gettysburg Address. Boy, are you susceptible to the power of suggestion!) Anyway, it says "government *of* the people," not "government the people," although that is certainly what Democrats attempt to do. Why did they drop the "O"? It's not as if "FOTL" spelled something nasty, at least not in English. It's like the apple, grapes, and lemon told the orange they didn't need him anymore. Some marketing idiot did this. Probably the same guy that dreamed up "New Coke." Anyway, it took all the joy out *of* my new underwear.

. . . .

The inherent vice of capitalism is the unequal sharing of blessings; the inherent virtue of socialism is the equal sharing of miseries.

...

However beautiful the strategy,
you should occasionally look at the results.

...

History shall be kind to me, for I intend to write it.
Winston Churchill

. . . .

Here's a poem that I wrote:

Certitude

We seem to think we will not die.
We will live and make death a lie.
Exceeding our threescore and ten,
we'll cheat the grave and somehow win.

Then suddenly our fate we meet,
and at last we know defeat,
when death comes knocking at our door
to tell us we have lost the war.

Yes death comes knocking at our door,
carries us to a foreign shore,
removes us from within the pale,
transports us then beyond the vale

where death shall take and turn to dust
every love and every lust,
and all that is or went before
shall be known by us no more.

Beholding death with our own eyes,
we depart in great surprise –
odd that the flower of our grief
should yield a fruit of disbelief.

No matter how many have gone before,
when one we know passes through that door,

we, more stolid than the ox,
are dumbfounded by the locks

that bar us crossing to and fro –
they let us come, but cannot go.
It matters not how much we yearn,
'tis not allowed us to return.

Do we not see the passing tide;
can one's destiny be denied?
Not for me, the insistent way,
I shall live another day.

I shall not cease to struggle and strive,
by sheer resolve keep life alive.
I shall fight 'til the battle is won,
keep on living after life is done.
I shall make death my slave –
be banished, death, to the grave.
I shall make myself immortal,
passing not through that dark portal.

Rewrite the rules, just for me,
empty the tomb and set me free.
To what end I do not know,
but I intend to make it so.

I do not want eternal rest,
to lie in peace among the blest.
Better to wander throughout time,
than to sleep in rest sublime.

So let me live life without pause,
no matter if it breaks the laws.
If only others would do the same,
perhaps we would not strive in vain...

but things are not as I had thought,
life alone is life at naught.
Is one star a constellation;
can life be lived in isolation?

No, it is not good to be alone.
Perhaps 'tis best if we go home,
give our place to those who come,
who think the battle can be won.

Let them push against the gate,
try to keep at bay their fate,
'til they, like me, can understand
that death is part of a greater plan.

. . . .

Maturity begins when you are content to feel you are right about something without feeling the need to prove someone else wrong.
Sydney J. Harris

. . . .

All my adult life, I have worn a size 9½ shoe. Since junior high, I have worn a size 9½ shoe. I do a lot of running. Whenever I play golf, I always walk the course. I play a lot of tennis, and I play hard... I run down balls that greyhounds and Labrador retrievers couldn't touch. All my adult life, I have shed toenails like a snake sheds skins. When I trained for my marathon, I lost eight out of ten toenails. I lost so many toenails playing tennis that I eventually made a necklace out of them, kinda like an Injun making a necklace out of bear claws. Whenever I would get behind in a tennis match, come the last set, I would pull out the necklace and slip it on. Sooner or later, your opponent just has to know what that thing is... yellow flakes with black and purple-crusted stuff on one side. When you tell him it's all the toenails you've lost chasing down balls while playing against people like him, it's usually enough. The one's that don't lose their lunch at least lose their concentration... game, set, match. Once, as I sat on my deck, adding my most recent addition onto the necklace, one of my daughter Megan's friends walked up. "What's that?" she asked. When I showed her and explained what it was, she literally hurled straight over the rail into the shrubbery, the Technicolor yawn. When that happens, you know you're onto something special!!

But this year, I finally became a complete cripple. I couldn't even walk. Diagnosis: Morton's neuroma, which is a medical term for having a white-hot, sixteen-penny nail driven between your second and third toes with every step you take. It throbs every time your heart beats, even in your sleep. Three shots of cortisone relieved the pain just enough to reveal that I also had severe capsulitis of my second toe. This results in a condition called hammertoe, so named because it feels like your toe has been smashed by a hammer. Fortunately, my good friend and former deer-hunting partner, a full-blooded Eyetalian and sculptor named Dario

Rossi, has a son who was smart enough to become a podiatrist. I was smart enough to let him fish in my mother-in-law's lake. I talked him into one more shot for the capsulitis. Since he wasn't charging me anything for any of the shots or office visits, I figured one more shot was pretty cheap. He told me not to bother coming to the office, because he was coming out to fish that afternoon and he'd just bring the shot stuff with him. Now these shots are touchy affairs. You have a good nerve supply in the foot and a couple of mine were pissed. In addition to jamming a needle in there, the real art, once the needle's in and you are back down from the ceiling, is to wiggle it around inside the joint, and really stick it to the hot spot. This procedure is made slightly less unbearable by the use of chloromethane (freeze spray) applied to the target just before harpooning you.

Mauro arrived that afternoon, just as I finished jogging, and I proudly presented him with a sweaty, August-afternoon foot smattered with sweat-sock lint. It wasn't any stinkier or slipperier than the catfish he was about to catch. He told me he had good news and bad news. I went for the good news first... he had remembered to bring his shot bag. The bad news? The can of freeze spray had exploded in the trunk of his car due to the summer heat. He gave me a choice, I could have the shot, *au naturel,* or I could wait for an appointment at his office. I broke off a dogwood limb to bite on, grabbed a tree trunk in each hand and told him to get on with it. I had an out of body experience – I leapt out of my body. I even saw the Great Light... it was a lightning bolt passing from my toe and out my right eye. While he was waiting for me to regain consciousness, Mauro studied my discarded running shoe. When I came to, he asked me what size my shoes were. All my life, I told him, I've worn 9½. "You might wear 9½, but your feet are 10½." No, I explained, I've worn 9½ ever since junior high. "In junior high, you might've been 9½, but whenever you've come to the office, you've been wearing a 10½," he said. That was pretty observant, I thought. But what he didn't know was... *those weren't my shoes!!* They were hand-me-downs from my father, and since they were good shoes, and since I am cheap, I wore them. They seemed to fit ok, even if they weren't the right size. Mauro asked me about my golf shoes. He asked me about my tennis shoes. Six hundred dollars later, with all new shoes in my closet, I haven't lost a toenail in five months. Good thing I already had my necklace made!

. . . .

Life being what it is, one dreams of revenge.
Paul Gauguin

I'm all for turning the other cheek, but I only have four of them, and when they're all spinning, something's wrong.
Coleman Hood

. . . .

2004

Youngest daughter Megan got a kitten this year, our first-ever male pet. She wanted a pet all her own (again). She complains that all her other pets become my pets. Now I have another animal sleeping in my bed. This kitten went several weeks without a name. I wanted to name him Jack, because his back legs and feet are big as a Jack Rabbit's. Everywhere he goes, he looks like he's walking downhill in snowshoes. But Megan finally named him Nemo. He's never seen another cat, so he thinks he's a dog. The dogs, on the other hand, are a neurotic mess. Nemo attacks them, grabs them around their necks, and drags them to the floor where he pummels their tummies with his snowshoe hind feet. When we first got Nemo, I sat down and had a talk with each dog individually. I even had to speak to one of them twice. They know they're not allowed to really defend themselves, so if Nemo gets too rough, they have to go hide somewhere. MacKenzie especially played epic war games with Nemo, which I fortunately captured on video. And Zoe loves to play war with him as well. They run at full speed throughout the house, with Nemo eventually sliding to safety under the couch or the bed. Actually, the dogs could probably fit under the bed, too, but they'd have to face those claws going in!!

I have personally witnessed Nemo chasing down and catching a full-grown squirrel! He spends countless hours outdoors, day and night, and could not care less if it's raining or freezing or both. His favorite pastime is to sit beneath the suet feeder in the yard and leap at the woodpeckers (I lower its height about an inch a week, just to make this interesting!). Since Nemo thinks he's a dog, he drinks out of the toilet just like they do, although he has to crouch on the seat to accomplish this. And speaking of toilets, that's really his favorite distraction. Although he thinks he's a dog, Nemo reminds me of an Alaskan brown bear... whenever he hears a toilet flush, Nemo rushes to jump up on the toilet seat, fascinated by its swirling contents as they retreat and disappear. He then starts dipping his paw in the "current" to see if he can "gaff a salmon." I've seen him catch one of those, too! I love this cat!!

. . . .

A baby is born with a loud-speaker on one end,
and no sense of responsibility on the other.
John Shelby Sponge

. . . .

2007

Well now, hold onto your hats while I go off on some tangents. Here, in shotgun fashion, is a bunch of stuff that just gets in my mind, and keeps me from discovering the cure to cancer. Why do women dye their hair for the "natural look?" Isn't the natural look exactly what they are trying to avoid? I love The *Andy Griffith Show*, probably more than anybody, ever. But for almost fifty years it's gnawed at me... at the start of every episode, Andy and Opie are walking along the shore of Myers' Lake, going fishing, yet neither one of them has a tackle box, not even a can of worms or a spare hook.

There is no such thing as a good time for a shoestring to break. You should rotate your shoestrings, just like the tires on your car, to maximize their useful life (left-to-right, right-to-left, never front-to-back). It might not be a 100% increase in lifespan, but it's at least a 50% increase (Who can contradict me?).

Another thing that drives me nuts is people at golf tournaments that run to surround a golf ball after an errant shot. They all stand just alike, with feet spread and arms folded behind their backs, hands crossed, palms down and out. What are they, Hitler's golf ball Nazis? Where do they learn this behavior? Where do they think the ball is going? Has anyone ever seen a golf ball jump up and run away? They can't be trying to keep the ball from becoming lost, because they can all see it perfectly well. If they're trying to keep someone from stepping on the ball, they might try pointing towards it and saying something like, "Hey, don't step on that golf ball lying over there (only they would say "laying" over there)." If they're worried about someone stepping on the ball, they'd cut the odds of that happening way down by just keeping their fat asses where they were when the ball landed. Just once, I'd like the TV cameras to catch Tiger walking up to this circle of jerks and saying something like, "Thank God you surrounded my golf ball before it could jump up and run away! And you did it without stepping on it! There are twenty-five thousand people on the course at this moment, plus a national television audience, and we all came out today just to observe your athletic proficiency in golf ball surrounding. Nice job!"

The Weather Channel has a program series entitled *When Weather Changed History*. I studied history at Furman and Wake Forest Universities, and I was pretty good at it ("History shall be kind to me, for I intend to write it," Winston Churchill). The subject of history, in my opinion, was not as academically rigorous as organic chemistry, differential equations, or thermodynamics, so I subsequently may have actually learned some of it. One of the things I remember best from my study of history is that *it happened in the past!!* History has already occurred – you cannot rewind the tape, you do not get a Mulligan or a do-over. Ergo (which is historical talk for "therefore"), one cannot change history, even if one is the weather (unless, of course, one is Mother Nature, in which case, being a woman, it is your prerogative to change history). And by the way, why hasn't The History Channel ever run a show about *When History Changed Weather*? If The Weather Channel wants to run a show about *When Weather Influenced The Way Stuff Happened*, or *Weather's Role In The Occurrence Of Historical Events*, perhaps even *Whether Weather Mattered*, then I could go along with it. But under no circumstances has weather, or anything else for that matter, ever *changed* history.

How many of you remember when bottle caps were not "twist-off?" How many decades has it been since you needed a bottle opener? Why is it then, that Swiss army knives (and now Leatherman multi-tools) still include bottle openers? Back in the day when you did need them, how many of you remember that, when you removed the cap, there was cork on the underside? I wonder how many hours I spent nibbling the cork from the underside of Coca-Cola bottle caps? I sure hope that cork is not a carcinogen!

Well, let's polish off this category so that we can move on to stuff that doesn't matter as much. I have a Rule: there are *two* sets of nail clippers on my desk. Is there anyone out there that doesn't see where this is going? One is for *finger*nails, and the other for *toe*nails. Why do you buy green olives in a jar, but black olives come in a can? And while we're on the subject of olives, what exactly is a pimiento? Most of you couldn't even spell it, much less define it. Obviously, I know what one is, or I wouldn't have asked the question (I might have wondered it, but I wouldn't have asked it!). Why don't we call a very safe driver, one who's never had a wreck, a wreckless driver? If someone starts talking to you about "climate change," run the other way! Possibly, they are attempting to refer to the question of "global warming," but if they don't know any more about the subject than to refer to it as "climate change," they are an idiot, to be ignored at all costs. Let me assure you that the term "climate change" is meaningless, as climate has never been static. Indeed, the concept of a "stable climate" is an oxymoron.

. . . .

Well, I thought that was the last of the maddening things I needed to get of my chest, but I was wrong. As I write this, it is December 20th, the Saturday before Christmas. I started working on real estate this morning at 8:00 to find a home for a kid that waited until 5:00 yesterday to begin looking for a house that he has to have by January 1st. I made it home this afternoon at 4:00, having no lunch or bathroom breaks. I walked in the house, and told Carol Jeanne that I was going to change clothes and wash her car. After tending to emails and a few voice mails, at 5:00 I walked out the door to start washing her car, a Toyota Sequoia that requires a step ladder and a solid hour to wash and dry. And, by the way, the sun sets at 5:28 here on the 20th of December, Solstice Eve. Now my usual car-washing hose bib is out front at the well-head. But this faucet I have to shut down and drain around Halloween, because a deep freeze (We've had several nights in the 'teens already this Fall, with another due tomorrow.) will bust those pipes in a heartbeat. So, once I had backed her car out of the carport and into the driveway, I had to drag the hose through the yard up to the carport faucet, which is what I was doing when Carol Jeanne came walking out. She announced that she was running up to see one of our neighbors, and asked if she could drive her car. I said, "Sure. I'll just try to run alongside really fast while I wash it, but I'm not sure how far the hose will go." She gave me a cold look of indignation, and replied tersely that there was no need to "act like that." So I ask you, is it any wonder husbands die fifteen years ahead of their wives? Is it any mystery why men have heart attacks?

And one more thing. We went to church this morning (It's Sunday, now.), a church we have been visiting for a while. We're moving cautiously before we commit to membership this time around. We want to be part of a local congregation. We don't want to go into town, to an Athens church, but one here in our own community, Oconee County. But we've been burned our first two times out with country churches, so this time around, we're taking it slowly. This church, Oconee Presbyterian, is pastored by a lady named Pam Driesell. Her daddy, Charles Driesell, is more readily known by his nickname, "Lefty." As a kid, I attended his basketball camp at Davidson College, where he was the coach. Anyway, we are terribly fond of Pam, but there's a whole lot of stuff that goes on in her worship service that I don't understand, and that her daddy wouldn't tolerate for one minute.

This is a fairly traditional church. They don't have six services, just one, and it is not a "praise" (i.e., modern) service with awful music. But it ain't traditional either. Is it just me, or does any of the following strike you as "different?" In the summertime, there are grown men who come to church in short pants and a shirt with no collar. Some do not wear socks (So far, I haven't seen anyone who did not wear shoes.), and no man wears shined, leather shoes. I saw one man who was wearing a "Tommy Bahama" T-shirt. There are men with ponytails, earrings, and tattoos. Last Sunday I sat behind a man who wore a hat into the lobby, into the sanctuary, and kept it on throughout the entire service. Both men and women bring coffee into the service, maybe even lattes; and what's more, they think nothing of getting up in the middle of the service to go out to the lobby to refresh their cups, and saunter back in the middle of a sermon. Is it any wonder that the kids in the service run rampant? They are in a constant flow to the lobby, bathrooms, and coloring books that are provided to them at the door (and which they could have picked up on their way in, with half-a-second of planning and half-a-brain). They constantly stand in their parents' laps, and conduct loud conversations. With God as my witness, I have never heard a parent in this church say "Shhh!!" I've never heard a "grownup" tell a kid to get quiet; indeed, I've never heard an adult refrain from responding just as loudly and just as uninhibitedly as the kid. I'm just not sure that I'm cut out to worship with the rest of you. I long for the good ol' days, when you could've back-handed one of these brats all the way into the narthex, and no one would have blinked an eye. I rue the fact that the adults have no sense of shame or decorum in their own deportment in the house of God. There should, quite simply, be a difference in attire, attitude, and behavior in attending a movie at the Cineplex as opposed to a Sunday morning worship service... but there ain't.

In the arena of college athletics (Nice double-entendre!), how many of you have ever heard of a player making an All-America team, of having received All-America honors? There are any number of such rosters: AP, UPI, coaches, *Playboy*, pre-season, post-season, all-time. Well, if you, a simple sports fan (I just love those double-entendres!), have heard of the All-America team, why is it that almost no "professional" sports writers (I don't know what's professional about them. So far as I know, they do not have to receive a particular degree or pass a licensing exam to be a sports writer, and goodness knows they have no professional code of ethics. I think they ought to be called "paid" sports writers.) have? Anyway, it's an "All-America" team, as in a "national" honor... you are recognized for all-country or all-nation performance in your sport. At the state level, here in Georgia, we call it the All-Georgia team. We could call it the All-Florida team, but that would get confusing, because someone else is already using that title. But the point is this: we wouldn't call it the All-Georgian team, not even the All-Floridian team (Would it be the All-New Mexiconians or the All-New Mexicans?). Well, it ain't the All-American team, either!! You are not named an All-American, you are named All-America. The Hardy Boys were All-American, so were Clark Kent, apple pie, and a lot of the folks in Norman Rockwell's paintings. But college athletes are not All-American (When was the last time a professional sports writer read the arrest blotter in a university paper, for crying out loud?!). So why these twits, who write this crap about that drivel, can't get it right is beyond me.

Most nights around 10:15, Carol Jeanne sticks her head out of our bedroom door and says something like, "It's bedtime," or maybe "When are you coming to bed?" or "Are you going to stay up much longer?" In the great husbandly tradition, I try my best to ignore this. I might nod, might grunt, might gesture towards the TV. As a fifty-two-year-old man, I feel I have earned the privilege (It would be a privilege, not a right. You cannot earn a right, despite the claims to the contrary of almost every idiot one hears in the media having claimed to have done so.) of coming to bed when I want to. I don't mean that I'm going to stay up all night. If I stayed up until 11:00, I'd be in a coma the next day. But if I want to stay up until 10:30 in order to finish watching an episode of

Married With Children, or finish reading the newspaper or a chapter in a book, then that shouldn't be a big deal. At the end of sixteen- to eighteen-hour days for her and for me, I assure you that there is nothing happening at 10:15 that requires the presence of both of us in the bedroom! So, of course I was delighted a few months ago when she announced, "I've thought of a compromise. Some nights you can come to bed early, and some nights I will come sit up late with you in the den." Talk about a win-win solution!

I have just completed an inventory of bottles/jars/cans/tubes in our bathroom. Not counting things that we either have in common or share (e.g., a bar of soap or a tube of toothpaste [and why isn't it "teethpaste?" I'm not going to brush just one]), the count is alarming. I have three containers (shampoo, aspirin, and shaving cream). In round numbers, Carol Jeanne has thirty. I say round numbers, because I'm only counting once the things she may have by the dozen, such as lotions and fingernail (fingernails?!) polish. There are containers that I cannot decipher; I have no clue as to their content or intended use. I'm not sure what any of this means, but clearly I must resolve this matter before I can move on to thinking about the implications of negative gravity on quantum mechanics and the resolution of the Theory Of Relativity.

By the way, I received some great personal news. Barrister Ugwabe Natombi, Minister Of Finance for the Federal Republic Of Nigeria, emailed me to say that my case had come to his attention. I hadn't even known that I had a case! Thankfully, the New Central Bank Of Nigeria ruled in my favor, awarding me $8.5 million dollars (U.S.) in delayed inheritance funds. They will be wiring these funds directly into my personal bank account. All I have to do is provide them with my account information, and then I'm headed to my new address on Easy Street!

2004

My Grandmother's Mansion
My Eulogy To Corille Avant Porter, My Mother's Mother

I never knew my mother's father, Corille's husband. Charles
Alexander Porter died before I was born. My father's father, Cy
Hood, was the best friend I ever had. At the age of sixteen, I was
totally unprepared for his death twenty-six years ago. I attended
his funeral and put up a brave front, but just did not have a clue as
to why this had happened. When his wife Gladys died twenty-two
years later, and in the fullness of time, she and I were both prepared for it. She had lived a long, beneficial, and happy life. Certainly, her mind was sharp enough to realize that her body was
failing her, and at any rate, she was ready to go home. My only
regret in attending her funeral was that no one who had known
and loved her spoke at her service. Her final voyage was commis-
sioned at the hands of strangers.

And so I fear that it shall be when my Grandmother Corille is
laid to rest today. People who never knew her will pray prayers for
the departed and sing hymns of mourning. Some poor cleric, fulfilling the duties of his office and well intentioned – but a stranger
nonetheless – will deliver a funeral service, not knowing the level

102

of grief to which he should appropriately target his audience. Under the best of circumstances, it will be detached and generic. It could not possibly be personal. Like my Grandmother Gladys, there will be no eulogy from a loved one. We shall entrust to the professionals the disposition of funeral and burial, hearse and casket. My conscience protests this sterile, antiseptic departure, but out of respect to family wishes, I too shall remain a silent spectator for these last brief moments of presence.

But I *will* remember. I will remember my Grandmother Corille, and I will remember her mansion.

Like my Grandmother Gladys, Corille also had a long and beneficial life. Actually, she lived too long. I cannot imagine that I am the only person who ever prayed, however fleetingly, that God would be merciful and let her die. And of course, as soon as such a thought crosses your consciousness, the guilt withers you. Who was I to think such things, to petition Almighty God over life and death, to offer the unsolicited benefit of my wisdom as to what was best? Her body, strengthened by a lifetime of struggle as a widow with three children to rear and genetically conditioned for tenacity, marched resolutely on years after her mind had retired from the field of battle. Even after time had stilled her limbs and numbed her senses, her vital core refused to yield. But of course, we all do yield, eventually. Corille's time has finally come. Corille's time has thankfully come. In the end, there was no life left to mourn... all that remains are the things that are to be celebrated and recalled with thanksgiving.

The first thing I would like to recall, if in fact I ever knew it, is how to spell her name, which, like the woman herself, was enigmatic. Of my two grandmothers, Gladys was my favorite, the realization of which caused me some angst as a child. It was understandable, of course. I spent nearly every weekend with Cy and Glady, sometimes longer in the summer. It was Glady who would pick me up from kindergarten, stopping at Hunter's store to buy me sour grape bubble gum and Cokes. Corille was a less frequent and more distant grandmother. She was almost my "holiday" grandmother, as so many children's grandmothers are today, although we never lived more than fifteen minutes apart. You could hug Corille, as all her grandchildren did, especially when returning home after having left the nest. But I don't recall her initiating any hugs. It's not that she was uncomfortable hugging and being demonstrative. Rather, she was comfortable in their absence, which teaches me something about myself. It would not be until many years later that I would come to realize that I didn't love her any less than Glady, only differently.

It is ironic that just two weeks before her death, I wrote in our family Christmas letter of my remembrances of Thanksgiving and Christmas at Corille's house. She was always in the kitchen, always in an apron, always churning away at her KitchenAid Mix Master making up a batch of her crescent rolls (made with yeast and left to rise underneath a warm, moist towel on the back porch) and which were truly divine. Her house would be invaded by her three children, her sons- and daughter-in-law, and their twelve children. And yet, never once did I hear her express concern about her carpets or her furniture, which as my Christmas letter documented, were frequently thrown-up on. She never once exclaimed about her hallway chimes being banged (loudly) against her wallpaper. She never once complained about the tribe of hellions sliding down her banisters. Quite simply, the woman never ex-pressed the first concern about the damage inflicted upon her material world or her magnificent house. Maybe it was the bourbon her sons-in-law kept slipping in her punch that kept her so loose on the limb about the destruction being wrought about her, but a more likely explanation is that her real house was built on a more substantial foundation.

When I was a child, I thought Corille lived in a mansion. Her house was three stories tall, not counting the basement. It had huge, cherry sliding doors, ceilings that were twelve feet high, a wrap-around porch, a portico, cypress-shake siding, and a whole other house in the side yard. By comparison, Glady's house was more of a cottage, something Cy had built, in fits and starts, with his own hands in his own good time. Once he finished it, he even turned the whole thing ninety degrees to hide the mistakes. I don't know if it's factual, or if I really ever heard it, but buried deep within my memories of Corille's mansion is the original cost of the house – a whopping $11,000 in 1923. You just know Charles Alexander Porter paid cash. Today, 11K wouldn't buy the sidewalks that border that mansion.

When her clan wasn't about the business of destroying her home, it served as a haven for a number of other residents and enterprises. Again, as documented in my Christmas letter, Corille ran a boarding house for "nursing" students. I don't know what they were nursing, other than maybe a hangover, but Corille was a pushover for a girl in need, as long as they didn't hanky-panky under her roof. And just to make sure they didn't, she eventually moved her roof to the basement, from whence she could guarantee its sanctity. And sanctity was important to Corille Avant Porter, along with righteousness, humility, and all the other Biblical virtues. To make sure that she was up on the Bible's commentary on one's spiritual walk, Corille arose daily - *daily* - at 4:00 AM to read her Bible and talk with her God. I don't recall that she spoke a great deal about her spiritual beliefs, but then again, she didn't have to. You knew.

In addition to her boarding house, Corille ran the first time-of-day service over the telephone. When you wanted to know the correct time, you called the number (It was Edison 23859), got Corille's switchboard and a brief commercial message. She ran an early version of both telemarketing and the Internet! Another of her enterprises was the Welcome Wagon for new-comers to Charlotte. That was in a time when you could see them coming one at a time. She had two sponsors in this enterprise. The first was Biltmore Dairies, whose milk was delivered to a box on our front porch three times a week. Biltmore also meant free ice cream and popsicles in Corille's freezer, which she would bring home packed in dry ice and which we would inevitably get our fingers and tongues stuck on while playing with it. The ice cream came in those little cardboard cups that you pulled the tops off of and ate with a flat, wooden spoon. I would give up cold beer for the banana-flavored "fudgesicles" they once made. Her other sponsor was the automobile dealership that provided her Welcome Wagon car. It was a Chevrolet dealership. I can't remember their name, but it should've been NASCAR. The woman could drive the hell out of a car. The last cop that could catch her clocked her at 98 in a 35, but she had already started to slow down by then, both physically and behind the wheel.

Eventually the unavoidable time came when Corille had to be moved to a nursing home, a luxury she had not been privileged to in the care of her own mother. Pink Grandmama, as we called her, was the recipient of her great-grandchildren's unremitting cruelty as she rocked herself catatonically in her bedroom, gnawing aimlessly on the webbing between thumb and forefinger, muttering, "num num num num... num num num num." But in her eyes, accustomed as I was to the ways of the elderly, thanks to my many hours at Cy's elbow, I read a stark message that said, "As you see me today, so will you also be one day. Better luck to you when it's your turn!"

Corille's grandchildren were solemnly paraded through her cavernous mansion, strangely empty without her and her girls in residence, to pick over her belongings and treasured family heirlooms (At least the Hoods got a crack at them. I can only hope that the Porters and Darnells did as well). I distinctly remembered a jar in her "office" in the front, ground floor of the house, that contained someone's tonsils, but I couldn't find it. Gone too from the office was the old adding machine of Charles Porter's, with hand crank and paper tape, that had fascinated me for endless hours as a child. Also missing was Corille's .22 rifle, with which she waged a holy war against the pigeons nesting in the hundred eaves of her mansion. Lord I pray it was turkey we ate on Thanksgiving, but the portions were so small! I did find a box of ammunition – .22 bird shot, not bullets – and it is with me to this day.

I did walk out with two treasures, and no relative or attorney will ever pry them from my possession. One is the circular, poker-chip holder (with red, white, and blue chips and two slots for decks of cards in the middle) that we *all* played with as children. The other is a spindly hybrid between a stool and a ladder that OSHA would condemn on sight, and that is a liability lawyer's dream-come-true. It is covered in red vinyl and has a center section with two steps, three inches wide, that fold out, proffering an invitation to climb on board for the ride of your life and possibly a broken neck. It was this stool-come-gallows that Corille used at 5:00 AM, after an hour of Bible study, to stalk recalcitrant light bulbs and belligerent cobwebs.

If I were to be honest about it, I don't know that Corille ever had the opportunity or the energy to be as happy as Glady. By happy, I mean a state of mind as opposed to isolated moments of experience. Certainly, she had happy moments. She was happy whenever one of her grandchildren married, which was the only time I ever knew her to buy an article of new clothing for herself. Mostly she was happy doing for others. I know she was happy when she bought a thousand-dollar bond from me, when I was eighteen, so that my church could build a new sanctuary. I know she was happy when she loaned me three thousand dollars after I quit my job to pursue my graduate degree in engineering. But I couldn't say that I knew her to be a giddy, bubbly persona. She was a simplistic woman, which is not to say she was simple or simple-minded. If anyone that survives her understood her, it's not me, nor any of her three children. If anyone knew her, it is her son-in-law, Frosty Darnell, who ate lunch with her every day (Ruth's Salads: chicken salad, egg salad, pimento cheese) and fixed her appliances and carried her trash and balanced her checkbook.

All of which makes me wonder, if God is indeed a God of mercy, why He left such a Saint-novitiate to languish so long after her personality was gone. Why have her three children had to place their emotional closure on hold for the past decade? I am no great Seer of Mansions, but if He is indeed preparing one for each of His children, and if it is in any way proportionate to their earthly stewardship and servitude, my guess is that God needed the extra time to get hers ready.

· · · · · · · · · · · · · ·

God comes to you disguised as your life.
Paula D'Arcy

· · · · · · · · · · · · · ·

2005

Last year I shared with you my eulogy for my Grandmother Corille. That got me to thinking about my other Grandmother, Gladys. I wrote a eulogy of sorts for her, too, which I used one Sunday when I was superintendent of the Seniors' Sunday School class at church. I fished around in my files and found that devotional. I thought it would be equitable to share this about her with you as well.

Last week Reverend Revels preached a sermon on death, and it has been my intention to speak with you on this topic as well, ever since Laylege Stone asked me three weeks ago if I would speak with you this morning. I think this is an appropriate topic for us to consider, since this is the *Seniors'* Sunday School class, and you are *Senior* Citizens. Saying someone is a *Senior* Citizen is a polite way of calling them old! Let's face it, y'all are old! Not as old as you hope to become, but older than you used to be. There's a saying that goes "You can't help growing older, but you can help growing old." I like that. Of course, growing older beats the alternative. Once you turn sixty-five, I imagine sixty-six starts to look pretty good!

How many of you are grandparents? How many of you *had* grandparents? Just checking to see if you're awake out there! Three weeks ago, I helped bury my Grandmother, Gladys Kennedy Hood. My first-born child, Rachel Kennedy Hood, is named partly in honor of her. She was my father's mother, and she and my grandfather Cy pretty much raised me. I didn't spend the majority of my time at their house, I grew up in my parents' home. But I was raised (*reared!*) in Cy and Glady's home. And I called them Cy and Glady. They were the first adults with whom I was on a first-name basis. I went from six to sixty and skipped all that troublesome adolescence in between.

Every weekend I was at their house, from Friday after school until it was time to go home and watch *Lassie* and *Walt Disney* on Sunday night. Most all of the summer was spent at their house. I was my Grandfather's shadow, and we were best friends. We had an established Saturday morning routine, starting with the dry cleaners, which was next to the A&P grocery store and was run by a family of Greeks who called me "Little Cy." Next stop was next door at the hardware store, followed by the Post Office, then a visit to Harris-Teeter (For some reason, Cy didn't shop at the A&P, which was next to the dry cleaners and hardware store.) for chewing tobacco (Reynold's Natural Leaf), cigars (Muriel El Producto), and pipe tobacco (Granger Rough Cut). Our final stop took us all the way downtown to the bank. And we knew *everyone* we saw, or at least everyone knew Cy! When we weren't in town, we were at "the farm," a few acres of fescue, cows, scrub pines, and a fish pond in the next county. Most everything I know about life and human nature, I learned on those Saturday morning journeys with Cy, or on that farm, or on the thirty-minute drive from town to the farm. Later on, when I got my driver's license, I learned it was just a fifteen-minute drive for a teenager. I think the old man was stalling, taking his time so he'd *have time* to teach me things. Plus the fact that thirty minutes in front of that old Ford heater was usually enough to put me out like a light by the time we would pull into his driveway.

But my grandfather wasn't the only one who gave me rides. Glady took me on many a trip in her old Plymouth, which had a steering wheel the size of a garbage-can lid and no power steering. I can remember her wrestling that big steering wheel through curves and parking spaces with every ounce of strength she had, and I can remember the wrist-shattering velocity with which that wheel would spin when freed from the bondage of her desperate grip! She would peer over the high dashboard, almost needing to sit on a pillow to see out. On Sunday, she would drive us to church at Sardis Presbyterian (I would walk home, because she always wanted to stay and "visit."), and often during the week she would pick me up at the church when I got out of kindergarten. While she piloted me home in the Plymouth, she let me be the navigator, telling her what turns – any turn – to take, trying to get her lost, which I never did. Somehow our twists and turns always took us by Hunter's, a country store, where I would get SourGrape bubble gum, or sometimes the orange-speckled SourApple.

Glady taught me all the birds: their songs, their nesting places, their food sources, and the different plumage of the males and females. Our favorites were the cardinals, who each Spring would build a nest in the rose arbor by Glady's bedroom window, so close that you could reach out and touch the eggs, which I was admonished not to do, but always did, surreptitiously, and then spent the night agonizing whether the mother really would desert the nest. Glady and I agreed that the subtle beauty of the female cardinal's plumage was the prettiest of all the birds. In the winter, it was my responsibility to keep the bird feeders filled. Summer and winter, I kept the two bird baths scrubbed and filled. On Saturday nights I would bathe in her cast-iron tub, then watch *Gunsmoke*, followed by *The Lawrence Welk Show*. I knew the name of every cast member on *Lawrence Welk*, and every week Cy would wait to see if Arthur Duncan would break his neck tapping out windmills on top of a piano. Glady taught me poetry ("Sweetest little fellow, everybody knows, don't know what to call him, but he's mighty like a rose."), and every night she'd tuck me under a twenty-five-pound quilt with the benediction of John Greenleaf Whittier's "Blessings on thee, little man, barefoot boy with cheeks of tan, with thy turned-up pantaloons, and thy merry whistled tunes."

Eventually, of course, I entered my teenage years and began on weekends to take my place among my peers. My weekends at Cy and Glady's became less frequent. Cy died on a Friday night in our driveway, November 10, 1972. In such a short time I was off to Furman University for the start of my college career. As is the normal course of life, I saw less and less of Glady, holidays and such, but eventually she moved to live with her daughter Melissa at Cape Hatteras. By then, I was occupied with marriage and shortly thereafter with a house full of babies. And not only did I see less and less of her, but it seemed that there was now less and less of her to see! Although her mind was as sharp as ever, she seemed shorter and smaller each time I saw her, as though she were shrinking. Physically, she began to appear frail, with the bumps and bruises that are visited upon the elderly. Now when I would see Glady, I would find myself wondering if it would be the last time I would ever see her. And, of course, eventually it was. I can picture Glady perfectly, standing on the front porch of Melissa's house in Shelby, where they had moved just down the street from my cousin Shannon (who married second-cousin Chip Blackley... we're that kind of people!). She waved us down the drive and out of sight around the curve, and I never saw her again.

Her death was a good one. She was aware of her mortality. She was prepared for her immortality. She had been a widow for twenty-two years. She had had relatively good health, although she had a perfectionist's bent that caused her to be plagued by migraine headaches throughout her life. She was the eldest daughter of eight children, the first of the girls to die. She didn't suffer. She died quickly, mercifully, and with grace. At her funeral, there was no need to ask "Why?" There was only thanksgiving when she took her place next to Cy in the Sardis Cemetery.

The heart has reasons that reason does not know.
Blaise Pascal

2003

This summer my older brother Ren and I went to see Garrison Keillor at the Fox Theater in Atlanta. It was almost perfect, but our wives went. Carol Jeanne runs the other direction on Saturday night at 5:55 PM when I start dragging out my extension cords and boom box so that I can listen to Garrison anywhere on our fifteen acres. I usually have radios dialed to National Public Radio, simultaneously, in the barn, the patio, the carport, on my computer, in my pickup truck, in my shop, and in the living room. She thinks this is excessive. So why she wanted to drive all the way to Atlanta and frown at me whenever I would pour myself a fresh Scotch while swaying over the Fox balcony and whistling at Garrison is beyond me!

After the show, Ren and I slunk down to the stage and slipped behind the curtains to nab some memorabilia... cue cards and scripts and such. I was dragging mine out of the trashcan, which wasn't exactly a high security zone, and frankly I didn't think much of it. Until, that is, I heard some woman screaming, *"Stop that man! Somebody, stop that man!!"* The man in question was Ren. In his best impression of a Chris Hood-like state of innocent oblivion to Ruth, Ren was plodding doggedly toward the exit about one step in front of this NPR femi-Nazi dyke, and trying for all he was worth to ignore the shrieking shrew. She finally managed to grab his papers and start a tug of war over them. I figured

Ren would probably win that contest, but then again, she was an NPR dyke, so call it a toss up. Personally, I wasn't waiting to find out. I slid my collection back in the trashcan. Just to the side of the stage was an exit door onto Peachtree Street. I took it.

2001

Well January, which was young when I started this tome, is sliding into February, and we're well into winter. It's chilly and damp. It generally takes the clothes two sunny days to dry on the line outside. In our family, we fight over the laundry – over who *gets* to do it, not who *has* to do it. I do most of it. Therefore, most of it gets hung on the line. The women in my house would rather dry the laundry in the clothes dryer, and when they do, they throw in something call Bounce Dryer Sheets. As it says right there on the box, these are fabric softeners with a fragrance. What it doesn't say is that the fragrance is a blend of urinal cakes and French bordello. I have found that nothing enhances the manly musk of a flannel shirt and blue jeans like Bounce. I wouldn't recommend it in a biker bar or at the rodeo, but if you're cruising the latest Monet exhibit at the art museum, this smell is for you.

The girls complain that when the laundry is dried on line, the clothes pins leave pucker marks on the shoulders of their shirts (Which, number one, how critical can that be on a T-shirt, and number two, why don't they pull their things inside-out before putting them in the laundry like I've told them to do for fifteen years, and number three, like pucker marks on the shoulder are any big deal compared to the fungus growing on anything I don't pick up [with tongs] to wash?). The girls complain that towels off the line are too stiff and rough. Pardon me, while all the kids in Somalia that have never had a steaming hot bath, much less a large, 100% cotton, clean, air-fresh, sun-dried, too-rough towel to dry their swollen tummies with, cry.

Even Carol Jeanne gets in on this. She complains that she doesn't want me hanging her underwear out on the line for "all the world to see." Two observations. First, I've been married to her for almost twenty-three years, and I ain't never seen her underwear, much less her not wearing it. Second, I hang out the laundry on a line on the basement patio in the backyard under the porch, and since we live over 500 feet from the edge of our dead-end street (Note: Our Dead End Street sign, honest, has been taken down and replaced by the politically correct "No Outlet" sign! To me, that sounds like we don't have any electric plugs on our street), with a pack of six dogs to protect it, and in the middle of fifty acres between us, her mother, and her sister, who in the world does she think is going to see it?! An escaped murderer from Atlanta has no chance of seeing her underwear on our clothesline. If one of the towel-heads escapes from Camp X-Ray in Cuba, they will no doubt make a beeline for Eastville, Georgia (Our motto: "Just wait 'til next year's map!") where they hope to see Carol Jeanne's Wal-mart unmentionables (modeled by Thelma in accounts receivable) hang-ing on the line. Woe unto you, Camp X-Ray wannasees... those briefs are lined in lead (No wonder there ain't any in my pencil!). There'll be no undercover underwear infiltration on this clothesline, thank you!

Did I say our laundry was protected by a pack of six dogs? (*One* dog that I intentionally brought home as a Christmas gift from Ruth and Chris, three that have adopted us, one that belonged to a neighbor but refused to live there, and two that belong to Carol Jeanne's sister, but live at/in my house, because that's where the big dogs hang out.) I meant fifteen. This past Thanksgiving, on the extended family's annual trip to the mountains, Carol Jeanne and Megan conspired to bring home yet another "stray" dog. Her name is Zoe. I did not go on this trip, so the vote to bring this orphan back was unanimous... which would have been the case even if I had been there and voted against it! Most stray dogs I have ever seen will eat anything that isn't nailed down. Not this puppy. She eats only meat. Not dry dog food, not cat food, not milk, or cheese. Only meat. Wherever she was getting her stray dog meals, they had pretty high culinary standards (What French poodles call *haute cuisine!*).

Anyway, this dog is still a puppy. Very young, very playful. Very gentle (except for when she ripped my face off when first introduced to me from under Megan's bed, from whence she launched herself like a scud missile!). She is back under that very bed at this very moment, very pregnant, and just beginning to go into labor. She must have conceived this litter approximately five minutes before wandering into the family's mountain campground, looking for steak tartare. She is so young, this has to be her first litter, if not an out-and-out virgin birth to commemorate the season. Thus, with my luck, she is bound to have at least as many children as Jesse Jackson. As we say in Georgia, "Go Dawgs!"

P.S. If any of you are looking for a wonderful pet to bring fulfillment and happiness into your life, please give me a call about March 1st (my motto, "Free to a good home!").

***

We interrupt this broadcast to announce the whelping of Zoe's first puppy at 7:15 P.M. Zoe has been in labor for about fifteen hours, ever since she woke me up at 3:15 this morning, panting, pacing, and anxious. More on this breaking story as it develops.

***

News bulletin... this just in. Zoe has just delivered pup #2. Zoe, who is as black as night, as is her first puppy, has just produced the most perfectly golden parcel you could imagine.

#3 Chocolate brown!

#4. Black, again.

#5. Golden, again.

#6. Solid white.

Whatever other things Zoe might have practiced in her former life, racial profiling was not among them! Zoe whelped these puppies. She even nursed them, briefly. God found them homes. Everything else in between was *me*! First, I had to build them a pen, and this had to be inside since it was winter. This I placed on the linoleum floor of the laundry room. This I did after renting a carpet-cleaning machine to disinfect the area in Megan's bedroom that served as Zoe's delivery room (Helpful hint: It is best if you do *NOT* add Clorox, which, as it turns out, is chemically very similar to bleach, to the carpet cleaning solution, even it is only a cup full and even if you had only the best of intentions.).

Every morning, in my efforts to houseclean around the puppies, I would have to fend off Zoe, who would attack anything that dared enter her room. She would even maul MacKenzie, our Jack Russell Terrorist and the undisputed alpha dog of the entire street. (MacKenzie is highly motivated and assertive, but just because she's a she, everyone calls her a bitch.) After luring Zoe outside with fresh steak, I had to roll up the newspapers that had

116

served as the previous day's bedding, and bag it up outside. By the time I would get back in, all six puppies would have had the bright idea to deposit on the linoleum what they should have been doing on the newspapers in the preceding twenty-four hours. After cleaning that up (Helpful hint: the use of Clorox is totally acceptable on linoleum... go figure!), I would go outside to find Zoe, who had inevitably, following some primordial, maternal directive, dug into the garbage bag to ingest the contents of the newspapers I had just deposited. I eventually wised up and started using the puppies as the bait to get Zoe outside, pausing only occasionally to stop my bleeding. The newspapers went straight into the wood stove for sterilization.

I had been having Scotch and orange juice at breakfast for just a few weeks when it came time for the first puppies to leave. I only thought I cried after sending Rachel and Rebecca off to college (After all, they would come home again, as they do every weekend, even though they're both going to college out of state when they could go here in Athens for free, and the private college tuition is nothing compared to the cost of filling up their gas tanks.). In those six weeks, I videotaped more footage of the puppies and all the other canine clan than all three of my children put together. Thankfully, four of the six puppies were adopted in pairs. The other two went to excellent homes. We still see four of the six from time to time... stunningly beautiful dogs. Zoe immediately went to the Vet for Planned Parenthood counseling and an old-fashioned, state-sponsored "appendectomy." In just a few days, she too was again a puppy. She couldn't have been six months old when she went astray. (Like Mae West, she started off pure as the driven snow, but like the snow, she drifted.) She now sees her life duty as sensing when my alarm is going to go off... about ten minutes before it does. She leaps onto the bed, pirouettes onto my head, curls up, and spends the next ten minutes flea biting and licking... sometimes her, sometimes me. Life is good.

*It is more instructive to allow someone to touch the fire
than it is to tell someone to not touch the fire.*

Anonymous

. . . .

Here's a poem that I wrote:

Intercession

Some somber saint from vespers rose
as evening birthed the stars.
His knees from hours of constant toil
bore witness through their scars.

I heard his whispered prayer take flight
up through the darkening sky,
pleading deliverance from some plight...
a loved one soon to die.

And as it passed me in the air,
t'was joined by another cry.
The two thoughts seemed to linger there,
petitioners asking why.

Then came a chorus of passing pleas,
each more urgent than before.
All of them were reasonable needs,
each requesting more.

A spirit groaning in its ache
bares itself, soft and sore.
A burdened heart, about to break,
reveals its brittle core.

Where is his God? Does He not hear
the pleading of a saint?
Will He not deign to intercede
Before the faithful faint?

Shall they, like Gideon, cast their fleece
upon the threshing floor?
Who shall ransom their release,
buy peace forevermore?

How shall they run and not grow tired;
how shall they mount on eagles' wings?
From whence shall come their saving grace;
cares He not for votive things?

Does God hold me in His hand?
Is each breath designed by plan?
On His wings do I fly?
Can He drop me? Will I die?

"This generation seeks for signs,
they do not seek My face.
They do not find Me or My peace –
they search in the wrong place.

They see their death as dread defeat,
though they shall live again.
They lay their wishes at My feet,
but keep their fears within.

They make requests, but do not know
for what, or how, to ask.
In order to refine their gold,
I've given them this task.

They do not know nor understand
how boundless is My love –
that I hold them in My hand,
in this world and above.

If they just could trust what I know,
of what's to come and what's to go –
how I shall come to set them free
and keep them through eternity.

Then they could live with fate assured,
seeing things as I do...
with all of life's travails endured,
I never did forsake you.

For I have washed you in My blood,
you stand before Me without spot.
Your body reaps the fruit of sin,
but by My grace your soul shall not."

So do not barter with your God,
rather trust Him with your soul,
and He will guide each step you trod,
redeem you safe and whole.

. . . .

There is no glory in outstripping donkeys.
Marcus Valerius Martialis

. . . .

2000
————————

Well, what else do we need to talk about from this past year? The Boy Scouts stunned the Nation by somehow getting the notion that "*...homosexual conduct is inconsistent with the values it seeks to instill.*" The Scouts argued before the Supreme Court (the Federal one, not that bunch of pretenders down in Florida) that requiring them to accept a homosexual scoutmaster "*would significantly burden the organization's right to oppose or disfavor homosexual conduct.*" The hell you say?! The fruit in the suit (Sounds like a Dr. Seuss line, doesn't it?), James Dale, said, "People don't join the Boy Scouts because they're anti-gay. People join the Boy Scouts because they want acceptance, they want community." The point that Chip 'n Dale seems to be missing is that this behavior is *not acceptable* to this group, they do *not want* that type of behavior in their community, they do *not want* him to join/lead their fellowship, and let's pray that no amount of political correctness can force the Scouts to abandon their right to an opinion on the matter. At the heart of it, this not about – or even against – homosexuality. It's about the right of a private organiza-

121

tion to establish moral guidelines that govern the beliefs and behavior of its members, including proscribing certain acts. When it comes to standing up for its beliefs, it seems the Boy Scouts might have more moral fortitude than the Church.

Setting the issue of homosexuality aside, momentarily, where in the world did the Boy Scouts come off thinking they could take a stand on morality, ethics, and principals and get away with it? Draw a line in the sand between right and wrong in America in the year 2000 P.C. (Politically Correct)?! Take a night-and-day stance on good and evil?! I don't think so!! You know who the Boy Scouts ought to be forced to accept? *Girls!* That'd teach them. You are entitled to support the values that the Boy Scouts seek to instill. If not, don't join!! If you don't like the sound airplanes make when taking off and landing, don't buy a house next to an airport, and then complain about the noise! Of course they are permitted to take a moral stand. No, I take that back... they are *required* to take a stand. Otherwise, they're not what they claim to be.

Of course, The Gay Scouts can't be far from inception (as opposed to conception, which will take considerably more time). I can just imagine the merit badges they will earn: baking, sewing, flower arranging. Oh wait, they already have all that. It's called the *Girl* Scouts!! The biggest problem with the Gay Scouts is that the Lesbian Scouts can't be far behind. Gays and Lesbians. Lesbians and Gays. Let's set the record straight (no pun intended) on homosexuality. (By the way, if a heterosexual person is "straight," why isn't a homosexual person "crooked"? It's like the abortion dichotomy, pro-life versus pro-choice. Shouldn't that be pro-life versus pro-death? Either that, or pro-choice versus anti-choice?). Anyway, science comes closer every day to proving what I have maintained for at least twenty-five years. Sexual preference is a genetically determined trait, much the same as alcoholism is. (Medically, does that make homosexuality a disease, as alcoholism is considered to be?). That does not make homosexuality desirable or acceptable (or, necessarily, undesirable or unacceptable) any more than it makes alcoholism desirable or acceptable. Nor does my heterosexuality make it acceptable for me to attempt to practice my preference with every woman I meet. (You'll get slapped a lot if you do, and it hurts!) Discovering the biological truth of homosexuality does, however, begin to make it understandable and addressable. That is the role of science. Determining whether it is desirable or acceptable is the duty of society… three cheers for social intercourse!

Well this is getting dangerously close to the precipice of religion, so perhaps it would be advisable to retreat. And speaking of religion, I'm disappointed in the Baptists. Not for the same reasons as Jimmy Carter, who up and quit the Baptists this season because they didn't win enough football games. Oops, my mistake, that was the Bulldogs, not the Baptists. But Jimmy did quit the Baptists because of their stance on women in the church. My position on women (or at least as close to them as I can get) is that I'm fer 'em. The more the merrier. I'll tell you this much, if it weren't for women, men – don't ask me how men would've got here without women (I know that's poor grammar, but if there ain't no women, who cares?) – anyway, if it weren't for women, men would be crouched naked and unshaven in a cave, waiting to pounce on their next meal. However, since there are women, men sit on the couch, naked and unshaven, waiting on a woman to bring them their next meal while they flip through the TV channels (They don't actually watch TV, not even sports. They just like to flip channels. It suits their attention span!).

Baptists, who are about as noted for being well-read as George Bush is for being well-spoken, have managed to read both Corinthians and Ephesians (which makes three "books," although they're more like short stories, so it doesn't exactly qualify you for being widely read). Baptists read that business about wives being in submission to their husbands, and got so excited they forgot to be literal and inerrant, all at the same time. THE BIBLE – my question is *which one?* People talk about "the" Bible as if there were only one. There's not a single comma left of a single original manuscript. What we have are translations and interpretations that have passed through cultures, societies, and languages for five thousand years. Now I'm not about to limit the power of the Almighty (Pretty big of me, don't you think?), but God originally made the world, including us, and it was perfect when it was finished. It was mankind (both sexes) that fouled up that arrangement. As far as the Bible goes, it weren't all written at once, under one cover, and published by Simon and Schuster (even if they were a fine Hebrew printing outfit before Schuster got dumped for Garfunkel, also a good Jew but he couldn't hit the low notes). Man-kind spent five thousand years piecing the Bible together: voting, fighting, and murdering over who got in on the original copyrights and royalties. I don't know anything that mankind has had its hands on for five minutes, much less five thousand years, that it hasn't made a total mess of. I can't grant the Bible an exception if perfection is the standard, and it don't matter if you're talking about The Living Bible, King James Version, American Standard Version, Revised Standard Version, Tyndale or Scarsdale – whichever is the true, one-and-only, literal, inerrant Bible, and don't pretend that they all same exactly the same thing. Do you believe the Bible is the literal word of God? Here's a test: Has your tongue/eye/hand/mind ever caused you to sin? Is it still attached to your body? Have you ever committed adultery? Are you still anatomically complete? 'Nuf said. (There is, of course, a subtle difference between whether the Bible is the literal word of God and whether you *believe* it!)

There is one peace (that's intentional, not a mistake) of Good News. None of those books is the Word of God, as much as that would please Baptists, who would fight you to the death over the validity of something they haven't even read. The fact of the matter is that we're not satisfied with a Trinity. We want a Quartet, and the fourth member is gonna be something that we can hold in our hands, place boundaries on, and control. Go ahead, but The Word of God is right where it's always been, except for that brief busman's holiday that precipitated, after all, the occasion of this epistle. How do I know? The Bible tells me so!! (John 1:1-14)

Anyway, the Baptists got themselves confused, which wasn't exactly difficult, and started thinking that *my* wife should be submissive to *all* husbands, whether she was married to them or not, which would technically make her a Mormon, not a Baptist. Well clearly once you start down that slippery slope, it doesn't exactly require a Divine revelation to see that *all* women should be submissive to *all* men, whether married or not, much less to each other. Wide is the path that leads to perdition, and there's plenty of women drivers on it! Jimmy didn't want Rosalyn answering to Billy Bob, especially since she doesn't answer to Jimmy, so he up and quit. What the Baptists need to do is to outlaw *all* activity of *any* sort by *every* woman in *each* of their churches. They'd be out of business in a week. So would Methodists, Lutherans, and Presbyterians. I'd say the Catholics, too, but they've excluded women for centuries and you see where it's gotten them (see above, *United States of America vs. Boy Scouts of America*). The fact of the matter is that women are responsible for about 99.44% of anything pure (or was that Ivory soap?) that gets accomplished in the church, including men's attendance in the first place. Tell the truth, if there were no women, would you come out of your cave, naked and unshaven, just to go to church? The number of men in a womanless church would equal the number of men at Christ's tomb on Sunday morning.

But as I've said, that's not the source of my disappointment with the Baptists. That would be the *Sunday New York Times*. They have an ad campaign out that's possibly running in your area also (I find it difficult to believe that any New York enterprise has developed an ad campaign just for the Eastville, Georgia market.). This ad starts off with a *Times* subscriber intoning that, "Sunday morning and *The Times* were made for each other. In the *Times* I learn things that I won't hear, see, or read anywhere else" – like in a Sunday School class! The ad then proceeds to display a demographically diverse sampling of its subscribers lolling about on Sunday morning in various stages of Gnostic orgy with their copy of the *Sunday New York Times*. The ad concludes with a vignette featuring a young couple devouring their *Times* while a background voice informs us that, "When the *Times* arrives, she goes straight to Arts and Leisure, he goes straight to Travel." They're both going straight to Hell! I'm somewhat mystified as to why the Baptists haven't mounted a Disney-like boycott of the *New York Times*, although there is that reading thing involved!

. . . .

Forgiving you would be easy, for I truly like you. The problem is that I have your number, and people's numbers seldom change.
William Alexander Percy

We have met the enemy, and he is us.
Pogo **(Walt Kelly)**

. . . .

2002

Well let's talk about the year's best news story, this idiot woman, Martha Burk. Ms. Burk is the president of the National Council of Women's Organizations, which, as I understand it, has no male members. Perhaps I should qualify that; they have no members who are Men. Maybe they do have a member hiding a Y chromosome underneath a training bra and panties, a member who doesn't have to sit down to pee (he simply chooses to), but let me assure you he is not a Man. You pull his finger, and the only thing you'll hear is him saying is "Ouch!" Silly boy.

Ms. Burk, it seems, has decided that it is terribly important to the furtherance of women's rights (as if they didn't already have a monopoly on all the ones that count) for a woman to become a member of the Augusta National Golf Club. Hootie Johnson, Augusta National's chairman, basically quoted that famous line from General McCauliffe at the siege of Bastogne, and told Ms. Burk, "Nuts!" I don't know how you get the name "Hootie," but I can tell you that "the Johnson" is a stand-up guy, if you catch my drift. To demonstrate how utterly clueless this woman is, someone pointed out to her that her membership issue was with Augusta National, while her threatened protest was against the Masters' Golf Tournament (It's a *tournament*, not a championship.). Ms. Burk insightfully observed, "Well, maybe we'll just get them to play it somewhere else." All of which goes to prove an old saying: *The difference between genius and stupidity is that genius has its limits.*

Let's get a grip on this real quick. Augusta National is a *private club*. The Declaration of Independence recognizes the rights – note, it does not *grant* these rights, it *recognizes* them – of American citizens to liberty and the pursuit of happiness. I am here to tell you that having to tolerate this frigid witch for even one hour would be an infringement of any man's right to pursue happiness. A woman once told Winston Churchill, "Sir, if you were my husband, I would poison your tea." To which Churchill replied, "Madam, under those circumstances, I would drink it." I wonder, in all this furor, what *Mister* Burk has to say? My guess is that "he" is being recharged in an electric outlet.

This is a private club. They can do whatever they want. They can discriminate against women, hermaphrodites, convicted felons, lawyers, left-handers, left-wingers, tree huggers, and tree frogs. Why don't Martha Burk care about the rights of poor people? Augusta National discriminates against them, too. There's not a single member who is poor, that gets a single food stamp, a single cent of welfare, a single unit of public housing, or a single mother. I say that Augusta National ought to be forced to admit a poor person. This will be a thankless task, but in the interest of protecting the rights of us po' folks, I am willing to sacrifice myself on the altar of opportunity. The Glenlivet, please.

Let me ask you something, do the Girl Scouts allow boys to join? Do the Boy Scouts have girl members (other than a few scout masters they're trying to get rid of)? How many white girls are eligible for the Miss Black America crown... how many boys, black or white? Have you ever listened appreciatively to the Vienna *Boys* Choir? How many men play on the LPGA... okay, bad example. If you go into any Federal office, anywhere in America, do they not discriminate on the basis of sex? To wit, do they not send you off to either this restroom or that, based solely on your sex? The best part of this sordid mess is that the Rev-uh-rund Jackson has announced that, come April, he will be in Augusta to support this protest. I'll just bet that Martha Burk is gonna welcome Jesse with open arms. He's just what she's looking for... a man to steal her thunder and share her stage.

Here's my response to Ms. Burk. I predict that the Master's will be played in April. I predict that a television network will cover it, preferably CBS if they have a brain in their corporate head. I predict that I will watch it. To that end, I mailed Hootie Johnson a check for $100 to cover my share of the broadcast expense. Now I know what some of you are thinking... it will cost more than $100 to broadcast the Master's. Let's check the math. The Master's has a worldwide audience of 20 million, including the women viewers. Let's say half of them support Martha Burk (yeah, right). Of the remaining 10 million, let's say half are unemployed. Of the remaining 5 million, let's say half are cheapskates. Of the remaining 2.5 million, let's say half are willing and able to contribute, but are absentminded and forget. Of the remaining 1.25 million, if they all contribute $100, that's $125 million, just over a tenth of a billion dollars. I think I could pull it off for that. I think I could pull it off for free. The rest of you have two choices. Either send me a check for your share of the $125 million, or send Hootie your check for $100. Just tell him Coleman asked you to send it. He'll know what you're talking about.

2006

———————

This past summer, everybody but me went to the beach, and they all went at the same time. Not just Carol Jeanne and the girls. Not just her parents. Not just her sister and brother, and their spouses and children. Even my brother and his family went to the beach, though not the same one (How is it that you can refer to it as "the" beach when there are so many of them?). Everyone went but me. That's *MY* vacation. I don't mind staying home; I collect the mail and newspapers, keep an eye on things, read a year's worth of *National Geographic* in peace and quiet (just like Andy Griffith!), and I care for all the critters. But this time they left me in charge of a menagerie. I was the vet, nursemaid, cook, head bottle washer, and warden to my three dogs (one of which is supposed to be Megan's), my cat (also supposed to be Megan's), my sister-in-law's two dogs (that live at my house anyway), my daughter Rachel's two cats (Miles and Kramer), my brother's new puppy, and 24 ducklings. In the category of cleaning-up-behind, the ducklings out-produced everything else combined. Rachel admonished me to not dare let her cats venture outside; they didn't know about dogs and the wild. They spent the entire week outside, generally chasing the dogs around the yard.

The one that worried me was Rennie's puppy, a wiener dog

named Ruby. I think she was only eight weeks old, weighed less than a pound, and was so little I couldn't see her on the floor, so I stepped on her a number of times when she crept up under my feet. To keep her from whining at night, I threw her under the covers where she slept blissfully. During the course of her stay, I was working on expanding my duck island in the pond, preparing it for the arrival of my 24 ducklings. I would stick her in the shade of a tree on the bank, while I rowed out to the middle of the lake in my boat. Imagine my surprise when I looked back from the island to check on her, only to see these two giant ears swimming toward me, nose poking out of the water like a submarine's periscope! "Please Lord," I prayed, "don't let a largemouth bass get her before I do!!!" That would have been soooo difficult to explain to Anne when they returned!

. . . .

God is a disc jockey, life is a dance floor,
love is the rhythm, you are the music.
P!nk

. . . .

Here's a poem that I wrote:

Senescence

O noble ship, whose bow has braved so many waves
on your voyage of countless tides,
your decks once washed in glory,
trailing honors in your wake –

now moored at uneasy rest
in a port that is not your home,
your crew in fitful slumber lies
in the watch before the dawn.

How you yearn to cast away,
to be free from the hawser lines,
your sails unfurled in splendor again,
the wind against your spines.

But there is no breeze now stirring,
your keel in the doldrums lies.
Your riggings hang in disarray,
your hull is a thin disguise.

Oh for the gift of Youth again –
faithful servant, trusted friend,
equal to the task at hand,
able on your own to stand.

No quarter given, none is asked,
no need to drink when the cup is passed.
Enduring longer than the day,
post the bill, glad to pay.

But were it so, our fate would never be reached,
our final berth would remain unknown,
and it is fulfillment that we seek
as we face the gathering gloom.

So when the Master of the Deep
bids us slip beneath the waves,
shed not your tears of vain remorse –
we have had our younger days.

. . . .

To sin by silence when they should protest
makes cowards of men.
Ella Wheeler Wilcox

People who believe absurdities will eventually commit atrocities.
Voltaire

. . . .

2005

The women in my family – which is everyone in my family but me – gain some deep satisfaction from rolling their eyes at me whenever I make a new "rule." That's their term for a life-guiding principle that I selflessly share with them in the hope of making their passage through this world less stressful and more productive, courtesy of my tremendous ability to observe, analyze, quantify, and maximize. Rest assured that there is a reason – stunningly brilliant in its simplicity – for each of my "rules."

I have a rule that there must be two laundry baskets. (Actually, I have four laundry baskets, but two are stacked one-inside-the-other to form one really heavy-duty basket. Utilized individually, your average RubberMaid won't last a single year of toting wet, heavy towels to the laundry line; the sides will split and the handles will rip. But double stacked, they'll last a lifetime... I've had my current set over twenty years.) Anyway, the rule is that one basket is for taking dirty laundry down to the washing machine, and the other basket is for hauling it out to the line and then back upstairs. "Why?" you ask. Because I don't want my freshly washed T-shirt (What does the "t" stand for?) being dumped into a dirty laundry basket that mere minutes ago held my dirty underwear, jogging shorts, and sweat socks (Why do you think they call them "sweat" socks?), all of which contained fairly water-soluble soils (not the dirt variety). Why not take a nice, fresh hand towel and swab the filthy basket out, then hang it on the towel rack?! Not me. There are two laundry baskets, that's the rule. And by the way, every time you empty out the dirty laundry basket, you have to spray it down with Lysol...that's the rule.

This year we have come into open conflict over the dishwasher "rules." I personally selected our family's dishwasher, and I picked it solely for maximum load capacity. I didn't research Consumer Reports, I didn't watch the ads for a sale. I went to Lowe's, I went to Best Buy (great selection and prices, world's worst service), and then to Sears (I still shop at Sears whenever I can, in hope that it will delay Walmart's takeover of the world. I remember growing up in Charlotte, North Carolina, when there wasn't but one Sears store, and it was way downtown. That was where our Daddy would do most of his shopping. If there had been a University of Sears, it's where he would have sent each of his kids to college. Sears was where he would buy us cashews, choco-late-covered malted-milk balls, and maple nut goodies [For those of you who don't know what a maple-nut goodie is, and I suspect it would be most of you, you can find them in a Brach's candy bag on the candy aisle of your local grocery store. Go ahead and look, they're there and they're good!] At the Sears candy counter, if you pushed up on the glass cover of the cashew bin, it had some give in it, and you could finger the ones closest to the edge out for free if the clerk wasn't looking. Back then it was Sears and Roebuck. I guess Roebuck must've died, but thank goodness Sears lives on, because he's the only thing standing between us and Walmart, and he's gotta be getting on up there in age by now. I guess this is getting pretty long for a parenthetical, so I return you now to our story.) This dishwasher came from Sears, and you can cram more dishes into it than the next two brands combined!

Our dishwasher's silverware basket runs down the right-hand side on the bottom rack. Not down the middle like my in-laws' dishwasher, which has the worst dishwasher layout in the history of dishwashers. Since they don't get *The Newsletter* anymore, I can pretty much lay it on the line about their dishwasher. I know their dishwasher intimately, since it is my responsibility to load it every Monday evening after we have had our weekly supper with them. The silverware basket in our dishwasher doesn't load along the front, or worse yet, on the inside of the front door. It runs down the right-hand side, and doesn't interfere with maximum load capacity. The silverware basket has eight compartments. The only drawback to this arrangement is my family. When you open the dishwasher door, you can only see the first two compartments – really just one and a half. This, of course, means that the four women in my house do their dead-level best to cram eight compartments worth of silverware into two, thereby saving the massive exertion it would take to slide the bottom rack out and expose the six empty compartments just begging for a shot at dirty fork or spoon! No, my women would much rather stick sixteen spoons into the front compartment, preferably "spooned" together, so that the front of the first spoon and the back of the last spoon come out immaculately clean, while every surface in between is covered with lasagna, peanut butter, and really sour cream.

The second source of conflict in my dishwasher rules concerns the upper rack. It's mostly for glasses and Tupperware, maybe a cereal bowl. The problem with this is my family. If they have an exceptionally heavy item – say a mixing bowl, a casserole dish, or a dirty cinder block – they like to stick it in the upper rack.

Not at the back, mind you, but right at the very front. They obviously wish to test the maximum shear strength of the upper rack when pressed into service as a cantilevered beam. As a consequence of poor upper-rack loading technique, they will one day manage to rip the entire dishwasher from the wall and crash it face first into our hardwood floors. On that eventful day, I fully expect them to look at one another (in disbelief), then at me (in awe), and solemnly exclaim, "*So that's why he had rule about how to load the dishwasher!*" It's a pity that that will be the exact day that Hell freezes over.

. . . .

I find myself going to bed earlier and earlier, because I can't wait to get up the next morning and see what I'll have to say.
Lee Trevino

. . . .

2014

Well let's find something a little more cheerful to begin wrapping this thing up. How about a little potpourri? Let's bounce around here like a pinball! I have four toothbrushes. Two for morning, two for night. Two of them are always a light color (say pink or yellow), and the other two are dark (say red or purple), so that I can tell the morning ones from the nighttime ones. Why four? So that they can dry thoroughly in between uses. Carol Jeanne has just the one, and after she uses it, she doesn't even thumb the bristles out, which drives me crazy. Her toothbrush is more soggy noodles than bristles. On the rare occasions that I travel, I carefully wrap my toothbrushes in several layers of toilet paper, like little mummies, before putting them in my shaving kit. Carol Jeanne just shoves hers into her makeup kit, and moves on. Drives me crazy!

When we remodeled our house, we went ahead and put a "handicapped" toilet in our bathroom; it's taller than a standard toilet, about wheelchair height. Now I cannot sit upon a regular toilet without almost breaking my neck... it's a two-inch dead man's drop!

December 28th was the 48th anniversary of my mother's terrible car wreck; I can still remember her sister, my Aunt Carolyn, coming to the house to collect my older brother and me (My younger brother and sister were in the car with my mother.). As I recall, it was mid-morning, drizzling, and she was wearing a red dress and wringing her hands through a pair of black gloves. I wonder if that's really what she was wearing. I can remember when we were kids, our parents would often take us to McDonald's on Sunday night (We'd have to be back in time for *Lassie* and *The Wonderful World Of Disney*.). There was only one McDonald's in all of Charlotte, and it was on Independence Boulevard, next to the Capri Theater and just a couple of blocks from Oven's Auditorium and the Charlotte Coliseum. I think that a hamburger at the Golden Arches was fifteen cents, but my older brother Rennie always ordered the cheeseburger, which cost an extra nickel, and he always ordered a milkshake in addition to his Coke. I couldn't believe how profligate he was with my father's money! After we finished, there was a giant red-clay hill behind the parking lot, and we would climb it and slide back down on nothing but our britches – it was wonderful! Thank goodness cars had vinyl seats (but not air conditioning).

Also when I was a kid, we'd think nothing of walking home from elementary school, or hopping on our bikes and riding up the highway from the house to the shopping center across from the school (There was a 7Eleven there, and we'd buy Icees. My dog Kobuk would usually run alongside me all the way, so when I finished my Icee, I'd take my dog and my cup around back to the spigot to get him a drink of water. They wouldn't refill my used cup with water from the tap inside the store.). I had it in my mind that it had to be a good four or five-mile trip, one way. One of the last times I went home, I drove out to the old house, then up to the old school site (The school is long gone.). It was only nine-tenths of a mile! Still, that was a pretty good poke on a very busy highway for a ten-year old kid... plus it was uphill both ways! And thinking of Sharon Elementary School, I remember that we used to have "milk break" midmorning. Did any of you do that? On Monday, you'd bring your lunch money for the week, and an extra nickel for milk break each day. The teacher kept a little brown manila envelope with your name on it. On the outside, the envelope had these little lines printed on it, like an accountant's sheet. She'd write the date and how much change you put into your account for the week, and she always marked the sum with a "¢" sign. Even if you were in for the whole tilt, you didn't nudge over into the "$" range! At milk break, you had your choice: a fudge popsicle, a banana "fudge" popsicle, or a carton of milk. If you went for the milk, you could choose plain or chocolate. The carton was a little square box, and you'd fold the top edge back and pull it apart to form a spout to drink from. At one point, they switched the milk carton from the little square to a tetrahedron (a pyramid-shaped thing), and it had a little tab at the top that you had to pull off, then stick a straw in it to drink it. I didn't like that, so I stuck with the banana popsicles.

When Carol Jeanne is out of town, I don't have to put the plastic crate that holds my cereal boxes back in the pantry every morning. A roll of paper towels and a roll of toilet paper will last an entire week. Without her or any kids around the house, I don't generate enough dirty dishes to justify running the dishwasher, but my inventory of acceptable cereal bowls (I won't eat cereal out of just any old bowl. There are five in the house that are the proper size and design.) is too scarce to last a whole week, so I end up having to wash them by hand. For shirts that button up the front (i.e., not a pull-over like a golf shirt or a T-shirt), you should only unbutton the top two buttons. That way, you can treat your dress shirt like a pull-over, and once you have it on, you will only have to button one button (or two if you're going to wear a tie). I do not know how much time this will save you over the course of your life, but I do know that I have better things to do with it... perhaps drink Scotch. Also, for men, it is extremely important to know how to tuck your shirttail in. You don't just stuff it in your trousers like a paper sack. On each side of the shirt, you should take the medial hem (the one between the underarm and the hip), pinch it high and low between the thumb and forefinger, then fold it rearward, securing it with the waistband of your trousers and then your belt. Do this and you'll look sharp, like a squared away Marine, and not like a sack of coal.

Finally, on a personal note, 2014 was a year of misery. I was just recovering from a torn adductor muscle on my right side when I tore my hamstring on the left side; I have the MRI to prove it. In June, after five years of nightly torment and sleeping in a brace, I broke down and had carpal tunnel surgery on my left wrist. My symptoms, including awaking *every* night by 4:00 AM to walk the floor until morning, were gone the next day. Unfortunately, within a week, I began to rapidly lose the use of my left hand. Although I am mostly right-handed, some things I do left-handed, and in a matter of just a few weeks I could not pick a dime up off of the floor, hold a razor blade, hold a toothbrush, button my pants or shirts, tie my tie for church (I still wear one), empty an aspirin into my left palm and roll it down to my finger tips to flip into my mouth, pinch the bottom of a page in a book or newspaper to turn the page, or remove the gas cap from my car. Not to be indelicate, but I could no longer use toilet paper, and that is not a good position to be in... don't know which hand you employ, but just once try doing it the other way 'round! A nerve conduction study revealed that I had "severe ulnar neuropathy." That's your "funny bone" nerve, and mine was dying, fast. If there is any such thing as "emergency" orthopedic surgery, I had it. The surgeon said it was in either my wrist or elbow, but since I didn't have time to find out, he was going to operate on both places, knowing that one of them was unnecessary, which is a heck of a thing for a doctor to admit to today. Well, one of them worked! I lost a lot of muscle tissue to atrophy, but I'm slowly climbing my way back, and very gratefully so!!

. . . .

In an abundant society where people have laptops, cell phones, iPods, and minds like empty rooms, I still plod along with books. Instant information is not for me. I prefer to search library stacks because when I work to learn something, I remember it.

Harper Lee

. . . .

2004

Usually, I peck along at this thing all through the year, but I never finish before January. However, today is the 29th of January, and I'm just sitting down to start. I was going to jump on this over the Christmas weekend, but the day after Christmas my little Jack Russell Terrier, MacKenzie, was killed, and I just haven't had any desire to write anything. My heart is broken.

I had taken MacKenzie and Zoe in the pickup truck down to the street while I raked up pine straw. You have to understand we live on a dead-end street in a rural, residential area – it's not a highway. I left Zoe in the truck, because she wasn't as street-savvy as MacKenzie. MacKenzie didn't chase cars, and she didn't run out in the road. She was standing on the edge of the road, wagging her tail and sniffing the neighbor's dog, which was being walked on a leash by a little girl, when a woman down the street ran her over. At 5:00 on a Sunday afternoon, the day after Christmas, this woman probably couldn't have told you her own name, or seen her own hand in front of her face. She was stoned out of her mind. MacKenzie was already dead before this woman ever touched her brakes. Thank God she didn't kill the little girl.

When you first pull into our driveway, and look up toward the house, there is a little mound landscaped into the yard, a promontory of sorts. This was MacKenzie's perch, the spot she would occupy from the time I left the house until I returned. She knew the sound of my truck's tires and transmission, and always knew I was home before I came into view. By the time I would make the turn, she'd be up on her feet at full alert. As soon as I was in sight, she would take off barking at anything and everything, exhorting all the other dogs to get up and get going. She wanted to look busy. I buried her on top of the little mound, facing the driveway, so she'll always know when I've come home.

For the ten years and one month of her life, MacKenzie slept at my feet, under the covers, and snored loudly. She would wait until I got into the bed before she would jump up. Then she would scratch and paw the ear off the side of my head until I lifted the covers for her to descend into the depths. Once at foot level, she would turn around once, then land with a thump at my feet. Religiously, at the count of three, she would heave a sigh of greatest contentment. On the rare occasions that I was out of town overnight, Carol Jeanne would have to drag her in from her perch on the mound. On those nights, she wouldn't sleep in the bed. She would go to the front bedroom and sit in the window seat, where she could look out over her little mound toward the end of the driveway where she knew I would eventually reappear.

MacKenzie was the queen of our roost. In ten years, she ran unknown *thousands* of miles, *literally*, with me. For every one mile I ran, she ran three – up and back, left and right, chase a squirrel up this tree or a chipmunk down that hole, a quick dip in the lake or creek. She was the master of our runs, deciding what order the other four dogs would run in each day, and how close to the front of the pack they could approach, constantly running back to nip and bark at the others to keep them in formation. She would have been in great shape even if she never ran a step, because in all her life, I never went up or down the stairs in my house without her between my feet. I never went from one room to another without her getting up to see where I was going.

A few things in life were sources of unceasing vexation for MacKenzie... vacuum cleaners, water hoses, and wheelbarrows all drove her into a frenzy. She could dart in on a Hoover upright vacuum that weighed twice as much as she did, grab it by the rubber bumper, and lift it off the floor. She would inhale gallons of water with every car I washed as she chased the nozzle spray. She would swim after our ducks for hours on end, even though she was a terrier, not a spaniel or retriever. The fact that she never caught one deterred her not in the least. She weighed fifteen pounds and would fight anything she saw, from possums to otters to the horse across the street or the bull in the pasture and dogs five times her size. She hated cold weather and loved heat. She would stand in front of the wood stove until her fur smoked, *literally*. On cold winter afternoons, if I were in the house, she would follow the path of the sun from room to room in search of the best nap spots. She taught all the younger dogs the boundaries of our land, as well as the boundaries of acceptable behavior. Whenever the other dogs found some cause for barking and dashing outside, it didn't become a matter of official canine concern until MacKenzie would deign to rise and scratch at the door. If she went to the trouble of joining in the chorus, the other dogs would go all the more berserk. She could tree a possum in the grape vines at dusk and bark in cadence through the night. Still barking at sunrise, she would be hoarse and her bark would sound as if she had inhaled helium. She loved pistachio nuts, and could crack them as neatly and empty them as cleanly as any human. Although MacKenzie was a girl, for her entire life she marked her territory by lifting her leg like any boy dog you ever saw.

In the wake of MacKenzie's death, each of the other dogs has been upset and somewhat lost. After I buried MacKenzie, when I went to bed that night, Zoe jumped up onto the bed. She curled her body around my head like a pair of ear muffs, her rump on one shoulder, her head on the other. She slept there all night, never moving. She had never done that before, never done it since. In the absence of their leader, they are all undergoing personality changes, trying to establish a new social order. MacKenzie was my third great dog. I wonder if she has met Georgia and Kobuk. I wonder if I shall ever see them again. God, I hope so.

MacKenzie
November 27, 1994 – December 26, 2004

....

*Your vision will become clear only when
you can look into your own heart.
Who looks outside, dreams; who looks inside, awakens.*
Carl Jung

*They who dream by day are cognizant of many things
which escape those who dream only by night.*
Edgar Allen Poe

Not all those who wander are lost.
J.R.R. Tolkien

....

2021
———————

I was adopted again this year. Each evening, when I make my way around our pond to feed my ducks, I put out a bowl of dog-food kibbles at the end of a bridge. I tell myself that this is a bribe for the foxes and coyotes to leave my ducks alone. I keep a good supply of plastic bags in all of my vehicles, and if I come across a clean road kill of squirrel or rabbit, I'll scoop it up, and leave it on the predator altar along with the kibbles. I generally keep a trail camera on this spot, so I see the foxes and coyotes making their rounds. But then, this little yellow dog started showing up in the pictures. Then I started catching glimpses of her from time to time, but they would be very brief, because she would high-tail it as soon as she saw you, and I mean to tell you, she was fast!

Several of the neighbors on the far side of the pond (my lake, not the Atlantic) were aware of her (She was probably living off of the food they would leave out for their pets, something I never do.). On the trail camera, I eventually noticed that this dog was showing up about five minutes after I set the food out. She had obviously learned my routine, and was no doubt lurking somewhere nearby, waiting on me to leave, so that she could beat out the foxes and coyotes. Then one day, one of the neighbors said that the little dog had started coming up in their yard to play with their dog, Mae (Mae has since passed away from lymphoma.). Mae had an underground wire and collar that kept her on a pretty short leash, so this little dog had to come up near the house to play. Then one day, the neighbor told me that the little dog had approached her husband while he was reading a book in a lawn chair, and that he had been able to pet her head. She also told me that two other neighbors were trying to catch the dog, so that they could take her to the humane society.

She said that they had even managed to catch her once, but after they put her in the passenger side of the car, then walked around to get in the driver's seat, the little dog had bolted out of that car like she was shot from a cannon! The neighbor who had managed to pet her head called her Flash, because she was so fast and could disappear so quickly! I told this neighbor that the next time he saw her, to please call me. I didn't want her going to the pound, and I said that I would let her adopt me. Well, that's pretty much what came to pass. One day they called me, I drove over, managed to slip a leash over her head while she was eating a can of tuna fish, and we went back to the house. I opened the back door, she trotted straight in, and jumped up on the top of the sofa!! Not just on the sofa, not on the cushions, but the very top edge of it. She's like a goat, in that she wants to be on the top of whatever perch she finds, including your head, if she has jumped in your lap. She can jump straight over your head, if she wants to. She was home, by golly! When I went to bed that night, she followed me back to the bedroom. When I raised the sheet and covers to slide in, she leapt up on the bed, and down the rabbit hole she went. I'm still trying to train her to sleep with her back to me, paws outward. They're sharp!

All along the way, I had been telling Carol Jeanne about this dog. The day I brought her home, Carol Jeanne was out running errands. When she came home and saw the little dog, she froze, and said, "NO! No way." It took the dog about two seconds to jump up on the countertop, place her front paws on Carol Jeanne's shoulders, then curl up in her arms. That was the end of that! This is the sweetest, fastest, smartest, softest dog I've ever known. The family went through a series of names, all of the girls getting in on the process – and by the way, every one of my girls wants this dog for her own.

She leaps into your lap, and melts onto your chest. She loves to give out kisses. I've never had a dog that was big on that, but she will lick you to death, often in the middle of the night (But no licking the face!). She has a tongue like an anteater. She is a barrel-chested Feist. She absolutely craves love. She is twenty-five pounds of pure love. And our other dog, Raleigh, absolutely loves her, too. They have epic "wars," snapping and snarling, and running tirelessly throughout the house or yard. She can be sound asleep, and if Raleigh happens to pick up a chew toy or stuffed animal, she awakens immediately. She will get this intense scowl on her face, brow furrowed, and will be laser focused on whatever it is that Raleigh has innocently picked up. She can't stand this, and will leap to the floor to steal it from Raleigh, or to play tug-of-war with him. That look on her face is priceless!

Eventually, I deduced the little dog's karma, and recognized that her true identity is Bonnie (Although "Pinball" would pretty well describe her usual state of being.). She is full of herself, and mischief. One day shortly after she arrived, I was working at my desk, when I realized that things had become deathly quiet, that kind of quiet that you encounter when you have very young children, and they are awake in the next room, and no way should things be that quiet. So I arose to see what was going on. Bonnie had discovered the grandkids' play chest in the recreation room, and was having a party!

Who wants to play?!!

Don't mess with it. I'm not done, just resting!

Man, I'm beat!

．．．．．．．．．．．．．．

No matter how hard you push against the envelope,
it will remain stationery.

Anonymous

．．．．．．．．．．．．．．

2002

Without doubt, the worst news story of 2002 was the news media. I have just absolutely had it with these guys. I watch none of them. They are more out of touch with what "news reporting" and "journalism" are supposed to mean than the Democrats are with the function of "government." (Political note: It is really not

Maxine Waters' place to declare that the people receiving the largest share of the tax refund, who incidentally are the people who actually *paid* taxes by virtue of actually having had a *job* and *earning* income did not "deserve or need it."). What Muddy Waters is conveniently overlooking here is that those people *made* the income and they *owned* it. It was their *property*. Before she tells America what those people deserve or need, she might want to *ask them how they feel about it!* But what is most alarming in her statements is her tacit assumption that if, in her opinion, you do not need something that you have earned and that is clearly yours, she is empowered to take it away from you and give it to someone else who has not worked for it. Or, as ultra-liberal columnist Molly Ivins puts it, the rich pay more taxes because "...they have more money." They *have* more money, not they *earned* more money, not they *owned* more money. Which brings to mind the definition of greed: "*Greed is the desire for the unearned.*" It's not what you have, but how you got it, that defines greed. Anyway, let's get back to bashing the news media.

There was a time in this land when Geraldo Rivera was a reporter. He worked on *20/20* with Hugh Downs and Barbara Walters. Then Geraldo went over to the Dark Side, interviewing Andy Kaufman about rasslin' and stuff like that. The News Media, and the rest of America, snickered behind his back. Looks like Geraldo will have the last laugh, because all the rest of The Media, including Barbara Walters, have joined him. Listen closely to this fact: there is not one penny's worth of difference between Katie Couric and Geraldo, between Tom Brokaw and Jerry Springer. They are employees of the entertainment industry whose job it is to sell advertising, period.

What none of them understands is that news consists of "who, what, when, where, how." When they crossed over into "why" they gave up all pretense of reporting and entered pure entertainment. They don't just tell you that a postal employee shot six co-workers, they tell you *why* he did it. What he was feeling, what he was thinking, how he responded emotionally to rejection. They don't get this as a quotation from the killer, because the last person he shot in the head was himself. No, they piece it together by talking to a co-worker in a different department, then a neighbor two blocks down, then the wife of a third cousin. They ask insightful questions such as, "Why do you think he did it?" Or, "Did he ever exhibit behavior that indicated he was a mass murderer?" "How does this make you feel right now?" It makes me feel like the guy should have saved a few bullets for the Eyewitness News Team.

The most maddening habit that The Media have adopted (They always act *en masse* – they have a stronger herd mentality than a flock of sheep.) is the dual-reporter, simulated repartee. One guy can't do the job, so they have a second reporter – invariably in another city, preferably in another country – join in to co-report the story. Here's the maddening part. After reporter #1 finishes his report, reporter #2 poses some insightful follow-up questions. We are supposed to accept these questions as spontaneous give-and-take between these two journalists who have their finger on the pulse of the issue. Right. These questions are as staged as a working girl's moment in *extremis*. "Bob, is there any speculation as to why the Arabs seemingly hate the Jews?" "John, no one here is saying for sure how the Arabs feel, but what seems apparent is that this particular Arab is now spread from the Golan Heights to the West Bank." What I'd like to hear is, "Bob, considering the global implications of the tensions between the governments of the United States and North Korea, is there any possibility of the US granting a unilateral guarantee of non-aggression to North Korea in exchange for North Korea abandoning nuclear proliferation?" "John, damned if I know what you just asked, much less what the answer is. What I do know is that that wasn't what we talked about in rehearsal, and it's not on my cue cards right now. Back to you, John."

I couldn't make this up if I tried. MSNBC has been running an ad campaign this fall that is the most egregious example of modern media incompetence. It features some guy named Aaron Brown, whom I have never heard of before. Aaron, proudly and with a straight face, intones, "We want to be risk takers. Not with the journalism, but with the way we present the story." Can you believe this? What the hell does he think journalism is? Isn't it something like this: find story, investigate story, present story. How do you "take risks with the way you present the story" without monkeying around with the journalism? Did Cronkite or Murrow follow this philosophy? Aaron Whoever He Is, gets even more entertaining. He informs us that, "It's not enough to have a great story. We have to be great story tellers." Never mind having a *good* story, Aaron has deemed that it is not enough to have a *great* story! The Media have to be "great story tellers."

Well I have an exclusive for Aaron. When you get into "why" and interpretation and opinions and entertainment, you'll tell stories, otherwise known as lies, which is what ABC and CNN news divisions have apologized publicly for in recent years – after they got caught (see Tailhook lies, Agent Orange lies, eleven-year-old heroin addict lies, etc., etc., etc.). Forget the concept of letting the facts speak for themselves. This guy is scary. He's like Alec Baldwin or Leonardo DiCaprio thinking they are elected representatives instead of actors. Oh, by the way, all the while Aaron is waxing idiotic, in the background, if you look closely, there are two giant towers billowing smoke and falling down. That's the backdrop he chose for his advertisement... could I possibly tell you more about him than he already has? Aaron Brown, Archangel of the Modern News Media, scares the hell out me. The only thought that frightens me more is that some of you are listening to him!

. . . .

Celebrity is just obscurity biding its time.
Carrie Fisher

. . . .

2004

On the news front this year, I guess the biggest story was the presidential election. I voted for George Bush, even though John Kerry had better ideas. Didn't matter what the topic was, Kerry was gonna be better. Kerry's idea might have been better, but his ability to articulate it was even less competent than George Bush's! The few times he did try to get specific hurt him even more than being vague (e.g., "Let me tell you what I intend to do about Osama Bin Laden. I intend to find out where he's hiding, then track him down, and bring him to justice!"). Well, duhhh!! Why didn't George Bush ever think of that?! Earlier this month, we celebrated (much to the distress of the liberal media) the inauguration of the president, who arrived with one sleeve rolled up to his bicep. A reporter asked him if it was a gesture symbolic of rolling up his sleeves to get to work in his second term. He said no, he was "just ready to get on with the inoculation!"

But the biggest story in the presidential election was in the ballots. Not counting them, but printing them. This year, in Georgia, you could choose to vote for "the president" or for "el presidente." I kid you not. I don't know about the Hispanic culture in your state, because I don't know the nature of the poultry industry and lawn maintenance businesses where you live. We got lots of both in Georgia, so we have lots of Hispanics. If you have some menial, back-breaking, or very dangerous chore that you need done, you go down to the Home Depot on Saturday morning and pick up however many Mexicans you figger it's gonna take to get the job done. (Editor's Note: For those of you accustomed to going down to the feed mill or lumber yard and picking up blacks for the same purposes, you should cut your recipe in half when cooking with Mexicans. Just give 'em a pack of Marlboros and a liter of Mountain Dew, then jump back! For those of you who think that sounds bigoted, let's just spend a morning in front of Home Depot and see what happens. People go buy 2x4s, paint, cement, and Mexicans. You will see no whites, blacks, or Orientals standing in that line. And when you perform this reality check, don't forget to be there at the end of the day when those workers are dumped back on the curb... except for the ones who got hurt doing something that was too dangerous to begin with, so now they're at the emergency room with no health insurance. But don't worry, I've got them covered. It's a lot cheaper to pay for their X-rays and stitches than it is for all the little new Citizens they're giving birth to.)

At any rate, in Georgia this year, we printed our ballots in Spanish. If you go into the bathroom at Walmart, employees are admonished "bañarse" your hands before leaving the "baño." Every government bulletin board that tells you about Equal Employment Opportunities tells you in English and in Spanish. Purchase anything at Best Buy and the owner's manual is twice as thick as ever... once in English, once in Spanish. Driver's license test, take your pick. Even our public radio station has a Spanish program on Saturday afternoons. I'm not talking about a salsa music hour, which we also have and which I enjoy, nor am I talking about *Latino USA*, a highly informative, weekly broadcast that highlights features about Hispanic communities and culture. No, I'm talking about an hour-long, Spanish-only radio show on Saturday afternoon. I don't know what demographic the geniuses at public radio think they're reaching with this program, but I can tell you the demographic they're turning away in droves. Just how many Mexicans that are listening to a radio on Saturday afternoon do they think are listening to *PUBLIC* radio, for crying out loud?! How many Juans and Pedros do they think are reaching into their blue jeans to become a member of NPR? Well I've quit being a member, thank you very much. I still enjoy Car Talk, A Prairie Home Companion, and All Things Considered, but now I listen for free. ¿Comprendes?

My point is this. Throughout the history of this nation, we

have had two things absolutely in common. The first was our Constitution, our rule of law rather than men. Secondly, no matter how different, no matter how disparate we are, we have always shared a common language (unless, of course, you were from Brooklyn, or Mississippi, or the California coast, or the hood). If you lived in America, you learned to speak English, or some passable version of it. If you wanted to stay in your own little world and speak only Vietnamese or Pakistani, that was your decision. The Federal Government, the local school system, and for darn sure your employer didn't fall all over themselves trying to accommodate your mother tongue. We still don't, if your native language happens to be Polish, French, or Italian. Hell, we didn't even go that far for the perpetually victimized African-Americans, printing stuff in Nigerian or Kenyan or some such thing (Possibly because it would do no good to print something if your target audience could not read it, and which only goes to show that, for all their activist whining about their culture, them folks weren't going to the trouble of learning no foreign language once they got established in America, and English became their mother tongue.). Throughout the world, English is the language of commerce. Thanks to Wilbur and Orville Wright, anywhere – everywhere – in the atmosphere of earth, if you fly a plane, you have to speak English in order to get your pilot's license. It is the singular language of flight.

But when it comes to Spanish, we're setting this country up for a cultural clash that will fundamentally change our course of history as no terrorist will ever be able to do. Our school system can't even teach English anymore, and now they are systematically being burdened with becoming bilingual. Your schools can't afford a nurse or a gym teacher, because they're paying for interpreters and EAASL (English As A Second Language) teachers. I have nothing against Hispanics as people, and I have nothing against Spanish as a language, but if you're in the United States of America, you better by golly get with the program and learn English! English is the international language of commerce. When I am

President of the United States of America, I will make it illegal to print any government document in any language other than English. I will also, as President, make it illegal for Mexicans to blow grass clippings and leaf litter into a public road and all over my freshly-washed car while I'm sitting at a red light!! Furthermore, I will make the owner of the business that was paying them to blow the trash into the street come out and re-wash my car!!!

. . . .

We are all here on earth to help others;
what on earth the others are here for, I have no idea.

W. H. Auden

. . . .

2004

On the home front, our oldest daughter, Rachel, is engaged to be married this June. With any luck, she will make it from here to June without ever having had a cavity, and thus her dowry will be in tact. Since she is getting married, we had to replace our kitchen countertops, which were in just as good a condition as the day they were installed. Why we did this is, I hope, obvious to all of you, because I really don't want to have to explain the obvious. In the process of replacing Formica with granite, one of us tore their rotator cuff while trying to twist apart a plumbing connection under the kitchen sink. Since everyone else in the family was on a cruise to the Bahamas, the affected party must have been me. And be-cause the new sink hardware did not arrive with the new granite countertops, I spent my week as a bachelor without the benefit of a kitchen. Fortunately, I was able to lug all my dishes back and forth between the kitchen and the basement slop-sink with my one good arm, so I only lost ten pounds that week. Anyway, "we" eventually managed to complete this project, so the wedding can proceed as planned.

Did I mention that Rachel is getting married? This of course meant that we had to tear out all the carpet in the basement, including the stairs. Before we could lay the new carpet, one of us had to move all the furniture onto the patio, tear out all the old carpet and pad, sweep/vacuum the whole basement, and seal the concrete with Kilz. I forget which one of us it was. Oh, by the way, as long as the flooring was all pulled up and the furniture out of the way, it was the perfect time to replace the baseboards and paint the basement (two finish coats, but only one of primer!). Anyway, "we" eventually managed to complete this project, so the wedding can proceed as planned.

Did I mention that we replaced the downstairs carpet? I have just walked through the basement and taken an inventory: On top of my brand-new carpet, there are NINE RUGS! I am sure there is a perfectly logical explanation for putting a rug on top of a carpet... if you're a woman!! Speaking as a man, which is the way of speaking with which I am most familiar, I just don't get it. Three of the "rugs" are actually carpet scraps (from the new carpet, not the old) that Carol Jeanne has put down as runners. When I (foolishly) questioned this, she patiently explained, "Shut up." She pointed out that by keeping a carpet scrap at the back door, the scrap would receive all the traffic and soil, and that the carpet underneath would remain like new. It crossed my mind that if it's perpetually covered up and out of sight, the condition of the underlying carpet is pretty much irrelevant. And since no guest has ever, in the past two decades, driven up to our house, walked around to the back yard and down to the basement, and knocked on that door for admittance, what's the point? This same line of reasoning compels me to not use floor mats in my vehicles. What's the point of keeping a car floorboard carpet protected if you're never going to see it? I say use it, see it, get it dirty, clean it when necessary, wear it out, then replace it. Life is short. Take the plastic cover off your sofa and take a nap on the damn thing!!

Did I mention that Rachel is getting married? This of course means that the kitchen floor linoleum and the master bedroom carpet must be replaced with hardwood so that they will match the floors on rest of the main level. The great news about putting hardwood floors in the kitchen, entryway, pantry, mudroom, and bathroom is that the second layer of subflooring must first be removed so that the finished floor will match the height of the rest of the floors! Oh yeah, don't forget to rip out all the shoe mold! I guess "one of us" has quite a chore ahead of them between now and June. Since "we" haven't yet completed this project, the fate of the wedding hangs in the balance!

. . . .

*****NEWS FLASH****

This just in. As it turns out, the wedding, which has prompted all of these home renovations, is *NOT* to be held in our home. Carol Jeanne has just revealed to me that my assumption to the contrary is in error!! If the wedding is not to be held here, why in the world have "we" had to change out the countertops and flooring throughout the house?!! What does the carpet in the basement have to do with the wedding if 99.99% of the wedding guests will never lay eyes on it?!! The longer we are married, the less I understand my wife, but the more I understand what a man needs. A man needs four fundamental things in a woman. He needs a woman who is a good cook. He needs a woman who is a good housekeeper. He needs a woman who is a good companion. He needs a woman who is a passionate lover. These four women should never meet!

*We are here to awaken from the illusion
of our own separateness.*
Ram Dass

2004

Well, Katrina might have been the *national* news story of the
year, but it was not the local story of the year. That honor would
go to the marriage of our eldest daughter, Rachel Kennedy Hood
Elder, and new son-in-law, Ben. Now if Rachel ever has a cavity, it
will be Ben's problem. This was, quite simply, a perfect affair (And
if son-in-law Ben knows what's good for him, it's the last affair
he'll have!). Everyone was invited to come, and most of you did.
All were welcomed guests. All returned safely to their homes and
families, for which I was grateful. I gave the bride away, and forgot
to kiss her when I did, but I think that was the only hitch in the
entire weekend! We had an outdoor reception and the first drop of
rain didn't fall until the last car door had shut. The groom's family
provided an excellent band, and everyone watched the singer,
Marvin Gaye's daughter, shake her booty, then went out and did
the same. The next morning the rain stopped, and we hosted a
brunch at our house so that all of you could see our new hardwood
floors and countertops (The Christmas Letter 2004), which cost
me a torn rotator cuff. But I don't think a single adult went to the
basement to see the new carpet! At the rehearsal dinner, I had to
give a toast, which I was told of beforehand, and for which I was
therefore prepared. Of course, I recited a poem, and I'd like to

share it with all of you. I hope you will read this poem slooooowly, maybe even more than once.

Her Door
Mary Leader

There was a time her door was never closed.
Her music box played "Fur Elise" in plinks.
Her crib new-bought – I drew her sleeping there.

The little drawing sits beside my chair.
These days, she ornaments her hands with rings.
She's twenty-one. Her door is one I knock.

There was a time I daily brushed her hair
By window light – I bathed her, in the sink
In sunny water, in the kitchen, there.

I've bought her several thousand things to wear,
And now this boy buys her golden rings.
He goes inside her room and shuts the door.

Those days, to rock her was a form of prayer.
She'd gaze at me, and blink, and I would sing
Of bees and horses, in the pasture, there.

The drawing sits as still as nap-time air –
Her curled-up hand – that precious line, her cheek...
Next year her door will stand, again, ajar
But she herself will not be living there.

I amazed myself by reciting that poem without crying. I've never even read it to myself, before or since, dry-eyed. At the reception I also had to give a toast, which I didn't know I would have to do because my wife didn't tell me until I was supposed be walking up there to do it, and I don't perform well extemporaneously. Giving the appearance of intelligence without actually possessing any is my only great gift, and while I can bluff my way through life quite well, it does take a certain amount of planning, practice, and preparation. Thankfully, Sir Thomas Moore came to my rescue. His poem, *Believe Me If All Those Endearing Young Charms*, was later transformed into a song. Rafe Hollister (played by Jack Prince) sang a bit of it once on *The Andy Griffith Show*. But before that, the music made its film debut in *The Quiet Man*, starring John Wayne and the most beautiful woman to ever act in a movie, Maureen O'Hara. If you remember the part in the movie when the men have the horse race for their sweethearts' bonnets, the music playing in the background is *Believe Me If All Those Endearing Young Charms*! So, without further ado, I share it with you.

Believe Me If All Those Endearing Young Charms
Sir Thomas More

Believe me if all those endearing young charms
Which I gaze on so fondly today,
Were to change by tomorrow and flee from my arms
Like fairy gifts fading away,

Thou wouldst still be adored, as this moment thou art.
Let thy loveliness fade, as it will.
And around the dear ruins each wish of my heart,
Would entwine itself verdantly still.

It is not while beauty and youth are thine own,
Nor thy cheek unprofaned by a tear,
That the fervor and faith of a soul may be known,
To which time will but make thee more dear.

No the heart that has truly loved never forgets,
But as truly loves on to the close.
As the sunflower turns on her god when he sets
The same look that she turned when he rose.

Ben and Rachel took a honeymoon cruise in Alaska, then bought a house in Roswell, an Atlanta suburb. He initially worked for Kimberly Clark, but was soon hired away by Bearing Point, a consulting firm, and his sole client is The Center For Disease Control. Rachel works in the neo-natal intensive care unit at Scottish Rite Hospital. They have recently acquired two cats, brothers, that I told them to name Romulus and Remus. No one got it. I think they settled on Kramer and Miles. Oh well.

. . . .

Tact is the art of making a point without making an enemy.
Isaac Newton

Diplomacy is the art of saying "nice doggie"
until you can find a stick.
Will Rogers

. . . .

2001

Well it's flu season here, and many sick people have severe cases of the crud. The Bible says it is more blessed to give than receive, so everybody in these parts makes sure to go to church and give like crazy. There's just nothing a good, hearty virus loves more than to pack two or three hundred people into a sanctuary, let them cough into their hands (instead of at the floor like I taught my children) for an hour or so, then spend the next fifteen minutes shaking hands with people that thought they were well!

I ain't worried about it, though. For one thing, I don't shake hands. I nod and speak, but I don't shake. Second, I don't put my hand anywhere near my mouth, nose, or eyes, where a virus can penetrate the mucosa. Third, I routinely sterilize my hands with vigorous washing at every opportunity. Fourth, I sterilize from within with medicinal applications of Scotch. Finally, I got a flu shot, and this year I got one early. Last year when I went, they asked me to wait a few weeks and come back for my shot. They wanted "high risk demographics" such as the elderly to have the first chance to be vaccinated. Like a good neighbor, I deferred. When I went back, they were out of juice. Like an idiot, I got the flu and nearly died. I coughed for two months. I coughed until my hair hurt. I drank single-malt Robitussin by the barrel. Have you ever read a Robitussin label? I have – I had lots of time. It says that Robitussin is "for a more productive cough." I'm here to tell you that if I got anymore productive at coughing, I would've raised the gross national product (pardon the pun).

This year, it's every man for hisself. I went for my shot early, and when the nurse asked me about waiting a few weeks for the elderly to get their shots, I looked her in the eye and said, "Screw 'em. If they catch what I had last year, they're gonna die anyway. Now load that syringe up, Sister, and let her rip!" I don't think Nuns are used to being spoken to like that!

....

Brains are an asset – if you hide them.
Mae West

....

2006

A good number of you have shared with me that my ramblings remind you of Lewis Grizzard, which is, of course, a great compliment to Lewis. He left us too young (like Edna St. Vincent Millay, *his candle burned at both ends, and would not last the night*). When he did not make it out of surgery to replace a defective heart valve, I wrote this memorial to him.

IF I HAD KNOWN IT WAS GONNA MAKE ME RICH, I WOULDA DIED SOONER
In Memory Of Lewis Grizzard, To His Editor

Gerrie,

Well, I guess you're pretty surprised to be hearing from me. When you think about it, though, you shouldn't be. I know it's not very conventional, but when have you ever known me to be conventional? I thought I'd drop you a line to let you know everything's alright. So far this hasn't been anything like what I imagined it would be. I figured you'd go straight from being *there* to being either in Heaven or at Georgia Tech, depending on what kind of life you'd lived. So far things have been in limbo... kind of an adjustment period, no big rush. That's been nice. *Everything's* nice. I don't have to wear socks – they'd look pretty silly without shoes, which you also don't wear in these parts. Neck ties? The word around here is that the fellow that invented them is on the Georgia Tech side of the fence! Please tell everyone how pleased I was with the way they handled my funeral arrangements. Tell Jim and Ray I appreciated their lying on my behalf, and making me sound more interesting than I really am... or was (I'm still wrestling with that, but then verb tenses never were my strong point. I'm proud to say that so far no one around here has asked me the difference between a transitive verb and a pluperfect one!).

I was disappointed Willie Nelson couldn't make it to my memorial service to sing "Precious Memories." But when I woke up over here, one of the first folks I ran into was Tennessee Ernie Ford, so he sang it for me. We've hit it off pea-pickin' good, and we're planning on heading down to Augusta National together in a couple of weeks. He's got a spot staked out on the fifteenth green, but he says we've got to get there early... hey, some things you have to stand in line for even up here!! I'll keep an eye out for Furman and the gang, but I won't be able to speak to them. There's a pretty strict rule about that sort of thing, but tell them to look for a bluebird sitting on a low limb of the pine tree between the fifteenth and sixteenth greens. Furman will know the one I'm talking about, and we'll just let this be our little secret.

Well, enough of this rambling. Let me get to the point of this column. One of the things that has tickled me most in looking in on y'all the past few days has been book sales. I just can't get over the way folks are snapping up anything I ever wrote. I heard where the grocery list I had on the refrigerator when I left for the hospital went for fifty bucks! The bookstores are empty, and prices are going up when they get restocked. I'm making money hand over fist, or at least my estate is. Good for Dedra, God love her (God knows I did). The thought has crossed my mind that, as an author, I'm worth more dead than alive.

There's been folks buying complete sets of my books this past week who have never bought 'em before. And most of these folks

163

ain't got no intention of actually reading the things. They're buying on speculation, hoping to turn a quick profit should my stuff turn out to have any value as a collector's item. To tell you the truth, I'd just as soon folks wouldn't do that, and I'm gonna ask you to ask them to stop doing it as a final favor to me. For one thing, they're gonna be disappointed. And for another, it don't reflect well on them. You don't see Ludlow hawking "Lewis Was My Cousin" T-shirts for $9.95 on the Home Shopping Network, or least not so far. And what would you think of him if he did? But you won't see him doing that 'cause he was Raised Right, and I should know. So were most of them folks buying my books this week.

I'm going to ask them to cut that foolishness out, and start behaving like they were brought up to behave. Elvis has assured me that this isn't an uncommon occurrence in the death of a celebrity, and that things will settle down shortly... about six weeks in my case, about fifty years in his. Oh, there'll be another little flurry of this around Christmas time, but that'll be my publishers profiteering instead of individuals, and that'll be alright because that's what they're in business for.

I guess you've noticed that this hasn't been typed on an Underwood. Actually, it hasn't been typed at all. I've just been thinking it, and now here it is in black and white. I just have to figure out how to get this to you in a way that you can accept. You'll probably notice it has an Athens postmark. That shouldn't surprise you. THE University may not have Augusta's azaleas and Amen Corner, but then Augusta ain't got our coeds, and right now Athens is in full bloom, if you know what I mean. Actually, with Zeir coming back this fall, I'll probably just hang around here through the summer. I'd like to drop you a note from time to time, if you feel comfortable with that. I don't want this to seem to be in poor taste to you. Sincerely. It's just that I have a few opinions I didn't get around to expressing, and what with Zell running again for governor, it's just more temptation than I can stand, even up here! Let me know how you feel. You'll think of a way.

No matter how cynical you get, it's impossible to keep up.
Lily Tomlin

2006

I guess our critter story this year has been the arrival of a new dog. One morning last February – and I mean it was a *cold* one – I headed down to get the newspaper. The dogs have to go along as one of their "chores." This they don't mind too much, because they know that when we get back to the house, they're going to get their daily dog biscuit, an event they embrace with much jumping about, yipping, and quick pirouettes. Anyway, this particular morning, just after leaving the house, I heard this whining and yelping from down in the woods, near the creek bottom. Man, I'm telling you I knew exactly what that sound was and what it meant, and I hurried for the paper as fast I could go. The last thing I needed in my life at that moment was what was at the other end of those yelps. I was looking forward to everything having settled back to normalcy by the time I got back with the paper. No such luck.

We live out in the boondocks. They're not so much the boondocks as when we first built here twenty-four years ago, but it's still country. Folks are prone to drop their unwanted pets off in our area... it's how we got most of what we have. Just what these folks think is humane about setting their pets out to starve, or be hit by a car, or get shot by one of the locals, is beyond me. But I figured out pretty quickly that this pup wasn't a drop-off. The creek is in the middle of my land, at least a half-mile from the nearest road, and this puppy was clearly too young to have wandered that far from the road through pretty rough terrain. No, this pup had to have come from something closer by, and that closer by had to be a mobile home in a pasture over the next ridge, owned by a carpenter named James.

I met James' deer stand way before I ever met James. One winter day while jogging around the lake, I crossed the bridge at Carol Jeanne's sister's fork of the creek, and started up the hill. I happened to glance up where I know I had glanced a thousand times before, but this time something was different. I was looking straight into a deer stand, a self-climber, that I had never seen before. I guess the leaves had obscured it through the hunting season, but now enough leaves had fallen to reveal its presence. Deer season had just expired, so I was no longer jogging in my orange hat, orange shirt, and orange shorts. I finished jogging, got my golf cart and some supplies, and headed back to the deer stand. I fetched it down and stored it in the golf cart, and sat down with my supplies. I wrote a note explaining who I was, that I had confiscated the deer stand, that I would be glad to give it back, but that no way was whoever owned it ever going to put it back where I had found it. I signed my name, listed my phone number, sealed the note in a plastic bag, and tied it to the tree.

By the time my phone rang nine months later, I had completely forgotten about the whole affair. The fellow on the other end of the line was pretty hot. He accused me of stealing his deer stand. I asked him how he knew I had it, and he said he found the note. I pointed out that that didn't too much sound like theft. He got madder, saying the stand wasn't on my land and started quoting me the law about how close to a property line you could hunt. I told him that I was sure he was right, but that he just wasn't ever going to hunt in that particular spot ever again, that he was aiming straight down the hill into the center of my bridge, a bridge that my children walked across, that my dogs and I ran across, that my in-laws drove across. I told him he could have his stand back, but that he simply needed to understand that he would never put it back where it came from.

He pointed out once again, and accurately, that he wasn't on my land. I told him I knew that, and that I also knew the man that owned it, a very wealthy fellow who lived in the next county. I told him that I would have a word with the owner, which I did. I told the owner of the risk this deer hunter had placed my family in. I told the owner that I intended to send him a registered letter to that effect, and that if any misfortune should ever happen to any member of my family as a consequence of this irresponsible behavior I – or my estate – would sue him for every penny he had or could ever hope to see. On the other hand, he could tell the fellow to move the thing and that would be the end of it. He must have told James something pretty much to that effect, because the next day he called to ask permission to come get his stand back if it wouldn't be too much trouble. James arrived on schedule, and he really wasn't a bad fellow after all. He had calmed down a good bit, so I told him that I had plenty of other places on my land that he could hunt, places that he was much more likely to see a deer than on a bridge fifty yards from my sister-in-law's back door.

Anyway, getting back to the matter of the puppy, I knew perfectly well that he had come from James' place. I figured it had wandered off, got as far as the creek, couldn't get across it, and now it couldn't get out of it, much less back where it had come from. Sorta reminded me of myself. Well, off to the creek we headed. As we got closer, the puppy must've heard us coming because suddenly everything got real quiet. It was also still real cold, but I had no choice but to sit and wait for things to heat up again. Shortly they did. I thought I marked the location of the whining pretty closely that time, but it took one more round of freezing on a stump before I realized that the sound was coming from the creek itself, just a few feet away. I looked that creek over, up, and down, and still couldn't see a dog... then I noticed a big fern hanging over the bank. I swept the curtain aside and there she was, a big, fat, brown, caterpillar of a puppy with mud-crusted icicles clinging to her fur. I could easily hold her in the palm of my hand.

By now I was running way behind schedule. I took the puppy to my bathroom, washed a pound of frozen clay off of her, gave her a bowl of warm milk, wrapped her in a dry towel, and deposited her on our screen porch. It goes without saying that she repaid this kindness by making a number of deposits herself on my porch by the time I returned that afternoon. Not giving myself a nanosecond to get acquainted, I bundled that puppy up, threw her in my pickup truck, and off to James' mobile home we went. When we arrived, among the dozen or so assorted hounds, spaniels, retrievers, and collies that greeted us vociferously, I was delighted to see a litter of puppies scampering for protection amidst the ruins of their own mobile home. It lacked doors, most of its windows, and a portion of its roof, but I suppose it constituted sufficient housing for dogs.

James met me at the door and said yes, the puppy belonged to him. He pointed out the suspected father, a large shepherd/collie mix. The mother, he said, was a jet-black border collie who had begun taking long sabbaticals in the woods now that the puppies' eyes were open and their teeth were taking a toll on her underside in the winter cold. He pointed out that they were ready to be weaned, that they had been born the day after Christmas (the day that my dog MacKenzie had been killed by a car). He said that I was welcome to keep this pup if I wanted to. I gave James a friendly pat on the shoulder, and out the drive I went. When my youngest daughter, Megan, arrived home, I made the mistake of recounting the whole adventure to her. She begged and pleaded. I told her no way... all the way back over to James' house.

That dog hasn't been out from between my feet ever since. Today, she weighs almost eighty pounds, and I can't hold her in both my arms, much less the palm of my hand. She has the most beautiful coloring of any dog I have ever seen, and her fur is the consistency of a mink coat. She has any number of shades of brown, from fawn-colored shoulders and tufts in her ears, to a chocolate muzzle and forelegs that are darker than black. Her coat is as iridescent as any hummingbird, crow, grackle, or starling you have ever seen. Around her neck and shoulders is draped a mane like a lion. Across her chest she has emblazoned the most perfect, snow-white cross you will ever see, which prompted the receptionist at work to dub her my "Jesus puppy," which, under the circumstances, I suppose she is.

We were faced, of course, with the dilemma of naming her, a privilege previously reserved as my exclusive domain. I thought of "Fern," since I had found her under one, but that was soundly rejected by Carol Jeanne and Megan (the number of women in my home having been cut in half in recent years, so now the vote was closer to even, being only 2 – 0). I thought of "Moses," as in the bulrushes, again no good. I tried for "Otter," since I had found her in the creek near the scene of the epic otter battle a few years earlier. No go. Megan wanted "Lily," but I objected to that for what it was worth (nothing). I was saved only by the fact that Carol Jeanne didn't prefer it, either. And thus it was that "Bailey" came to be a part of our family. As it turns out, daughter Rachel's observation was most apt... we should have named her "Licker," since that it is what she is most proficient at. She can lasso your ankle with her tongue and bring you to the ground. When she was a small puppy, her favorite pastime was to lie in wait behind the laundry hamper and ambush you when stepping out of the shower. She would endeavor to lick your wet feet dry with a tongue that was, of course, wetter than your feet. As a small puppy, this was endearing behavior. But now that she's better than knee-high and given that she's fairly indiscriminate in her enthusiasm, I have had to banish her from the bathroom, lest one of us be charged with moral turpitude.

In addition to her stunning physical beauty and salivary proclivity, Bailey has one other remarkable trait – nuclear urine. Heretofore in nature, it has been the case that a patch of grass or other similar vegetation that was the recipient of some critter's water-of-the-wild has turned a darker shade of green and prospered above its neighbors. Not so in Bailey's case. Forget Agent Orange and RoundUp. They're no match for Bailey! Any patch of grass so unfortunate as to find itself underneath a squatting Bailey can kiss this earth goodbye. Its demise is both certain and exceedingly swift. Within twenty-four hours, that grass will have died and withered like the Wicked Witch of the East underneath Dorothy's house! Our yard is now pockmarked with dinner plate-sized circles of death and threatens to soon more closely resemble the lunar surface than a lawn of Centipede turf grass.

. . . .

A committee is a cul-de-sac down which ideas are lured, then quietly strangled.
Barnett Cocks

. . . .

2021

America is a very divided country, split just about down the center. That's apparent in our politics, everything from your local school board to the White House. But I'd venture to say that our longest standing source of division is in regard to race. That should no longer be the case. Race, as an issue, should have been put to bed long ago.

May I suggest that you quit being "black." It is simply a genetic phenotype. Quit being "white." It is simply a genetic phenotype. Your skin color does not define you. It should not limit you, anymore than it should entitle you. It does not determine your identity or your destiny. The color of your skin guarantees you nothing. Start being human – compassion, patience, understanding, empathy, love – these traits will be of help. Go watch – and listen to – George Burns and John Denver in *Oh God!* After the murder of George Floyd, have you noticed that it is now *de rigueur* to capitalize the word "black" (when referring to a race, as in the opposite of white, but not when referring to a color, as in the opposite of white)? They took a vote, and passed an Act to change the Rules of Grammar. This is the height of herd mentality, woke-ness, political correctness, hypocrisy, and kowtowing (although it escapes me as to what, or to whom, you might be kowtowing). I blame the media, which used to be comprised of journalists, for this stupidity. Just how false and pretentious is this practice? They can describe a suspected killer as being "Black" (upper case "B"), and the person he killed as being "white" (lower case "w"). Now we have "Black leaders" (otherwise known as ticks), "Black churches" (not Christian churches?), and one of the greatest myths ever foisted upon the American public, "the Black community."

I am here to tell you that there is no such thing as the Black community. Is there a white community? I am pretty sure that I am white, damn near 100%, or at least as far back as my wood-pile records go. I have never attended – never been invited to – a gathering of the white community. I have never attended any event that excluded any person of any other color, or excluded anyone on the basis of anything (except maybe my high school Honor Society, which discriminated on the basis of academic performance – a bigoted meritocracy). This being a fact, how can I know how to think/feel/act? My "community" has let me down! There is no white community, no white monolith. Get some white Catholics and some white Baptists, some white Alabama football fans and some white Notre Dame football fans, some white stockbrokers and some white car mechanics together, and you know what they all have in common? They're all white. That's it. End of story. Their "whiteness" connects them in absolutely, exactly, no other way. The white guy in front of me in a check-out line or a red light is just a white pain in my caboose (especially if he won't pull out into the intersection when the light turns green, instead of parking behind the stop line, with his white head up his white... oh well, never mind). If you are Black, then you are a black pain in my caboose.

Get over yourself, get on with life, and get out of my way.

Barack Obama was black, and probably still is, and is referred to as the first black President, even though he is just as white as he is black. Kamala Harris (who has, herself, pronounced her own first name as "comma-la" and as "kam-ala," but has castigated others for mispronouncing it – because they are racists), is referred to as the first person of color to be elected Vice-president. Her "colors" are those of an Indian (not the Native American type) mother, and a Jamaican father. As an added bonus, she is the first person elected to be Vice-president who also has a vagina (This is purely speculation on my part. She says that she is a she, but she has thus far not tweeted anatomical proof.). Either of these facts only matters, of course, if you are practicing identity politics. But here is the very important point you want to keep in mind: Kamala Harris is a person of color – you must refer to her that way. Do NOT, however, refer to her as a colored person. There is a distinction. Since I ain't woke, the distinction eludes me.

I want to be honest with you. I am sick of the subject of "Black." Not black people, not "people of color." Rather, it's the purveyors of hate and division that hide behind the mask of justice and equality. They speak of equity, not equality, which means giving them something in the way of reparations (something more than food stamps, subsidized housing, cell phones, free lunches, or Medicaid). They preach inclusion through exclusion, such as the Denver school that reserves its playground one night a week exclusively (There's that word!) for "people of color." Or University campuses that designate "safe spaces" to be used exclusively (There's that word!) for "marginalized" individuals (e.g., minorities, LGBTQWXYZ, and schizophrenics).

These people exploit the ignorant. They weaponize diversity to prevent unity. What they actually demand is conformity. They want to be treated equally by being treated differently. In Georgia, like everywhere else in the United (yeah, right) States of America, the month of February is designated as "Black History Month." It usually peters out in about a week. But in Georgia, we go the extra mile. In Georgia, we additionally designate the Friday after Thanksgiving as "Black Friday." There is no apparent movement afoot to designate a "White Saturday."

If you disagree with the woke, then you are a racist (I doubt that most of those folks could accurately define "racist" [Hint: Hitler was a racist.].). The word they should use 99.9% of the time, is "bigot." Your supposed racism is a consequence of your "privilege." I confess that I cannot accurately define "privilege." I guess I've been too busy busting my butt to earn a living and pay taxes to take time out to attend a privilege seminar. I do know this – privilege doesn't mean that I pay less at Walmart or Lowe's. They don't have "white" prices.

If I were in charge – as I should be – I would make it a crime to refer to a person's race, unless it was in a police report along with traits such as gender, age, height, and weight. Martin King famously said that one day people would be judged on the content of their character, rather than on the color of their skin. I think that most white folks are in favor of that notion, and maybe even most black people as well. But we hear from the activist, not the ordinary. We hear from the proponents of Black Lives Matter, Critical Race Theorists, Cancel Culture, and Antifa, not our neighbors. I would outlaw referencing any American using a hyphenated term. No African-Americans, no Mexican-Americans, no Native-Americans (even though I am one myself, having been born in South Carolina).

Racists, bigots, xenophobes, homophobes – these types of people do exist, and in every shade of skin you can find. But they are the exception, not the rule. They are not the majority. No one in America today is enslaved, or even oppressed (unless you are being forced to listen to Joy Reid). For the love of God, get over yourself. Keep your family intact, get a job and show up every day, generally mind your own business instead of the business of someone you've never met. Be nice to other people. Allow them to be nice to you.

I want to share an excerpt with you that is the most insightful item on race relations in America that I have ever read. It's from William Alexander Percy's *Lanterns On The Levee* (1941).

> ... [The American Negro] will grace in idleness the poolrooms and gambling halls of the colored end of town. None of them feels that work, per se, is good: it is only a means to idleness ("leisure" is the word in white circles). The theory of the white man, no matter what his practice, is the reverse: he feels that work is good, and idleness, being agreeable, must be evil. I leave it to the wise to say which is the more fruitful philosophy, but I know which best develops the capacity to wear idleness like a perfume and an allurement. A white poolroom is a depressing place where leisure does not seem excellent or ribaldry amusing. But Negro convocations, legal or otherwise, are always enjoyable affairs right down to the first pistol shot. No race probably has less knowledge of its own past, traditions, and antecedents than [the American Negro]. What African inheritance they still retain lies in the deep wells of their being, subconscious. They know not whence they came or what manner of life they led there. Their folklore, rich and entertaining, is American not African. Only in their practices in voodoo – their charms, potions, and incantations – can we catch glimpses of customs practiced by them in their mysterious homeland. This failure on their part to hold and pass on their own history is due, I think, not so much to their failure to master any form of written communication, as to their genius for living in the present. The American Negro is interested neither in the past or the future, this side of heaven. He

neither remembers nor plans. The white man does little else: to him, the present is the one great unreality.

I leave it to the reader to discern which path the author finds preferable.

Here's my solution for ending racial strife: interracial marriage. Interbreed until we're all mulatto, a nice high-yellow, a soft café au lait. Then we wouldn't know who to hate.

Peace from my front yard!

. . . .

A man often preaches his beliefs precisely when he has lost them and is looking everywhere for them, and, on such occasions, his preaching is by no means at its worst.

Philip Melanchthon

. . . .

The culture of sports brought us two illuminating insights in 2005. The first comes courtesy of one Barry Bonds, a professional baseball player for the San Francisco Giants. In the next year or two, Mr. Bonds will break Hank Aaron's home run record. Mr. Bonds was implicated in this year's steroid scandal. Since I can remember him playing at half his current body weight, I am certain there was more than a good work ethic at the gym involved here. At any rate, when questioned by reporters about his use of steroids and the implications it might have on the legitimacy of his soon-to-be home run record, Bonds responded, "You want to keep investigating this thing, we're gonna go way back, all the way back. We'll investigate everything and everybody. We'll rewrite it all. It's time to move on. I don't think that steroids improve eye-hand coordination so that you can hit a baseball better, technically." I guess we'll never know, Barry, since you pretty clearly used them to get where you are, which isn't where you wuz gettin' to before you started all this hype (-odermic). Barry sounds like he was tutored in self-defense by Bill Clinton and the Rev-uh-rund Jesse Jackson, who only I will remember counseled one another after being caught in adultery.

Our second sports insight comes courtesy of the NCAA, as in college athletics. This year, the geniuses at the NCAA have decided that come March Madness/Sweet Sixteen/Final Four schools with politically incorrect team names and/or mascots will not be allowed to refer to themselves the way they were allowed to all season long in every other NCAA-sanctioned basketball game, not to mention every other NCAA-sanctioned sport and bowl game. The most taboo transgressions, it appears, involve Injun monikers. If you're a Brave or a Warrior, if you're a Seminole or an Iroquois, if you play for INDIANa (duh!!) University, you're toast. I guess no one out there plays for the San Francisco Fruits, the Brandeis

Kikes, or the Mississippi Slaves. So the NCAA is pretty much stuck protecting us from teams named after the Red Man (I used to chew his tobacco... a little on the sweet side, but better than Beechnut.). Anyway, this has all got me to wondering when the NCAA is going to start worrying about protecting *me*. I'm a Christian (of sorts), and I don't like it when teams call themselves "Saints." I'm a bird watcher, and I don't like it when the Hawks/Eagles/Raptors are oppressed by having tens of thousands of people cheer beneath their banner (Why aren't any teams named the Chickadees or the Sparrows? I think we're on to a whole new form of discrimination here!). Should Hawaii be allowed to continue to host the Hula Bowl? Which people of color do the Cleveland Browns denigrate? Do not the Boston Celtics infringe upon my Scottish heritage and sensitivities? The NCAA has just managed to become, institutionally, a bigger idiot than Congress, and brother, that takes some doing!

While we're on the subject of sports, in last year's Newsletter we addressed the subject of diversity and told a story on NASCAR. This year, in a case of life imitating art, NASCAR has called for greater diversity. One can only assume that it means greater diversity among its drivers, as opposed to its fans. Just what is meant by diversity was unclear, but I assume they are looking for someone named Lance or Bruce to handle a hot pink rod (whew!), or perhaps a wheelman from the hood to drive a stolen BMW. Maybe they could do like pro rasslin' and have a hooded, mystery driver. Tell you what I'd like to see. I'd like to see a Muslim driver. Let him wear a towel on his head instead of a helmet. Strap him into a car, and let NASCAR fans cheer him on in their unique fashion. I bet he'd never lose a race! Is NASCAR considered to be a sport? I'm not sure. They don't play with a ball, there's no score, and no time clock. They prefer you'd "play on the field" (i.e., drive on the track), but it's more of a concept than a requirement.

At any rate, I have a couple of other sports issues to address. The first is Phil Mickelson. As I write this, the PGA tour is playing the Bob Hope Classic in Rancho Mirage, California. At last year's tournament, Phil Mickelson announced that he would donate $100 for every birdie he made to an educational fund for orphans of special ops servicemen killed in Iraq. He won the tournament, made 37 birdies, cost himself $3,700... but he won $810,000!!! That's 0.46%, *less than one-half of one percent*, about a ½ cent per dollar. Phil, who is a millionaire many times over, didn't have to donate anything, but it was his decision to do so and to make a public announcement about it. Phil could've donated $10,000 per birdie instead of $100 and still walked away with almost a half-million in winnings. While playing in the tournament, Phil didn't pay for a hotel room or a rental car or a meal. He didn't buy any of the clothes he wore or any of the golf balls he made those birdies with. He donated a whopping $3,700 to educate the orphans of dead special ops vets. That wouldn't pay for a single semester at the University of Georgia, and we're cheap as those things go. Nice idea, terrible execution.

And by the way, let me share this about that. I am not a Democrat. I do not support the government taking money I earned away from me to give to someone else who didn't earn it. But here is a "social spending" issue I would support, and this country would never know the difference, fiscally speaking. If you die while enlisted in the Armed Forces of our nation and you have children, we will pay for their college educations. You can go into the service of this nation knowing that you have our pledge to educate your children should you make the ultimate sacrifice on our behalf. That way, you won't have to count on Phil Mickelson making birdies to get your kid through community college in about fifteen years. Why don't we all agree to pay for the educations of orphans of our military? Limit the value to a four-year ride to the state university in their state of residence, then let 'em go where they want... Harvard, Yale, Faber. *Write a letter*. Why do I have to come up with all this stuff by myself?

Another pro sports story involves pro sports – more to the point, the *culture* of pro sports. Obviously, there are the drugs and steroids. Guys who did not – could not – earn a college degree,

178

and if it weren't for pro sports, they'd be asking you if you'd like fries with your order. Guys who can't beat the other team, but do beat their women, however many of them they have. Then there's what I call the ghetto mentality... a guy dunking a basketball and hanging on the rim like orangutan and running down court pounding on his chest like a chimp right past the guy that threw him the pass, ignoring him as if he didn't exist. Or a guy scoring a touchdown and going into a spastic orgasm of self-adulation in the end zone, as if he were the first guy to ever score a touchdown and is himself somewhat amazed that he has accomplished this complicated feat. Then consider the growing violence between athletes and fans, millionaire idiots versus blue-collar cretins. Fans who can't spend an hour in church on Sunday, but can spend two days and half a paycheck to attend a single game. You begin to get the picture. My theory is that the culture of professional sports is a barometer of how far down the path to ruin this country is, which is pretty damn far.

As a first step toward curing the culture of sports (or at least in accelerating its inevitable collapse), I recommend the following. Let the winner take all. You have a league (NL, AL, AFL, NBA), play for all the marbles. Lose a game, you're out, season over. Don't pay 'em a dime. Only winners get paid, only winners advance. It would shorten up these interminable seasons, and would quickly cure the professional indifference and malaise toward performance. Some player for the Minnesota Vikings was fined $15,000 for pretending to moon the fans of the opposition. On camera, in an interview, he laughed, he mocked the fine. "Fifteen thousand dollars, fifteen thousand lousy bucks. What's that to me?" To his father, it would have been a year's wages.

Well I hate to leave the subject of sports on a low note, so I invite you to consider this. As I write this, Tiger Woods is pursuing one of the longest lasting records in golf – the most consecutive wins. Golf legend Byron Nelson made history in 1945 by winning eleven straight tournaments (He also won eighteen for the year. Between 1944 and 1945 he won thirty-one of the fifty-four tournaments he entered, or just over 57%.). Winning twelve tournaments in a row is something I guarantee you Tiger Woods will never do. Never. Byron Nelson's record is the most dominant tour-de-force that the game of golf – or virtually any sport – will ever witness. But it wasn't *THE* greatest feat of dominance in the history of sport.

Edwin Moses, track star and master of the high-hurdles, holds the greatest, most unbreakable record in all of sports. As one who has little use for athletics, and even less respect for athletes, I must admit I stand in awe of Edwin Moses. Forget Cal Ripken and most consecutive games played... that's kid-stuff. Home run record? Frauds and cheats. Most points scored in a game, most money in a season, most championships in a career? Forget 'em all. Remember Edwin Moses: Bachelor Of Science in Physics, Master's Degree in Business Administration, two Olympic gold medals (would've had three if not for Jimmy Carter's Olympic boycott in 1980). He won 122 consecutive races in the 400-meter hurdles. He was undefeated for **nine YEARS, nine months, and nine days**. During that time, he set the world record. During that time, he broke his own world record three more times. He was so good, so superior, so unbeatable that the sports world virtually dismissed him. Moses once famously quipped, "It just so happens that my slow is faster than most athletes' fast." In 2006, I believe Tiger won four tournaments in a row, and is currently in the process of extending that streak in 2007. Call me after he wins the next 118 straight. No, on second thought, call me in a decade, in 2016, *IF* he goes undefeated in the interim. Edwin Moses, absolutely the best... ever!

. . . .

Sports don't build character – they reveal it.
John Wooden

. . . .

Well, all this terrorism stuff, along with a stagnant stock market, have pretty much put a damper on the annual Big Trip sponsored by Carol Jeanne's parents for their sixteen-member clan. No Grand Canyon, San Francisco, or Niagara Falls this year. But Ray and Peggy still sponsor a week at Hilton Head each June in the Boss-of-the-Beach, four-story, rental house. I can still remember our first trip to Hilton Head with Carol Jeanne's parents, which we didn't attend, or at least not completely.

I was in graduate school and Carol Jeanne was working at Athens General Hospital. Rachel was fifteen months old and her younger sister, Rebecca, was due that month. One day Carol Jeanne announced that her parents had invited us to Hilton Head for the weekend. I was pretty much sick of classes and labs and teaching and engineering, and a spring weekend at the beach sounded pretty good. That Friday evening, after Carol Jeanne got home from work and I had finished teaching, we loaded up the car with a baby seat, a baby crib, a playpen, a high chair… nothing but the essentials. I can still remember with a degree of clarity that rivals that of standing on the curb under the oak tree in front of Sharon Elementary School waiting for Mrs. Bishop to pick us up after school on November 22, 1963, the precise moment Carol Jeanne made her big announcement. We were on our way to Hilton Head, traveling east on I-20, just entering Augusta and passing under the first Bobby Jones Expressway sign. "By the way," she mentioned, "you know we're staying in the same room, don't you?" Well I should certainly hope so. We were man and wife, officially married and all. Why shouldn't we stay in the same room? "No, you don't understand," she said. "We're *ALL* staying in the same room." By this, she meant not only our family, but all of hers as well, including her sister.

I was driving a 1972 Chevrolet Monte Carlo that I had inherited from my father Chris. At the time, it had a bright orange body with a blue vinyl roof. Originally, the roof had been white, but I had to have it cut off with a torch after I went snow boarding on the roof in an ice storm. I put that Monte Carlo through the median of I-20 in a Hollywood-style bat turn that would have made a NASCAR driver proud. We were now headed west on I-20, back to home and my own bed. Carol Jeanne cried the whole way. I remember making the call to Ray, telling him we wouldn't be down that night. "No, no problem, we just won't be able to make it tonight, maybe tomorrow."

The next day, of course, I did have to cave into Carol Jeanne, and we drove the two hours to Augusta for the third time in twelve hours, then the other three hours on to Hilton Head. I awoke Sunday morning in a hotel room – not a suite, mind you, just your standard two beds, one john, and a sink hotel room – with my 8 ½ months pregnant wife next to me in one bed, my mother-in-law and father-in-law in the next bed, my sister-in-law at the foot of their bed on a roll-away cot, and my infant daughter at the foot of our bed in a crib. You have to understand that my wife grew up in a family that resembled *The Waltons*. If you went to the bathroom by yourself and closed the door, they whispered among themselves, wondering what you were mad about. The family I grew up in also resembled a TV family... the Bundys, from *Married, With Children*. Thank God that Carol Jeanne's brother and sister finally married and had kids, too. This wouldn't have stopped them all from packing into that same hotel room together like Mexicans crossing the border, but local fire codes usually prevailed and they had to begin splitting up into separate rooms.

. . . .

"Shut up," he explained.

. . . .

2005

————————

Since I am now in real estate, and since I now work 6 ½ days a week, at least twelve hours a day (Some of you will think that I have just employed a literary device known as hyperbole. You would be wrong.), it is now February, which is a tad bit on the tardy side for a Christmas letter, even by my dilatory standards. One benefit of my procrastination, however, is that it allows me to share this observation with you. The morning news idiots have just fallen all over themselves to "report" exactly the same story they report at this time every year, to wit, Groundhog Day. The Yankees started this stupidity, which ought to tell you more than you need to know about it right there. Almost three hundred years ago, Pilgrims (An Olde English term, which is translated into American as Yankee) got bored watching it snow. They were short on good weather, but long on rum, and thus was born Punxsutawney Phil. A few centuries later, some rednecks in Atlanta got suspicious that there was money in this gimmick. They went North, captured a groundhog (There ain't no groundhogs in Atlanta.), smuggled him back South where they have held him hostage ever since. Thus was born General Lee, which has, of course, proved to be a source of infinite confusion to fans of *The Dukes Of Hazard.*

Nonetheless, let me distill Groundhog Day, North or South, down to its essence. A bunch of tipsy Bubbas, North or South, drag a sleeping rodent from its den into the glare of a bank of Klieg lights sufficient to illumine (You could say "illuminate," but why use the extra syllable?) the glide-path of a returning space shuttle, toss it on the ground, then wait to see if it will either: 1. hang out for a while, or 2. run like hell back to its den. The rodent's reaction, since it has the highest IQ of any of the mammals present, is then interpreted in one of two ways (Please keep in mind that this is the second day of February.). Either there will be six more weeks of Winter, OR it will be only six more weeks until Spring! Just in case you've had more than your fair share of rum, let's run that by one more time. Six more weeks of Winter OR six more weeks until Spring. And they've been peddling this tripe successfully for almost three hundred years!!! How dumb can you get?

There is one semi-valid point that I, in my demented genius, can extract from this lunacy. Everyone in the world except me thinks of the Vernal Equinox, on or about March 21st, as the first day of Spring. This comes approximately twelve weeks after the Winter Solstice, on or about December 21st. The Winter Solstice relates to the day that the path of the Sun, relative to the tilt of the Earth's axis, reaches the Tropic Of Capricorn in the Southern Hemisphere, the southern most point in its annual pilgrimage. Subsequently, the Vernal Equinox marks the time the path of the Sun (Once again, the "path" of the Sun is an expression relative to the tilt and orbit of the Earth, a subtle point that cost Copernicus his membership in the Catholic Church for several hundred years.) crosses the equator on its "journey" back north.

Now, if you will analyze that process carefully, you will eventually come to realize that the Winter Solstice, the "shortest" day (It still has twenty-four hours in it.) of the year, is actually the center of Winter, the Summer Solstice (the "longest" day of the year) is the mid-point of Summer (sun at the Tropic of Cancer), and the first day of Spring is NOT the day of the Equinox. The Equinox (both Vernal and Autumnal) is the mid-point of both Spring and Fall (Sun at the equator). Spring actually began when the Sun was half-way back to the equator from the Tropic of Capricorn. Spring thus begins about the second week of February, about six weeks from the Winter Solstice and about six weeks before the Vernal Equinox. Therefore, Spring has always begun one week after Groundhog Day. Let those of you who have heretofore walked in darkness be enlightened!!

Ignorance is the mother of admiration.
George Chapman

I shall always cherish my initial misconceptions of you.
Anonymous

What you think of me is none of my business.
Terry Cole-Whittaker

2006

I am a dull and unimaginative man. I enjoy the rut. This is especially true in matters of cuisine. I have a particularly dull and unimaginative culinary habit that for some reason puts a burr under the saddle of all those around me. For breakfast and lunch, I eat exactly the same thing every day. Until the sun goes down, I am a vegetarian, eating only fresh fruits and vegetables... exactly the same thing, in the same numbers, in the same order, every day (Lunch is a banana, pear, tangerine, twelve grapes, three apricots, three prunes, three baby carrots, three olives, three cherry tomatoes, three slices of squash, a handful of mixed nuts, and a V-8.). When my friends (or at least people I know and work with) go out for lunch, I go with them and carry my sack lunch. This is not part of some spiritual quest. As I have already confessed, this is because I am dull and unimaginative.

But there are other reasons for such behavior. First, it is healthy; if I wait until lunch time, until I am hungry, to decide what I want to eat, I will be under the French-fry vat at MacDonald's, accepting direct deposit. Second, it really speeds up grocery shop-ping. I can make it through Kroger faster than any other human, because I buy exactly the same thing every week. If they move one of my items to a different shelf or location, Miss Stephanie, my cashier, or Miss Janice in customer service, or Jimmy Craft over in produce will tell me about it when I walk in the door. "Mr. Hood, we've moved the V-8 out of Health Food over to aisle #4 with the breakfast juices," Miss Janice will tell me. They call me "Rain Man" behind my back, and think that I don't know it. Third, this is the greatest weight control device in the history of the calorie. The more your caloric intake is identical from one day to the next, both in quantity and source, the more likely your weight is to remain the same. Forget all that crap on cable TV commercials and gro-cery store check-out line magazines. You want to lose weight, give me a call.

....

An act of mercy closes the book on a misdeed;
an act of revenge writes a new chapter.
Anonymous

....

2007

As I have previously reported, I despise network news. I turn the TV on in the morning for about an hour, and channel surf incessantly. During that time, I make coffee, then breakfast for myself and six dogs and one cat, and lunch for Carol Jeanne, and then I exercise and stretch (Ten minutes for food preparation, fifteen minutes for food consumption [two handfuls of Total cereal, one handful of Cheerios, one handful of raisins, one handful of blueberries, four strawberries, and a glass of pomegranate juice], fifteen minutes for pet care, and fifteen minutes for exercise, which means I waste about five minutes each morning, somehow.). Over the course of the hour, I watch The Weather Channel (just the regular, daily weather, not the type that changed history), maybe some History Channel (which has never had a show about when *History Changed Weather*). I check out The Golf Channel (if they're doing a rebroadcast of the old *Shell's Wonderful World Of Golf*, but usually at that time of the morning, it's infomercials). And, occasionally, I watch a little of CNN Headline News. CNN is bearable, briefly, so long as you keep reminding yourself that it has nothing to do with news. It is not even entertainment programming. It is only, absolutely, about two things: creating public opinion polls (not conducting them, but creating them), and exploring new business models to transition their network broadcast into the Internet age and audience.

First, they apply their liberal media slant (Yes, Virginia, there is a liberal media, with a stocking stuffed full of agendas. And yes, there is also a conservative media, also with agendas. The difference is, the conservative media purchases its time, and portrays itself as such. It is not well funded, nor is it subtle. The liberal media, insofar as agendas are concerned, is systemic and undisclosed.). Anyway, the liberal media at CNN applies their slant to the most ridiculously biased questions, then they ask you to log onto their web site (Where you can also conveniently purchase CNN coffee mugs, T-shirts, and – no lie – bathrobes! Does anyone know anyone who has ever actually purchased a CNN bathrobe? Would anyone with a higher-than-fifth-grade mentality admit to buying one? If someone *gave* you a CNN bathrobe as a gift, could it ever end up anywhere other than as bedding for your dog house?). Once you're logged in, they want you to answer their biased question, so that they can then turn it into a "news report" that advances their agenda.

Now, of course, they have moved you from the television to

the Internet, which was their intention all along, and while they have you there, in addition to answering their silly questions and buying cheap crap that you don't need, they get you to do more interactive stuff. This involves activities such as competing in their "current events" contest. Basically, they announce on the air that they're about to "open the contest" right after the next "news" report. They give you the report (i.e., the "answers"), then tell you to log-in and see what questions they ask (a real surprise, I'm sure!!). If you ever try this, and score less than one-hundred percent, go back to fourth grade.

There are contests to see who has the most interesting morning routine while watching the show, and contests to nominate "your hero." You can even register for a CNN wakeup call. If you happen to be the lucky winner, they call you one morning to wake you up. If you're not the lucky winner, oversleep and lose your job! There are countless other things to get you wrapped up in their system (which includes, of course, your giving them your email address and a treasure trove of personal demographics). CNN is pitched to a fifth-grade level of mental development, so you can't watch long, only a minute or two at a time, which is more than enough time to picture hot morning hostess Robin Meade in the buff (How many of you have ever done that? CNN wants to know. Text cnn/robinA for "yes," or text cnn/robinB for "no.").

I time my changing of the channel away from CNN by the broadcast of two of their daily features. The first of these is the *Salute The Troops* segment, which features some enlisted personnel's family wishing their loved one was safe at home, instead of in Iraq or Afghanistan. It was developed as a cheap shot by the liberal media to press home the fact that George W. Bush was at war in the Middle East and getting American boys (and the occasional girl) killed in combat, and therefore you should vote against John McCain. It is the same gratuitous, self-serving liberal media tactic that George Stephanopoulos uses on his *This Week With George Stephanopoulos* Sunday morning talk show.

Now most of you don't see George's show, because it airs while you are in church. But if you are in real estate, there are many Sundays (about 50 a year) that you have to work. That doesn't mean that I miss church 50 times a year, but I have seen George's show enough to know that every week, at about 11:50 AM, he airs a segment titled *In Memoriam*. He lists national politicos, world leaders, Hollywood liberals and Nobel laureates who have died in the previous week. This segment always ends like this: "This week, the Pentagon released the names of four soldiers killed in Iraq." They then proceed to scroll the name, age, rank, and hometown of each of these dead soldiers.

My question is, "Why?" To what end do they do this? They weren't necessarily killed in combat. They could have been killed in a traffic accident; they could've had a hangnail that turned sour. The only requirement for making George's roll call is that they died in Iraq or Afghanistan. They could've been shot when somebody's husband came home early, as long as it was in a desert tent, and they would still make the roll call. You get shot on guard duty serving our nation while stationed in Frankfurt, West Germany, tough nuggies, George don't give you squat for air time. If you're a cop or a fireman, and you give your life in the line of duty, George gives you nil, zilch, zero, the big bagel, on *In Memoriam*. If a sailor in the U.S. Coast Guard drowns while attempting to rescue survivors of a capsized fishing trawler, not a word. Killed in training exercises at Camp Pendleton, California? See ya. Why? Well, because their deaths do not enter into the political equation that ABC is foisting upon you (if you were able to watch it instead of singing the closing hymn and receiving the benediction). It is political programming that is consummately disingenuous and hypocritical.

You let Barack Obama get in office, and I predict these salutes and obituaries will become more endangered than glaciers at the North Pole (which has exactly nothing to do with Barack Obama). You let America get out of Iraq and Afghanistan, and you will never hear either one of these shows ever again mention some schmuck in the service who gave his all. Why not? Mission accomplished!

Anyway (and back to the matter at hand, which is still in the general category of crap that hacks me off, thereby preventing world peace), the second CNN segment that reminds me to change the channel is their *Travel Report*. In this fantasy, CNN pretends it is the FAA, and imagines itself able to tell you how many planes are currently in flight. This they do with a map of the nation and little airplane icons scattered about the country, say a couple of thousand at any time (And, I swear, they give a disclaimer that states that the airplane icons "are not to scale."). No kidding?! In the age of technical wonder, this map looks like a fifth grader's social studies project. They have airplanes the size of Delaware on it, and they have to disclose that the airplanes are not to scale?!!!! Give me a break!

But this is not why I am forced to change the channel. It is the absolute inanity of the segment's premise that forces me to surf. When was the last time you traveled through Atlanta's Hartsfield Airport? The people there who work for Delta cannot tell you when your flight is going to leave, even if you're standing in the ticket line that second. Hell's bells, the stewardess (who is now called a "flight attendant," so that "men" can also be one) can't tell you when you're going to leave, even when you have been sitting on the tamarack, twelfth in line to taxi to the runway, for two hours!! But you mean to tell me that the CNN weatherman, for the love of all that is holy, can tell me at 7:00 AM on the east coast that I can expect a thirty-minute departure delay in Portland, Oregon, at 5:00 that afternoon due to the approach of a cold front?!!!!! It doesn't take Fellini to forecast a delay on any day, at any airport, for any flight. And let me promise you, if CNN could even come close to being accurate on that point, it would mean that you were so close to the time to take off that the last place you better be is sitting in your living room, in your lazy boy, in your underwear, watching TV. You have to leave my house a MINIMUM of three hours before your flight, in order to travel the one hour to the airport if you plan on making it through security and onboard the plane.

Does anyone at CNN have any idea how much can happen in three hours? Can anyone at CNN guarantee me that their travel forecast is rock-solid, iron-clad, money-in-the-bank if I listen to it? As my wildlife biology professor, Ernie Provost, used to say, "The answer is not No. It's Hell No!" Uncle Ernie, as we called Dr. Provost, lectured while sitting on top of his desk, crossed-legged like an Indian. With his left hand, he would hold cigarette wrapping paper in his lap, while with his right hand, he would hold a little bag of tobacco above his head. Without ever looking at either hand, he would twiddle the fingers of his right hand such that the tobacco would trickle out into the wrapping paper. He never spilled a single grain of tobacco. He would then roll, lick, and light a smoke, never missing a beat of his lecture. Uncle Ernie gave multiple-multiple choice tests. If you failed to mark a right choice, you lost points, and if you marked an incorrect choice, you lost points. Not only was it possible to get a negative score on one of his tests, it was a common occurrence!

But I still have not gotten to why I have to turn the channel when they begin to broadcast the *Travel Report.* That would be because, *I'm not traveling today!* Or, if I am, I ain't flying. Probably, I'm driving. Possibly, I'm taking a bus, or a cab, or a train, or a ferry, but I'm not flying. Or, if I'm flying, I am going to be the pilot, which I am licensed to do, and their report doesn't apply to me or any other private pilot. But here's the greater point: audience demographics! How many people do you think fly on any given day? Let's say it's one million. Out of a total national population of 300 million, of the one million (three-tenths of one percent of us) that travel by commercial flight, how many of them do they think are going to fly to the six airports they cover? Out of that fraction, how many of them do they think are tuned in to CNN? Out of that fraction, as mentioned earlier, how many could receive their questionable information in time to act on it? By now, you're down to a crowd of folks that could cram onto an airport shuttle bus!! Why are they taking up my valuable time to get a worthless report out to a national audience that, day-in and day-out, has absolutely no use for it?!!! It's so dumb that it boggles the mind!

. . . .

Intelligence allows you to entertain three things:
a friend, an idea, and yourself.
Thomas Ehrlich

Millions long for immortality that don't know what
to do with themselves on a rainy Sunday afternoon.
Susan Ertz

. . . .

2006

I have a great wife, way better than I deserve, probably the best wife in the history of wives – but she's not perfect. Witness the fact that she questions my "rules" (See *The Newsletter*, 2005 for the dishwasher and laundry hamper rules.). I have a rule that toilet paper and paper towels must be dispensed from the top of the roll, so that they come off in the front. As is the case with all of my rules, there is a brilliant reason for this. If the paper comes off the bottom of the roll (i.e., the back), then your hand hits the wall behind it. If your hand is wet or dirty or greasy, then guess what happens to the wall? If you're a woman and you have big rings, then they smack the wall, too. Over time, this will mark up a wall. Since no one in my house is ever going to have to paint that wall, it's no big deal to them. But since I've painted every square inch of every wall in this house eight times in the nineteen years we've lived here, I have a rule, and life is simply better if you obey the rule rather than question it.

All of which leads me to share three life-long behaviors of my wife. In the twenty-seven years we've been married, every night she has asked me, "What do you want to do about supper to-night?" Every night for twenty-seven years my response has been the same – "I want to eat it!" What she really intends to ask me is what do I want to eat, but if I have to think about it, I'd just as soon make it myself (and frequently do). I am not an imaginative, exciting type of person. I am pretty dull and boring. I like "the rut" (see *The Newsletter*, 2003), and seek as a matter of course to stay in one... it means that things are safe, calm, and secure.

Carol Jeanne's second life-long behavior is that she has the habit of asking questions and then not listening to the answer. I do not mean that she simply fails to pay attention, although that is certainly true. No, what she does is ask a question, and as soon as I begin to answer, she finds something else to do. Start a blender or a vacuum cleaner, for example, or perhaps leave the room. Then, when something goes awry two weeks later, and I protest, "But I stood right here and told you..." she denies it vehemently. Upon further reflection, I guess that doesn't make her unique in the world of wives.

The third and final trait perhaps points to a fundamental difference between men and women, and the way they process information. I will ask her a question, and she gives me an answer, but the answer is to a completely different question!! For example, late most every afternoon I will get a call from her when she is on her way home from the hospital. "Where are you?" I will ask her. "I'm running a few errands. I'm about to return a pillow that I bought last week, then I'm going to stop by Michael's to get some fabric, and I have to pick up milk on the way home." All of this is terribly interesting information. It is the cement of a marriage. It has not, however, done anything to address the question I asked of her. The observant among you will have noted that I did not ask her what she was doing. I asked her, "Where *are* you?" (as in at this exact moment), and no hint of that information is contained in her answer. Had she said, "I'm just getting off the by-pass at the mall exit, and I'm going to stop by Pier 1 Imports to return a pillow, then run by Kroger's for milk before heading home," then I would know where she was and where she was headed and approximately when to expect her (as well as my supper). I'd know which way she was coming home, and which direction to work backwards from to find her if she didn't arrive safely. I'd still know a lot of other stuff I don't have the attention span to grasp, but at least I'd have the answer to my question. So I will invariably become impatient and point all of this out to her, and demand that she *just tell me where she is!* There will be a bruised silence on the other end of the phone for a moment, but for only a moment. Then she does it... she asks me what I want to do about supper!!!

. . . .

The trouble with talking too fast is that you may say
something you haven't thought of yet.
Ann Landers

. . . .

1999

————————

This year our nation began to seriously address the issue of drugs. Not cocaine... that's just Darwin's theory at work. I mean prescription drugs. Is it just me, or was 1999 the year of the pharmaceutical? I attended the 25th reunion of my high school gradu-

ation this summer. Now I know what most of you are thinking...
this guy actually *graduated high school?!* Well, socially speaking,
yes, but only after I lobbied for five-credit hours for detention hall.
At a ratio of 10:1 (hey, I was good at math), it seemed an equitable
arrangement, plus they didn't ever have to see me again. Anyway
(And please stop interrupting, or this letter's going to have more
sidebars than the OJ trial.), at the reunion I did not see one hus-
band/father (Assuming they're one in the same, which is certainly
not a safe bet with my senior class, and I told you to stop interrupting.) whip out pictures of the kids. They were too busy whipping out their Viagra, which only led to some really ugly whipping-
it-out scenes about thirty minutes later. Needless to say, I was
stunned! Twenty-five years after graduating high school, I assumed
my classmates would be like I am now – like we all were back then
– which is celibate.

And the drug craze doesn't stop there. Lift up a man's sleeve
and you'll see he's wearing Xyban, the nicotine patch. Lift up a
woman's skirt and you'll get your face slapped (That doesn't have
anything to do with drugs, but it's a handy thing to remember so
that you don't have to learn it the hard way like some people did.).
Nowadays we're taking Echinacea (testosterone), Folgard (cardio-
vascular), St. John's Wart (anti-depressant), Zomig (migraine),
ginseng (energy), Flintstones (out of habit, plus I really like the
fruity taste), and garlic (fleas and ticks... oh wait, that's for the
dog!).

However, in this year of the supplement, my all-time favorite,
the Academy Award Winner, the premier prescription in the land,
has to be (drum roll)... Xenical!! Have you heard the ads for
this??? I'll mail you a tape. The manufacturers tout this as one of
the modern class of "fat whackers." It supposedly inhibits your
body's ability to absorb fat from your diet, thereby allowing you to
lose weight. We know that it doesn't work, because if it did, there
would be no scientific explanation for Rosie O'Donnell. But that's
beside the point. You simply have to listen to the ad. (And I mean
listen, because there are no living people in them to watch. No

matter how much money they offered, no one would participate on-camera, not even a lawyer.). What makes these ads such a classic is the Federal-government-protecting-you-from-your-own-stupidity warning at the end. It's the same doctrine that causes Joan Lunden's ads for Claritin decongestants to caution you that they may cause drowsiness or nausea (like listening to an Al Gore speech), or that makes Briggs and Stratton caution you to not stick your hand under your lawn mower *while it's running!!* Just another example of where we need less government and more Darwin!!

Anyway, as the ad fades out and the government chimes in, the announcer solemnly intones (And again, in the honest-to-goodness words of Dave Barry, I am *not* making this up!) "Caution: Use of Xenical may cause excessive gas with oily discharge, an increase in bowel movements, a sudden urge to have them, and an inability to control them." *Is this the greatest drug ever invented or what?!* This adds a totally new dimension to the game of "pull my finger," which is now more like pull the trigger...in a game of Russian Roulette! Could there possibly be a real man on the face of the planet who will not immediately rush out to buy this wonder drug?! Forget Viagra, I wanna know where I can lay my hands on some Xenical!! Talk about an ice breaker at a party! Or how about that guys-night-out-and-poker-party combo: "I'll see your five aces and raise you... whew! where did *that* come from?! Sorry guys, hope you'll excuse that oily discharge... HAH! HAH! HAH!" Not only am I buying Xenical, I'm buying their stock. This drug is destined to bring more happiness to more people than any product since lithium.

. . . .

When turkeys mate, they envision swans.
Johnny Carson

. . . .

For some time now, I've wanted to introduce you to one of my neighbors, Big Johnny. I first met him when I worked for the local electric cooperative, or the "REA" as Big Johnny likes to call it. REA stands for the Rural Electrification Administration, but I'm confident he never knew that. For that matter, I doubt he could pronounce Rural Electrification Administration. For that matter, I doubt he could even spell REA. None of that mattered to Big Johnny, though. What did impress the hell out of him was that when the electricity went out in our neck of the sticks, which it did frequently, I could ride the line backwards from our dead-end street up to the crossroads in front of his mobile home and, once I was satisfied the lines were clear, I could take a slip stick and throw the switch back on in the recloser at the top of the pole and turn the lights on to every house for the next three miles. Big Johnny couldn't have been more impressed if I had personally discovered electricity, and then invented both the generator and transformer. From that moment ever after, if the lights so much as blinked, my phone would ring. It would be Big Johnny, asking if I had noticed the lights blink, and what did I reckon had caused it. If the lights went out, my phone would ring, and it would be Big Johnny asking when they would be back on. Quite understandably, he sought out my divine omniscience on these matters.

For my part, I always found it curious that Big Johnny thought of the loss of electricity only in terms of "the lights." It was always "Why did the lights blink," or "When will the lights be back on?" Never, "Why can't I watch rasslin' on my TV," or "Why don't my toilet flush?" And by the way, when you live in the boondocks and get your water from a well, water is the big thing you're out of when you're out of electricity. You can heat your house and cook with a wood stove or even a fireplace. Loss of the television is a blessing. In the old days, before the cordless/portable models came out, the phones would still work. But when you ain't got water, you ain't got squat! We've talked about this before, about how I have to tote five-gallon buckets of water up from the creek so the women can flush. But Big Johnny only speaks of "the lights" being out.

Anyway, it was through these phone calls that Carol Jeanne became acquainted with Big Johnny. More to the point, it was through the messages that he would leave on our answering machine asking about "the lights." One day I came home to find Carol Jeanne puzzling over the answering machine. "Listen to this," she told me. I listened. It was Big Johnny. His message said the lights had blinked that morning, and asked if I knew why. I looked at Carol Jeanne, and asked her, "What about it?" "Who in the world is that, and what in the world did he say?" I repeated the message to her, word for word. She played it again, and still didn't understand a single word of it – and I mean literally not one word. She replayed that message a half dozen times trying to identify a single, separate word, and never succeeded. You see, in speaking the King's English, Big Johnny does not find it necessary to actually move either his jaw or his lips – variations in the tone and modality, the amplitude and frequency, of various grunts and sighs are sufficient for communication. Neither is it necessary to remove, even temporarily, the half pouch of Red Man chewing tobacco permanently stored in his jaw.

Receiving – and saving – answering machine messages from Big Johnny became a great hobby of Carol Jeanne and the girls. On days that new messages were left, I would arrive home to a cluster of women waiting at the back door, imploring me to interpret them, to the delight of all. They would bet one another on what was being said, with points awarded to whoever discerned the most actual words. However, no credit was given for guessing "the lights." That those two words were imbedded in there somewhere was a given!

Understand that Big Johnny is the nicest guy you'd ever want to meet. If you had to set a sack of money down and ask somebody to keep an eye on it until you got back, Big Johnny would be your man. He wouldn't ask you where you were going or when you'd be back. He wouldn't ask what was in the sack, and after you left, he wouldn't peek. He'd just watch it for you, and it would be there when you got back, all of it.

Have I told you why we call him "Big Johnny?" He's just under five feet tall and weighs something north of four hundred pounds. Or he did when I first met him. These days, his blood sugar (That's country talk for diabetes.) has forced him to drop about a hundred pounds or so, lest they start having to lop off various appendages. He has a full, thick beard that drapes majestically to his chest and sweeps back over his shoulders. This beard serves as a preliminary filtration system for the tobacco juice that is constantly draining into it from the corners of his mouth. It must be pretty absorbent material, because I'm always on the lookout to see it emerge from the lower side, but it never has.

Any time other than Sunday morning, Big Johnny's wearing as many articles of camouflage clothing as he can support. From his boots, to his coveralls, to his shirt and hat, to the shotgun on the rack in the rear window of his pickup, he likes it camo (I don't want to know about his drawers.). He once told me, with great delight and a measure of pride, about sitting on a bench in front of the mall, waiting for Miss Ruby (his wife) to do some shopping. He had dozed off, but something disturbed him, and he halfway opened one eyelid to discover the mall security nerd reconnoitering him. Big Johnny waited for this kid to get right in front of him before lunging at him and shouting, "Boo!!!" That kid ran all the way to the cleaners! Big Johnny eventually dozed back off. He said the next time he was awakened, it was by an old lady tucking a dollar bill into his shirt pocket. He loved that!

In the twenty-something years I've known Big Johnny, he has never had a job. Once upon a time, he worked for the State Department Of Transportation, but he hurt his back and has been out on disability ever since. So from that day to this, since he can't work, in addition to his disability check he's had to get by plowing fields for the neighbors in the spring, bush hogging in the summer, and cutting firewood in the fall. In between, he's a welder and mechanic. Being disabled has been a terrible burden to bear.

In the winter, he hunts deer, or at least he tries. Big Johnny is the worst shot in the history of gunpowder. If he were shooting at me, the safest place I could stand would be square in his sights. I let him hunt the northwest corner of my land. He's too big to climb a deer stand, so he built a little "playhouse" that he sits in, with sliding windows on three sides of it (I told him he couldn't have a window that pointed out the back of it, toward my house!), and a recliner that swivels 360 degrees. It has two mini-propane heaters to keep him warm. You know when he's hunting, because he always calls the night before to tell you he's coming, and besides, you can see the top of his pickup truck from my kitchen window. Big Johnny don't walk far in his quest for big game... he parks about ten feet from his playhouse!

Anyway, sooner or later over the course of the season, you'll hear the crack of his rifle. That's when I look at my watch, placing a small bet with myself as to how long it will be before I see his pickup coming down my driveway. I know why he's coming before he ever gets there. Invariably, he will report that he had seen a big one, but he "couldn't get a good shot at him." Not that that ever prevented him from taking whatever shot he had!! "Must've nicked a limb," I know he'll say. Usually he does miss, but sometimes he hits the deer, just not where he was aiming, as a flock of buzzards in the pasture a few days later will reveal. But, in the true spirit of sportsmanship and good hunting etiquette, he will endeavor to search for a blood trail on every errant shot. The problem is that he's too heavy to walk the woods. And, if he should find whatever deer was so misfortunate as to walk straight down the barrel of his rifle, he can't drag it out of the woods by himself.

To that end, when he goes hunting, he doesn't go alone. He is always accompanied by Miss Ruby, as well as her mother, whoever she may be. In over two decades, neither Big Johnny nor Miss Ruby has ever acknowledged her presence, much less introduced her by name, but when that pickup rolls down the driveway, I know she's gonna be in it. The women-folk sit in the cold truck while Big Johnny sits in his heated playhouse. The three of them together couldn't pull a goat out of a ditch, but Miss Ruby and her mother are tenacious trackers... fresh meat isn't a daily feature on their menu. I know that two hours after they appear, I will have finished dragging back to his truck whatever victim he's managed to kill, and Miss Ruby's managed to find!!

After he's misfired at the day's victim, he'll pull up to the house, causing every dog inside and out to go into a frenzy of barking. I'll go out to the truck, he'll roll down his window, and he'll mutter something about not being sure if he "hit him or not... he was moving pretty quick, must've been running a doe." After a few more grunts, intended to be descriptive of the drama of the hunt, Big Johnny will lean over, pick up a Coke can, and spit a stream of tobacco juice into it. Then he passes it to Ruby, who spits, and then she passes it to her Mother, who proffers her own amber donation into the collection. You know what they say, "The family that chews together, stays together!"

....

Often we have no time for our friends,
but all the time in the world for our enemies.
Leon Uris

....

2005

I was kicked out of some of the finer institutions of higher learning in the Southeast... five of them at last count. One of them was Furman University. This past summer, I received the quarterly alumni magazine. The last page is always a column entitled "The Last Word." This issue's Last Word was from University President David Shi. It was entitled "Ode To The Oak." It paid homage to the many, massive oaks that adorn the Furman campus, especially those along the colonnaded drive into campus (Furman's campus is nationally renowned for its beauty. When I was there, we used to joke that they had two grounds workers for every student to rake and sweep behind them as they walked to class.). Anyway, the article had this Monet-esque shot of one of the mighty oaks, undoubtedly shot by a photographer lying on his back at the base of the tree and gazing up through its mighty limbs. I read the article and glanced at the photo. Something didn't seem right. I set it aside, but something kept picking at my mind. I went back and studied it again. And the rest, as they say, was history.

I share this story as a small memorial to my former dendrology professor, Dr. Charlie Fitzgerald, who died this past year. He taught me the difference between *Fagaceae* and *Aceraceae* over twenty-five years ago, and I believe his lessons stuck. What you see and think of as a poplar tree, is to me *Liriodendron Tulipifera Magnoliaceae*. The dreaded sweetgum is more poetically titled *Liquidambar Styraciflua Hamamelidaceae*. And no, I didn't he have to look them up to know their names. Between puffs of his pipe in the Oconee-Denmark Forest, Dr. Fitz taught us that a good taxonomist never has to look past eye level to identify a species. It was the bark in the photo, not the blurred leaves, which gave it away!

The wrong tree

Sharp-eyed reader Coleman Hood '78 caught us in an error on "The Last Word" page in the summer issue of the magazine.

Accompanying David Shi's article, "Ode to the Oak," was a photograph of a majestic tree. The only problem: It wasn't an oak.

As Hood pointed out, "The photograph accompanying this article is almost certainly not that of an oak (genus *Quercus* L., family *Fagaceae*). Rather, it is of a maple tree (genus *Acer* L., family *Aceraceae*.) While the photograph is by no means definitive, the tree appears to be one of *Acer saccharum Marsh*, the common sugar maple.

"I might be wrong. It wouldn't be the first time. At any rate, I enjoyed my brief time under all of Furman's canopy, the academic as well as the arboreal."

Hood attended Furman for two years before going on to the University of Georgia, where he earned his degree in 1979 — in forest resources.

We checked with biology chair (and botanist) Joe Pollard, who confirmed that Hood was correct. And we traced the error to a mix-up in communication (and lack of botanical skills) between editor and photographer.

So in an attempt to remedy the situation, we herewith try again to publish a photo of one of Furman Mall's mighty oaks. And we thank Coleman Hood for his good-humored letter.

— Jim Stewart

. . . .

It is better to confess ignorance than to provide it.
Homer Hickman

. . . .

2008

There's something I have to get off my chest that comes from last year's news, concerning the firing of radio talk show host Don Imus. As you may recall, Imus made a remark about the Rutgers women's basketball team in which he referred to them as "nappy headed hos." Fire and brimstone rained down on Imus as upon Sodom and Gomorrah! Tortured cries arose to the heavens, demanding everything from his job to his head on a silver charger. The Revv-ah-rund Jessie Jackson, the same man caught on tape referring to New York City as "Hymie Town," said Imus' prejudiced, insensitive, racially inflammatory remarks could not be ignored; Don Imus must atone for his sins (Don Imus, by the way, was *not* caught in an adulterous affair in which he impregnated a college professor, like some Revv-ah-runds I could name!). Jessie's self-righteous indignation was irksome (and, like everything else about the man, self-serving), but not unexpected. The one that really hacked me off, though, the one that got on my very last nerve, was Al Sharpton.

Sharpton, who also refers to himself as reverend (Although I do not believe he graduated from any seminary or ever pastored a single church, there are published reports that he was ordained as a minister in the Pentecostal church... at the age of ten!). Sharpton squealed louder and longer than anyone over this outrage. He proposed himself as the leader for threatened boycotts of program sponsors, a bluff no one had the guts to call. When Sharpton rolled out his bandwagon, all the politicians and celebrities who had flocked to the foot of Imus' throne, pandering to his prowess as king-maker, started bailing ship faster than lice off a road-killed 'possum.

In putting Don Imus out of business (If only temporarily... he is back on the air on the ABC Radio Network, and you won't hear a word out of Al Sharpton over it, because he's already milked it for all the media attention it's worth.), I wonder if Al Sharpton ever thought about how many other people he put out of work, some of whom may have been black, or female, or some other oppressed minority, or maybe just a lower-income white dude. How about the rest of Imus' broadcast team? How about the news director, news reporter, producer, sound engineer, cameraman, make-up artist, web simulcast technician, ancillary staff, and the list goes on? How many advertisers lost major accounts – and major income – over the protestations of this ostentatious windbag? Tell me, where does Al Sharpton, who as near as I can figure has never himself been employed in an actual job, come off demanding the unemployment of a dozen other people?

And let's take it one step further. Don Imus, and his program, are (were) huge philanthropic enterprises. To the tune of many millions of dollars, much of it coming from Imus' personal wealth, he launched, managed, and maintained the Imus Ranch for kids with cancer. He toiled endlessly for research into Sudden Infant Death Syndrome. He did the same for autism. The Revv-ah-runds Jackson and Sharpton couldn't rub two nickels together in comparison to the socially compassionate, personally responsible, and eleemosynary lifestyle of Don Imus.

Don Imus was sacrificed on the altar of political correctness and moral expediency. He was fired for doing what he was hired to do, for fulfilling his contractual obligation to be "outrageous and controversial." In this day and age, try doing that five days a week, on air, live, without ever offending anyone's sensibilities. Tell me this, where are the Revv-ah-runds Jackson's and Sharpton's outcries of outrage over the lyrics to rap music (where the word "ho" is ubiquitous), the blatant exploitation of black girls in music videos (where the depiction of "hos" is obligatory), or the vocabulary of comedians who are black (who are the only entities in our entire world entitled to use the word "nigger," a entitlement they exercise *ad nauseam*, to a degree beyond the pale)? Was Imus' comment the most sophisticated, best advised thought to ever make its way past his lips? Probably not. Did it merit the moral tsunami that it spawned? Hardly. My advice to every single personality vying for the spotlight in that three-ring circus of indignation is to put on your big-girl panties, and get over it. Remember, as I've already pointed out, those radios and television sets have dials on them, and you don't have to be a rocket scientist to learn how to use them.

....

A public-opinion poll is no substitute for thought.
Warren Buffett

It is because we have at the moment so many claiming the right of conscience without having gone through any discipline that there is so much untruth being delivered to a bewildered world.
Mahatma Ghandi

I never gave anyone hell.
I just told the truth and they thought it was hell.
Harry Truman

....

2002

It's Thanksgiving weekend. I am determined this year to get an early start on writing my annual epistle. Not necessarily finishing it early, but at least starting it before New Year's Day. Our Thanksgiving has been quite successful – so very much to be thankful for. Rachel came home from Furman the weekend before Thanksgiving; her tuition notice came the day after. Rebecca arrived from Presbyterian the Tuesday before Thanksgiving; her tuition notice came the day after. Collectively, I have laid my eyes on the two of them for a total of fifteen minutes, or about the amount of time it took to lecture them on the importance of checking the air pressure in their tires as the temperature begins to fall with the onset of winter. This was warmly received with the type of blank stare one would expect from a welfare recipient if you were to tell him about the great news of a job opening at Walmart. Apparently, if you want to communicate with college-aged girls, you must adjust your circadian rhythm to resemble the crepuscular habits of a deer... most active at dawn and dusk (as in come in at dawn and sleep until dusk).

We actually did have a wonderful Thanksgiving meal next door at my in-laws, Ray and Peggy. After our banquet, we all settled in around the fire to watch a tearjerker movie titled "Simon Birch." Every time I started to drift off to sleep, Carol Jeanne would stab me in the ribs and wake me up. It all got me to thinking about my own childhood. Thanksgivings, which, like Christmas, were always spent at my Grandmother Corille's. Every other day of the year, at any opportunity, I spent at my grandparents Hoods' house, Cy and Glady. But holidays were the exclusive domain of the Porter house.

I have an indelible memory of Louis Armstrong singing *What A Wonderful World* on a black-and-white TV with a small, circular screen in a console that probably weighed three hundred pounds while my Grandmother Corille rocked quietly in her chair and dabbed at her tears with a crumpled Kleenex. The Thanksgiving parade started at the corner of East Boulevard and Park Road, right in front of her house. Santa Claus was always the last float, but since it started right there at the front porch, we got to see him early. We watched the staid high school bands from East Mecklenburg and Myers Park warm up and practice their marching tunes. And we saw the jiving gyrations of the colored band from West Charlotte High School – cantilevered at the waist, bent low toward their shoe tops, but with heads thrust skyward, knees pumping high past their shoulders, snapping their fingers with the backs of their hands almost brushing the ground. They didn't have to warm up because they were cool.

As I have previously reported, along with the Hoods and Porters, there were also the Darnells, who ate pickled peaches and celery stuffed with cream cheese and pimentos. The Darnells, Hoods, and Porters shared Corille as a common grandmother (My Granddaddy Porter died before I was born, but I have a suspicion that I inherited from him, in no particular order, temper, tenacity, and honor.). Cy and Glady also came. So did the Darnells' other set of grandparents, the Darnells. In my entire life, I never heard them referred to as other than Granddaddy and Grandmomma Darnell, except my Aunt Carolyn (their daughter-in-law) who called them Mr. and Mrs. Darnell as long as they lived. Since my Uncle Frosty Darnell is actually Ira Gideon Darnell, Jr. (which does a lot to explain why he had a nickname, since nobody but a Gershwin could be an Ira, and also explains why Frosty was a boxer in his younger days) I know that Granddaddy Darnell was very likely Ira Senior, but only by the process of deduction. If you put a gun to my head, I couldn't tell you Grandmomma Darnell's first name. I do remember that she was possibly the most innocent human I ever met. [Editor's Note: One of my Darnell cousins, upon reading this story, called and informed me that Grandmomma Darnell's first name was – are you ready for this? – Elmore. I kid you not!]

Granddaddy Darnell was a quiet man, reserved and genteel, but absolutely a man. It was a time when a man had two choices of aftershave – Old Spice or English Leather (There was Aqua Velva, but nobody actually wore it... they just watched the commercials with Lani Kazan cooing "there's just something about an Aqua Velva man."). There were no "male fragrances" (unless you pulled a Darnell's finger after Thanksgiving supper) and the only thing you put on your hair was Brylcreme or Butch Wax, neither of which could be sprayed from a can. Anyway, at holiday time, someone would always manage to slip Granddaddy Darnell a glass or two of blackberry wine before dinner, and afterwards he was permitted, publicly, a shot of Old Overholt rye whisky. If you've never had a shot of rye, suffice it to say that it took a man of the Old World to consume Old Overholt. One shot was sufficient to put Granddaddy Darnell in a singing mood, which invariably resulted in this chorus, sung heartily by all the men folk:

> *I'm gonna start a graveyard of my own,*
> *If them niggers don't leave my gal alone.*
> *I've got a razor with a rusty blade,*
> *Gonna lay some niggers in the shade,*
> *If them niggers don't leave my gal alone.*

By today's standards, of course, this is politically incorrect, so much to my regret I will not be able to share with you what would have been a thoroughly quaint vignette. In the politically correct society of America today, when it comes to writing about our past, we could make the historical revisionists of post-World War II Japan yellow with envy.

Today's media, correctly and understandably, will not use the racial pejorative "nigger" in their own operating vocabulary. What is *not* understandable is why they will not repeat it when quoting someone. The Media have apparently received a memo from the PCP (Political Correctness Police). Across the board, without exception, The Media quote this slur as "the N word," a practice dating back to Mark Furman and the OJ Simpson trial. I'm serious. From National Public Radio to *Sixty Minutes* to the NBC Nightly News, whether they are reporting a racially charged circumstance or the latest comedy routine by Chris Rock, they will not verbalize the word nigger, even if Chris Rock is telling Ed Bradley (Ed Bradley, who appears to be black, by some quirk of fate is always the *60 Minutes* correspondent assigned to do the interview of anyone who is also black. Go figure.) – anyway, they will not verbalize the word even if it is Chris Rock telling Ed

Bradley, "You can't have nothing nice with niggers around." Of course, the only reason Chris Rock isn't banned from the entertainment industry for saying this is because he is a person of color – guess which color – and a comedic genius. If Jerry Seinfeld or Robin Williams used the word nigger in a comedy routine, they would be run out of the country. And so would I, if I used it in front of my mother-in-law, something I did not know when Carol Jeanne and I first started dating.

I am the only mostly white person of whom I know, in contemporary society, who ever freely used the term nigger in the presence of blacks and in reference to them. In fact, this occurred twice in my life. The first time was in the ninth grade, when the United States Supreme Court, in *Charlotte Mecklenburg v. Swan*, determined that our nation would be much improved if I were to attend Randolph Junior High School instead of my normal McClintock Junior High (and incidentally thereby denying me my long-awaited shot at dating Holly McClellan, whom I fully intended to summon the courage to ask out somewhere between 1970 and 1971). In a demonstration of interracial harmony, a small band of blacks, inevitably led by Excel Lineberger, would perhaps greet me in the bathroom and invite me to express my support for their civil rights by giving them my lunch money, or they might wait until I had spent thirty-five minutes of my forty-five minute lunch period waiting patiently in line for my turn at the trays and silverware before a dozen or two of them would step in front of me and break into line. On any and all of these occasions – obviously envisioned by our Supreme Court Justices as an opportunity for bridge building between the two races and cultures – I would inevitably fail our national heritage.

You'd have to understand that I was reared in large part in the shadow of my Grandfather Cy Hood, which is a story for another time, but the closest I could come to the olive branch of peace was to suggest that they shove it up their – well, it was a long time ago, and I don't recall exactly where I recommended they plant the branch of peace. But I do recall that I would couch my counteroffer in peaceful and loving terms, typically employing a sexual metaphor, even if it was onanistic in nature, and address them collegially using "the N word."

Invariably there would follow a brief but intense period of backslapping, handshaking, high-fives, low-twos, and the shedding of a slight bit of blood in the time-honored, blood-brother ritual. I am certain that I thus became brother to many of them, but I do not recall any of them reciprocating in this fashion. We generally retired to the principal's office following these induction ceremonies, but one time I became blood-brother to so many brothers at once that the principal's office couldn't contain the complete membership and we had to convene our meeting in the auditorium. The only other white boy in this particular induction ceremony was a Jew named Ted Geddings, who wasn't really even invited to the proceedings, but who had selected exactly the wrong moment to attempt to cross the quad outside the cafeteria. Unfortunately, he couldn't attend the services, because he was in an ambulance on his way to Memorial Hospital. Don Rodgers, our mighty principal, who had little principle, concluded that I had attacked thirty-four black boys, which was all the faculty could corral in the ensuing mêlée. He summarily suspended me, but none of them. But as I said, I was gettin raised by my Granddaddy Cy, and his brother Dan was on the Board of Education. I was in school the next morning before Don Rodgers.

The next time I used "the N word" in the presence of blacks, I was allowed to. I spoke not from my ignorance, but from my status as an honorary black man. It was a term of affection rather than anger. My roommate in my sophomore year of college was Travis Leon McKelvey, from Folly Beach, South Carolina. As is typical of most indigenous people of Folly Beach, Leon was a practicing Gullah. To wit, he was blacker than any asphalt, any eight ball, any midnight-in-a-cave you ever saw. In our room at night, after lights out, the glow of his Kool cigarette was the only indication of where in our room Leon was. Leon and I were the first-ever interracial roommates in the history of Furman University.

I remember the only time my parents ever set foot on any of the five campuses they paid for me to live on was the day they moved me to Furman for my sophomore year. When we arrived at my room in the basement of "C" dorm (which was *not* an acronym for Caucasian, it's just that the Baptists weren't going to throw a name on a dorm for free, not when they could wait for some wealthy benefactor to pass onto his – and their – great reward, and, in exchange for a small bequest of several million dollars, name a building after the dearly departed)... anyway, the rooms in C-dorm were desirable because they, uniquely, contained a sink and medicine cabinet with a mirror. Unfortunately, the sink that my room contained also contained a large number of short, extremely curly black hairs. My mother immediately noted this slovenly behavior. "Your roommate doesn't wash out the sink after shaving," she noted disdainfully. I walked over the see what she was talking about. It didn't have anything to do with shaving. It had to do with picking. As in using a pick-comb to coif one's Afro. This was 1975. My roommate, I informed my mother, seemed to have come down with a severe case of black. My parents were aghast. They offered to go to the Administration and have my room assignment changed. I couldn't believe them. No way was I giving up a room with a sink!

The rumor of the "Odd Couple," as we came to be known, spread quickly through the campus. This was a very small, very Southern Baptist University, and "liberal" only in terms of a liberal arts education. They had only allowed dancing on campus the year before (when, as freshmen, Pam Pinkston and I won the campus dance contest, which was before Dirk Carlson got accepted to medical school to become a rich Ob/Gyn with a license, as opposed to me, who couldn't get into medical school and didn't have a license for what I was practicing, and so Pam quit dancing with me and started marrying Dirk). But alas, our cohabitation (Leon's and mine) remained a rumor only. For three weeks, I never met Travis Leon McKelvey, who was as elusive as a virtual vapor, a veritable spook. Then one night, about three in the morning, I was awakened by a rustling within the room. From underneath the door of Leon's closet, I saw a crack of light radiating, and heard the distinct scrape of clothes hangers on cast iron pipe. Slipping from my bed, I tiptoed over to Leon's closet and threw open the door. At long last, for the first time, I laid eyes upon Leon. "Where the hell have you been?" I asked. "Around," he demurred. "Well why haven't you been around here?" I asked. "Why haven't you been to our room?"

Leon explained that he had come by our room the very first night. He wanted to see if it was true that he was having to room with a white boy. He had come in late, as was his wont, and I had gone to bed early, as I was inclined to do (think Odd Couple). He had inadvertently awakened me from a sound sleep. Leon said that I sat straight up in bed and summarily informed him that I did not allow niggers in my room. He had left and been afraid to return in my waking presence. Leon swore this to be true. I have no conscious recollection of it.

After that, we hit it off famously. As it happened, we weren't complete opposites. We both smoked and we were both poor. In the basement of C dorm, they had these ashtrays in the halls that were the stand-up kind, the tops filled in with what was a precursor to kitty litter. At night, after everyone else had gone to bed, Leon and I would cruise the ashtrays for butts. Since Leon smoked only Kools (or Salems if desperate), his smokes were hard to come by... only blacks smoked Kools, and both blacks and Kools were in short supply at Furman University. Since I smoked only unfiltered brands (Camel or Lucky Strike), my smokes were hard to come by... only Men smoked such brands, and as I said, we were at Furman University. We both also liked beer and chocolate-chip cookies for breakfast. Another common (and boy do I mean common) trait that Leon and I shared was that we were the messiest, sloppiest, foulest people on campus. We both worked in the school cafeteria, which gave us the opportunity to purloin a significant amount of food, plates, silverware, glasses, and trays into our room. None of it ever made it the three hundred yards back to the dining hall. I am fully confident that all of it still exists under a couple of beds in room C-103. I know for a fact that by Christmas break, there was stuff growing in our room that the Biology Department could not identify and the Ecology Department refused to examine.

At any rate, my co-habitation with Leon earned me a sort of honorary status among the two hundred or so black students (out of three thousand total students) required to field athletic teams, school bands, and have enough black females on campus to keep the black jocks from being tempted to date some white Senator's (redundant at that time) daughter. As it turned out, they could have spared themselves the trouble with Leon. As an added bonus to being the first interracial roommates on campus, Leon and I were also the first openly mixed-sexual-orientation roommates... I dated girls, Leon didn't. Actually, he would, sometimes. Leon dated anything. He practiced with vigor the philosophy of Woody Allen that, by being bisexual, one immediately doubled one's chances of a date on Saturday night. The consequence of all of this was that I was freely permitted, as a white man and with impunity, to call any black man on campus a nigger to his face, something the black men on campus routinely did to one another. As a bonus on the sexual orientation front, I was also allowed to call any homosexual on campus a fag, including the center on the football team, who was dating Leon at that time. Never once did they hold me down and fix my hair.

I know I'm getting long in making the point in all of this, but I remember George Carlin teaching us that there were seven words you could not say on radio or TV, and none of them started with the letter "N." Why do reporters think it is politically incorrect to say nigger, but morally acceptable to induce me into thinking that word by saying "the N word?" If it is wrong to say it, must thinking it not precede saying it in transgressing? How can the media cause me to think it, although not having themselves uttered it, without violating the principle of estoppel? Does the technical refrain from utterance absolve them of wrongdoing? Are they not complicit in my evil? Can you imagine Walter Cronkite having said, "Holy S, they blew his F brains all over the back of the limousine!"? Now who's responsible for what just went through your head, you or me? I apologize for making so worthy a point in so vulgar a fashion. But it is a worthy point. How do reporters know that I won't mistakenly take "the N word" to mean Negro, or Nazi, or Nerd, or Nice? There's a lot of room for subjective misinterpretation in "the N word" that just isn't appropriate in a news quote. If that's what someone said, and you think the complete story's journalistic merit warrants the rest of the report, quote it the way it was said. I believe they call it a "quote" for a reason.

There are four points to be drawn from all of this; make a note of the ones with which you disagree. First, political correctness has done got way outta hand. Freedom of speech extends only to the voice of a vocal few. A word in our language is being driven – at least publicly – into extinction (Is there an endangered species list for words? Are words like murder and poverty on it?). This is putting at risk the works of Mark Twain, as libraries and school boards are lobbied to ban his books; in this environment, Flannery O'Connor couldn't even get published, much less win a Pulitzer, or Faulkner a Nobel. Second, there is the implication that there is no such thing as a nigger, which is false (And yes, this statement begs a definition. *If you would converse with me, define your terms.* Voltaire). Third, there is the assumption that all blacks are niggers, which is false. Fourth, there is the assumption that only blacks are niggers, which is false. Anyway, I sure wish I could have told you that story about Granddaddy Darnell, because he sure did enjoy singing that tune... either that or the rye!!

While the story of me and Leon is fresh on your mind, I want to share an epilogue with you. In 2020, Furman University reached out to its former students with an offer to participate in the Alumni History Project. Alumni were solicited to submit their "Furman memories," and then they were offered the opportunity to purchase a copy of those memories, and by the way, that collection was by no means going to be cheap – the price tag was in the hundreds of dollars! So it was basically a fundraiser. Fair enough. I'm certain that Furman expected tales of meeting future spouses, fraternity brothers, and possibly a remembrance of an inspirational professor. I submitted my story of Leon, the same story I just shared with you. Several months went by, and I realized that while the charge to my Mastercard had been processed, I had not heard anything further from the marketing company in charge of the project. So I reached out to them, and was told that they would get back to me shortly. They didn't. So I reached out to them again. Same thing. I went back to them a third time, and was stonewalled. So I called the Alumni Association, and told the representative what I was experiencing. This person said that they would look into it. They did (I am not giving their name, or whether it was a man or a woman.), and very apologetically informed me that "the administration" had rejected my story. They had taken my money, but not my story. Eventually, I got my money back, and "the administration" at Furman got an earful from me. I would like to share my letter to them with you now.

July 10, 2020

President Elizabeth Davis
Dr. Lane Harris
Furman University
3300 Poinsett Highway
Greenville, South Carolina 29613

President Davis and Dr. Harris:

Dr. Harris, as the chair of the history department, I am including you in this letter. As an historian, I hope that you will find the treatment of "My Story" (attached) to be alarming. As a professor at a liberal arts university, especially one that claims to be both diverse and inclusive, I hope that you will be disturbed by the events that have transpired. Rest assured that my story is historically accurate and factually true.

Earlier this year, I was solicited to submit (and purchase) "My Story" for inclusion in the Furman Alumni History Project. I thought that my story was unique, and important both to myself and the history of Furman. To that end, on February 18, I paid my $438.63, and submitted my story.

Following my payment and submission, there were a number of months of non-response from client service at Publishing Concepts Incorporated (PCI), the publishing group behind the history project – a project that is essentially a fundraiser based on nostalgia. I will not bore you with all the details that followed, as they are not the point of this letter. Suffice it to say that I eventually enlisted the assistance of a member of the Alumni Association to help me find out what was going on with my story.

The outcome of this was that I was informed by PCI that my story was unacceptable, and would not be published. Specifically, I was told that my story "...contained language that PCI and Furman University are not comfortable publishing." I do not know who at Furman University consulted with PCI in reaching this decision.

I am shocked. My story has been censored by an anonymous group whose existence was not disclosed beforehand. Never was it stated that alumni contributions were to be scrutinized by un-named, unaccountable judges, to see if their stories met some un-defined performance metric. I wonder how many other submissions were subverted?

Please let me state the obvious. "My Story" contains the word "nigger." It is not used in a hateful sense. It is absolutely germane to my story, and it is utilized in an entirely appropriate context – I quote a black man who said that word. That man was my room-mate. While he was black (He is now deceased, having died of AIDS.), I am white. My story – our story – is the story of the first ever black-white roommates in the history of Furman University. If the people who censored my story were not so scared of a word, they would understand that our story is a love story, one of a platonic and brotherly nature.

The day after receiving notice of the rejection of my story, in a miraculous coincidence, I received an email from "Black @ Furman." President Davis, this email has your name on it, along with that of Chief Diversity Officer Michael Jennings. Since I am not a student on the Furman campus, what possible point could there be in sending me an email notice about "bias incidents," "perpetrators of racist incidents," "hostile acts towards others," and "disciplinary action." I have had no part in any of these behaviors.

This email goes on to conclude that, "Only when we have a campus community that values the inherent worth of every indi-vidual will we be able to fulfill our educational promise of prepar-ing each student for a life of purpose and consequence." Apparently, that sentiment does not extend to my inherent worth as an individual, nor the inherent worth of my story.

If the people who sit in judgment of my story – if the people who claim to value "diversity and inclusion" – could find their way past their hysteria over a word, and value the overarching narrative of my entire story, they would realize that my story represents a successful accomplishment of the very goals they struggle to experience today. And, quite remarkably, my story was experienced as a reality FORTY-FIVE YEARS AGO.

When I was a student at Furman, I took a class taught by Mrs. Ann Sharp (At that time she was addressed as "Mrs." not "Dr." as she did not hold a Ph.D.). She lectured on the works of Flannery O'Connor and Mark Twain. I suppose that these authors – along with countless others – have been stricken from the syllabi of every course on campus.

Why anyone would think it necessary – or themselves qualified – to sit in judgment of an alumni history story defies understanding. We are alumni making our way daily through the world, not children in a classroom. We are intelligent – and obviously well-educated – adults. We are capable of discerning for ourselves what merits our acceptance, or meets with our disapproval, and move on with our lives. To be able to do so is a significant reason for our having attended Furman University.

It saddens me to learn that freedom of expression applies only to a vocal few, and that at Furman, it is a carefully cultivated illusion. Dr. Harris, as an historian, I trust that you appreciate the great danger to truth – and its assured destruction – when the measure of that truth and the approved expression of it in an historical context is controlled by an agenda-driven oligarchy that is the antithesis of truth. The consequence of that is a well-worn lesson of history that, because we fail to learn from it, we are doomed to repeat it.

Finally, please note that not everyone on the Furman campus in 1975 approved of Leon and me being roommates, but I chose not to write about that. Can you imagine that there were white, Southern, good ol' boys that were threatened by this? Can you imagine what they might have called me? And the same was true on the black side of the coin. Leon experienced some backlash over our cohabitation as well. It wasn't always an easy walk, but it was my choice to take that walk, and it is a walk – a story – to be celebrated, not shoved under the rug of history in mindless obeisance to political correctness and "wokeness."

As Winston Churchill famously observed, *"Men occasionally stumble over the truth, but most of them pick themselves up and hurry off as if nothing had happened."*

With profound regret,
Coleman Porter Hood

. . . .

If you can wish but for one thing, let it be an idea.
Anonymous

Ideas may drift into other minds, but they do not drift my way. I have to go and fetch them. I know no other work, manual or mental, to equal the appalling, heart-breaking anguish of fetching an idea from nowhere.
A. A. Milne

It is better to entertain an idea than to take it home to live with you for the rest of your life.
Randall Jarrell

. . . .

2002

For those of you who missed it (apparently, there were none of you), there was no *Newsletter* last year. For some unfathomable reason (It's actually because I'm married to a woman.), last year, on the first Sunday of December, I began to paint my master bedroom and bathroom. This I was actually glad to do, since I spent the first twenty-one years in our home in a pink bedroom.

Carol Jeanne objects to this (as she does to every other opinion I vainly attempt to hold), saying that our bedroom was "mauve." I'm not sure what "mauve" is. I think it was made up by the catalog guy at Land's End. Now, I love Land's End. Most everything I own is purchased from a catalog, usually on-line (Shoes are the big exception.). If it doesn't say Land's End, LL Bean, Cabela's, or Woolrich on the label (.com), I probably don't own it. I have one or two items whose label reads "Orvis," but I've about decided that it is socially irresponsible to buy from Orvis. They have flannel shirts in their catalog (none of the ones I own) that go for $125 and up. I wouldn't dare repeat the price of an item of Merino wool or cashmere. If you're gonna buy Orvis, you have to wait until they have a "Season's End" sale. This is their code term for a "We didn't really think anybody would be stupid enough to buy this product at this price, especially when they can get its 75% equivalent at Walmart for 25% of the price, but hey, you never know until you try" sale.

Anyway, if you've ever perused a catalog from any of these fine retailers, you have to wonder where they come up with their colors. Nothing is "red" or "black" or even "white." Their colors are "red dawn," "midnight black," and "snowy white." At least I have an inkling (cerulean, actually) what these colors are. But what the hell is "burnt sienna?" How about dessert ochre, pewter heather, or bright pistachio? Well, like I say, I don't know what mauve is, but I know I've spent two decades in a pink bedroom.

I've always been partial to the notion of a green bedroom. The bedroom I spent my many nights in at my Grandfather Cy's and Grandmother Glady's house (once I graduated from a cot at the end of Glady's bed to a room of my own) was green. We even called it "the green room," after it got added-on to the rest of the house, along with a second bathroom (with green tile). So when Carol Jeanne and I finally found a shade of green that we could agree on (It was called *Nantucket Gray.*" Go figure!), I didn't even think about the calendar.

There I was, three weeks before Christmas – with all of the associated children coming home, guests, company holiday parties, gift-buying, gift-wrapping, and travel – about to begin painting the bedroom. Now, of course, one does not simply paint a bedroom, especially when one lives in it. There is furniture to be herded towards the center of the room and entombed in drop cloths. There are dust bunnies (tumbleweeds, actually, courtesy of six dogs and a cat and a home in the country) to be corralled. There are light fixtures to be taken down, switch plate and outlet covers to be removed, and cobwebs to be swept from long-neglected corners. And, if you happen to be married to a woman, there will invariably, inevitably be walls to be spackled. Nature may abhor a vacuum, but Nature ain't got squat on a woman when it comes to a virgin expanse of sheetrock. My wife (who is exactly like your wife, trust me) can't stand to see a solid, pristine wall. She is genetically compelled to violate its chastity with pictures and their accompanying hangers (i.e., nails in the walls). Once the paint has been deflowered, the woman quickly decides that "we" (meaning she) didn't hang the picture in the correct place, and so now "we" (I) must pound a new hole in a new section of the wall.

Anyway, once all of the pre-painting preliminaries have been completed, it is time to begin the painting preliminaries. In my world, this means everything must be primed. You cannot properly paint something without first priming it. Especially if, in the case of woodwork, you are switching from oil-based paint to latex paint, which you might as well do, since latex paint is so much easier to work with, and especially to clean-up after, and because oil-based paint, once the finest paint product on the planet, has now, thanks to environmental activists, become as worthless as horse urine. You can't put lead, mercury, arsenic, or anything useful in oil-based paint anymore, because children with rodent-like tendencies tend to gnaw on it after it has been applied to bed-posts, stairway balusters, and window sills. This, of course, doesn't do the paint any great wonders, but it apparently has even greater implications for the aforementioned infants, who, thanks to their lead-laced brains, are now destined to grow into near-idiots, living underneath bridges and out of shopping carts, and wearing full-length overcoats in August.

I painted four coats (not counting the primer) on all walls, ceilings, doors, baseboards, and crown mold. I even painted some-thing no human has ever painted in their own house, once they have moved into it. I painted the backside of the closet doors, and the inside of the closets themselves (I'm not sure if that statement is redundant. Do closets have an "outside?"). This meant transfer-ring the contents of all four closets in our bedroom to the beds in every other bedroom in our home. Have you ever tried to roll the inside-front wall of a closet? Half the performers in The Cirque Du Soleil couldn't curl themselves into the corners that I contorted into. Half-way through the closets, Carol Jeanne told me she didn't like the way her shelving was configured. She had pictures from *Home Beautiful*, *Southern Living*, and (I swear) *Southern Architecture* to illustrate her desired shelving configuration. So off to the barn and the mitre saw "we" went (There was a time I would have performed this carpentry in my shop, but I long ago abdicated my shop to extra female bedrooms and storage.). Anyway, what began on the first weekend of December, 2007, was concluded the first weekend of February, 2008, and there was, therefore, no 2007 *Newsletter*. I've heard it said that "absence makes the heart grow fonder," but then again, I've also heard "out of sight, out of mind." I guess I'll let you be the judge.

Greed is the desire for the unearned.

Anonymous

2006

Did I mention I have a great wife? Did I mention that this year we celebrated our 27th wedding anniversary? I celebrated it on our wedding date, June 16th. Carol Jeanne celebrated it in September, when she took her annual trip to New York City with a bunch of tennis women to watch the US Open (and Andre Agassi's booty for the last time). While she was gone, the house seemed emptier and quieter than ever. I was contemplating this one afternoon while hanging the laundry out on the line (Hey, just because my wife was out of town didn't mean that I was relieved of any of my domestic duties!). That's when it dawned on me that for the first time in twenty-four years, we were without a child at home. The last time that that was the case, I was in graduate school, and we lived on the *other* side of Carol Jeanne's Momma in our little A-frame house. But now Megan had departed for UGA and the dorms. We were empty nesters, or at least I was, and we would be, once Carol Jeanne returned from NYC. For some reason, this epiphany dawned upon me just as I was draping a pair of Carol Jeanne's Walmart panties on the line (See the laundry wars, Christmas Letter, 2001. And why is it that panties are a "pair" when there ain't but one of them?). Well there I stood, a fifty-year old man, about to have my own house to my own self for the first time in two and half *decades!!* That's almost 50% of my entire life. That's 89% of my married life.

I set that laundry basket down, got in my truck, and headed for the mall. There's a Victoria's Secret store in there, or at least there had been the last time I had been to the mall, several years before. I had passed by it, but never been in it. It was an experience!!! I don't know what Victoria's secret is, but I can promise you she ain't hiding it on her! But then again, I guess that that was why I was there. I had gotten this far spontaneously, which is not my natural inclination. I was a little nervous walking in the door, but I forged ahead. It wasn't until I ran into three (not one, but three!) sales girls standing in front of the counter that I suffered a full-scale anxiety attack!! "Do you have any older salesmen?" I inquired (politically incorrectly). None of them could have been over eighteen. "Why do you need someone older?" the head torturer asked. "Because *I am old*," I blurted out, "and I don't want to buy underwear for my wife from one of my daughters!"

This was exactly the wrong thing to say, as it began a chorus of giggles that wasn't going to do anything but get worse! As it happens, there was an "older" sales lady (She was almost twenty-one!), but she was already assisting another customer. "What are you looking for?" the little girl asked. I had hoped that that would have been intuitively obvious, but as it happened there was a plethora of panties to be previewed. I *briefly* (Sorry!) attempted to explain what I had in mind, but that quickly escalated the volume on the giggle meter. While the lead torturer continued to grill me, her two minions drifted off to gather every other available employee and even a few customers to witness my extreme discomfort.

The temperature in that store was going up in inverse proportion to the oxygen content of the air. Glancing about for a graceful avenue of exit, I spied a Victoria's Secret catalog. I grabbed it up and clung to it like a drowning man on a floating plank! Flipping it open randomly, I pointed to the first thing I saw. "Get me a pair of those," I implored, hoping to send the clerk off searching while I bought time to formulate a battle plan. This is exactly why spontaneity is never a good idea. "You want to buy your wife a pair of boots?" she asked. There was a photograph, there was a near-naked woman in it, she had on underpants and her bare arms were crossed over an equally bare chest. The only other stitch of clothes on her body was a pair of cowboy boots. That's what this particular photo was selling – cowboy boots! *What were the odds?!*

Finally taking pity on me, the girl took over control of the catalog, and began to point to various styles and colors of different undergarments. She made several recommendations, with which I complied gratefully. One-hundred and thirty-seven dollars later, I walked out of there with a completely new under-wardrobe. I went home, gathered up all of the old wardrobe, and tossed it in the trash. When Carol Jeanne got home, there were a half-dozen Victoria's Secret bags on the bed with fancy-colored tissue paper sticking out the top. Best damn money I ever spent!

. . . .

Courtship consists of a number of quiet attentions, not so pointed as to alarm, nor so vague as to not be understood.
Laurence Sterne

. . . .

2008

——————

This year I gained another son-in-law and another dog. Let's do the son first. As near as I know, Rebecca never dated a boy twice. Once-and-out was her policy. I called her the Black Widow. She occasionally introduced us to a date, but nothing stuck. Then one weekend she brought home Chris Davis. They both were employed in youth ministry at Mount Bethel Methodist Church in Marietta. Evidently, Rebecca had already disclosed some insider information to Carol Jeanne, but it was evident even to me that something different was afoot. Chris is a country-boy from Tennessee (And, yes, I know that that's redundant.). When he came to visit, Rebecca said he wanted to go deer hunting, so I outfitted him with my rifle, and one afternoon we set off across the back forty. As we reached the top of the ridge, I was attempting to explain to him where he should position himself the next morning for the best vantage point, while indicating to him where the deer would cross. Just then, he tossed my rifle to his shoulder, pulled the trigger, and nailed a young buck just past my ear. Now I'm as deaf as my father-in-law, but at least I knew we would hit it off (This fall, after the wedding, he came back for his second hunting trip with the rifle Rebecca gave him for a wedding present, and he bagged his second deer in thirty minutes, after oversleeping an hour past sunrise.).

Anyway, Chris and Rebecca were married this October, in their church in Marietta, and it was a perfectly wonderful event. My second tour as father-of-the-bride was much more relaxed than the first. Everyone arrived and returned safely, so I counted it a huge success. Chris's family is delightfully normal. They wear well, and I enjoy being amongst them. At the children's request, we held the rehearsal supper at a BBQ rib joint, and we all ate with our fingers while listening to a blues guitarist. It was magnificent. The day after the wedding, the Hood side of the affair retired to my brother Rennie's home in Duluth. This included a strong contingent of Porter cousins, nieces, and nephews, who made the long trek down from Charlotte in support of their clan. Little Charlie, who signed on to attend the festivities, promptly reserved rooms at the same hotel he stayed in at daughter Rachel's wedding. Fortunately, my sister Amy had a dental appointment with him the week before, so he was able to change the reservations from Athens to Marietta in time for the service! He and brother Eddie arrived at the reception, and stuffed my tuxedo jacket pockets with high-dollar, single-malt scotch. At the time, I thought this was pretty considerate. However, the next morning I awoke to discover that the Russian army had washed their socks out in my mouth, then dried their feet on a piece of shag carpet they had glued to my tongue. And, oh yeah, I also had some vague recollection of accepting a challenge to a tennis match against some Porter offspring.

Katie Kournikova Porter is about thirteen-going-on thirty. She takes private tennis lessons every day, except for the ones on which she is being chauffeured by limousine to her next match or state tournament. She did not marry off her daughter the night before. No one, especially not her Dad and her Uncle, plied her with single-malt scotch until two in the morning. She is not fifty-two years old. She has not had reconstructive surgery on both knees. The wind was angry that day, my friends (*"like an old man trying to send back soup in the deli"*). That did not play well into my slice-and-dice game, but it seemed to suit her rocket-from-hell forehand just fine. To her credit, I couldn't get between her ears, not even when I brought out my toenail necklace, made from all the toenails I've lost running opponents' shots down over the years, and which I keep in my tennis bag at all times. To my credit, I picked a few games off of her before we had to forfeit our court to an Alta league match. I'm pretty sure that if Rennie had been able to supply me with Budweiser, rather than Miller Lite, for brunch, I would have won a few more. Anyway, I am completely satisfied that I have set myself up for some pretty heavy betting by the time daughter Megan strolls down the aisle. I know I'll be wagering heavily – all of it on Kournikova Porter!!

Chris and Rebecca accepted a call to a church in Dahlonega, Georgia, so I was invited to move their furniture the week after all the groomsmen returned to Tennessee. I am proud to report that I can still lift my half and then some of anything any woman can think of to cram into a house, and still run three miles the next day. Chris has received the seal of approval from both of Rebecca's sisters, and from Rachel's husband, Ben. Chris and I have rotated the tires on his truck in my barn, and I have showed him how to change the oil filter on Rebecca's car (the trickiest filter to reach of the nine vehicles I maintain). I think it might work out. I must say that in the field of sons-in-law, I have done exceedingly, abundantly well.

I am now just a little older than my father was when I was married. He was very much a middle-aged man at that time. But I feel so much younger today than I remember him being back then. Am I really that old now, myself, and then some? There's so much living been done since the day I was married (thirty years ago in June), but I try to think back on it, and it's just a blur. Do I really have that much more living in front of me? Is there that much more of life to take me to where my father is today? And will it pass that quickly, perhaps even more so? I look at Rebecca and Chris, and I think of the words of Rainer Rilke in *Letters To A Young Poet*:

> You are so young, so before all beginning, and I want to beg you, as much as I can, to be patient toward all that is unsolved in your heart, and to try to love the questions themselves like locked rooms and like books that are written in a very foreign tongue. Do not now seek the answers, which cannot be given you, because you would not be able to live them. And the point is to live everything. Live the questions now.

Well, I believe I told you I also acquired a new dog this year. She wasn't completely new, just slightly used. One hot day last August – one of those Georgia August afternoons where the heat and humidity combine to slap you in the face with a shovel as soon as you stick your head out the door – I had to drive out to the middle of nowhere to take a picture of a subdivision entrance for a client. It was so hot that I was dreading getting out of my van, and I even let the motor run (along with the air conditioner, which is totally unheard of for someone as cheap as me) while I assembled my digital camera, clipboard, and "stuff." While doing so, I happened to glance out my window, and over in the weeds I saw a head that had to belong to a very large dog. The head was all I could see, but the word "wolf" popped into my mind.

I am a dog person, so of course I wasn't overly concerned, but since we had not been properly introduced, I made a mental note to keep an eye on this fellow for signs of misbehavior. I went about my business, and was squatting down to get a good angle for a photo of the entrance to this subdivision, when the thought of that dog popped into my head. Whirling about, I glanced hither and yon for the dog, and saw nothing. Please keep in mind that this was the middle of nowhere. If you get a dictionary and look up the phrase "middle of nowhere" there will be a picture of the entrance to this subdivision. I could see, quite literally, for miles in any direction. No dog, nowhere. I got up and looked behind the entrance sign, one of those ostentatious stone affairs that set the developer back the cost of three or four lots. Nothing. I went over, and looked in the weeds where the dog had been. Nothing. As I was panning the horizon, I happened to glance past my van, the door of which I had left open in case I needed to beat a hasty retreat. That dog, a purebred Malamute, or Husky, or sled dog, or whatever they're called, was sitting in the front passenger seat, panting, and very clearly saying to me, "Hey man, it's hot as hell out there. Hurry up with that camera, and let's go home!"

Jogging over to the van, I was saying in my most pleasant dog voice, "No, no, no, puppy. You can't stay in there. I have appointments to keep (*and miles to go before I sleep*), and work to do, you can't go with me." As I reached for the door handle of the van, that dog went over the seat, over the next seat, and finally over the last seat into the rear of the van. As I reached for the dog, and tried to lift it up, that dog turned into 100% liquid, deadweight. I had to drag it over the seats and slide it out the side door. I did try to get it some water at the irrigation spigot behind the entrance, but the water hadn't been turned on yet. Looking completely humiliated, the dog dashed across the highway, narrowly missing being hit by the only car other than mine that would pass down that stretch of road all day. Getting back in the van, I reached over for my trusty phone book, called the county animal shelter, and told them about the abandoned dog, a dog that had obviously been someone's pet. I asked them to please send someone out to get the dog before it was killed, or worse yet, seriously injured, and left to die.

That evening, as I was telling Carol Jeanne about my adventure, the biggest lightening storm of the summer blew in. It even had hail. Thinking about that poor dog, I told Carol Jeanne to get in the van – we were going looking! We drove the seven miles out from our house, and while I dodged lightening bolts and hail (I don't know if it was golf ball sized hail, ping pong ball sized hail, dime sized hail, or what – and why isn't there any such thing as hail sized golf balls?), I called and whistled for that dog. Well, I got bad news for all you Lassie fans out there. No dog turned up. Eventually, before I drowned or fried, I had to toss in the towel, and head for home. The next morning, bright and early, I was on the phone to the animal shelter. They were proud to inform me that they had recovered the dog that I had abandoned the day before! I calmly explained to them why they were idiots, and then, since they were idiots, I asked them to describe the dog they had recovered.

They described this dog perfectly, a Husky and all that. They said it was a three-year old male. I asked what their procedure was: seven days for someone to place a missing dog ad in the paper, then seven days for adoption, then *Twilight and evening star, and one clear call for me.* I told them to not let the dog be put to sleep, but to call me when his time was up. A couple of days later, I called back to check on him. He was still there, and I asked how much exercise he would get. They said not any, unless someone came to adopt him. There just weren't enough workers to go around. But, they said, I was welcome to visit him, and take him for a walk if I wanted to. Well, the animal shelter is thirteen miles from my

231

house, like I was going to do that at $4.00 a gallon for a dog that wasn't mine and that I needed like a (nother) hole in my head. So all the way down there, I'm trying to figure out what I'm going to name this thing, if no one else adopts my dog.

Once I get there, and get reunited with the Wild Thing, I discover for myself that he's a she. So then I check her belly, and a little ridge of scar tissue tells me that she's already been spayed, so she was definitely someone's pet, at some time... I don't think Mother Nature carries major medical. When she sees me, she bounces off the ground, all four feet at once, like a seventy-five pound pogo stick! No way I am going to leave her fate in the hands of the Einsteins at the pound. I drive twenty-six miles round trip each day until she's mine (minus a side-trip to the Vet for de-worming and, since she was already spayed, a dental cleaning, no lie!). Since she was down to three-strikes-and-out, and since I was her last hope, I named her Hope. I brought her home, and let her in the back door. She stopped by the hall toilet for a quick drink, then loped into my bedroom, and hopped straight onto the bed. If I'm lying, I'm dying!! Carol Jeanne was not impressed.

Even though she is visually very intimidating, Hope is the smartest, softest, and most gentle dog you could imagine. Her sense of smell puts a bat's sense of hearing to shame. She has a unique marking on her nose that looks like roots at the base of a tree; the trunk then slides up her nose, and the branches arch out over her eyebrows. She fit right in with all the other dogs with very little adjustment needed. She does have two behaviors that I'm assuming are peculiar to Husky-type dogs. Although she never barks, when she gets excited, and wants to play with one of the other dogs, she has a very spooky growl. Then she shows her teeth in a way that looks like a snarl, but it isn't. Neither of these behaviors are displays of aggression. She'll do them both while rolling over on her back and wagging her tail. I've tried to explain to the other dogs that this is just the way her people act up North, but they ain't buying it! The only real problem area has concerned the cat. Hope and Nemo have *not* hit it off famously. Hope is inexhaustibly curious about Nemo. Nemo is incurably suspicious of Hope. Nemo is right! It's been four months, and we've made about one-half step of progress. This has frayed Carol Jeanne's nerves, and would have put Nemo's mistress, Megan, on Prozac, if she were here instead of being away at school. So it has fallen to me, and petitionary prayer, to buy time for the lion to lie down with the lamb. Please pray for peace!

. . . .

I'm suspicious of people who don't like dogs,
but I trust a dog when it doesn't like a person.
Bill Murray

. . . .

Hope

233

On a personal note, I lost two close acquaintances these past two years. My neighbor, Big Johnny (*The Newsletter*, 2006), finally succumbed this autumn. He beat more odds, more times, than just about anyone I've ever known, but he finally drew the short straw. In 2009, my daughter Megan's cat Nemo (*The Newsletter*, 2004) died. This was the greatest cat I ever knew. He loved the outdoors, hot or cold, rain or dry, and he was a hunter. He was bitten by a tick that carried a virus that is endemic in the bobcat population, but not fatal (kinda like the parasitic worm, Giardia, in a Central American). It is, however, incurable in a domestic cat. He fought a valiant fight with dignity, and he broke our hearts when he lost. On the rare occasion that he wanted to come inside the house, he would jump up on the window sill next to the front door, and meow. I buried him just below that window, facing into the house.

Nemo

Memory loves Time.
Anonymous

2010

As mentioned at the outset of this edition, there was no *Newsletter* in 2009, because I am married. As previously alluded to, Carol Jeanne one day asked, "You know what *WE* ought to do?" Unless they are hiding a mouse in their pocket, what wives truly mean when they speak of what "we" ought to do, is that they have something in mind that *YOU* are going to do, if you want to stay married, and rest assured your life will not be worth living until you have complied fully!

Actually, Carol Jeanne has entertained grandiose visions of remodeling the house for years. Her initial impetus was my fault. When I drew the blueprints for our house, twenty-two years ago, I wanted to maximize the adage, "function over form." I was an engineer, not an architect (An architect is an engineering student that couldn't pass the four courses required in calculus.). Anyway, to that end, I designed the ground level of our home with no hallways. Each room spilled into the next, either through a doorway (or two), or a cased opening (or two). Thus, our master bedroom was located directly off of the living room, with no long, narrow hallway to walk down to get to the darn thing. This drove Carol Jeanne crazy. She didn't like the idea that someone sitting in the living room could look directly into her bedroom (like there was anything going on in there worth seeing!). She conveniently ignored the fact that the bedroom had a *door*, which many people have historically used to occasionally separate one area from another. As a matter of fact, doors are powerful enough to separate the *out*side from the *in*side, so separating a living room from a bedroom wasn't even particularly challenging, as door duties go. This, of course, was of no consequence to my wife.

All she wanted to do was knock out two exterior walls of our home, which were roughly half of the four exterior walls we have (or *had*). She wanted to knock out the back wall of the house where our kitchen is, and where our thirty-foot long deck *was*. In its place, she intended to build a giant gathering/dining hall. And she wanted to knock out the wall at the far end of our house, where our master bedroom was, and where she intended to erect a new master bathroom. The biggest engineering obstacle to this dream was the fact that, stepping out of either of the old spaces into the envisioned new spaces, one found oneself fifteen feet in the air, the old spaces being inconsiderately located above a full basement.

Fortunately for me, like every other married man, I have a wife with a magic finger. If there's any such thing as reincarnation, I want to come back as Shirley MacLaine, or any other woman. Then I, too, will have a magic finger. Every husband knows how they work. The wife, who is in possession of the prized digit, simply points it a something, anything, and says, "just do this," or, "just do that." Magically, even the physical laws of the universe will be temporarily suspended, while some poor slob such as myself accomplishes the impractical, if not the impossible. And so it was that I came to accept what I had long known... I was beaten.

Carol Jeanne works very hard, very long hours. She earns a good salary (much better than real estate agents these days!). She's generally low-maintenance as wives go; she doesn't ask for much, and demands even less. She doesn't care about clothes or jewelry. She has had exactly one new car in our thirty-one years of marriage. She tolerates my bringing into the house, if not into the bed (ok, usually, the bed, too) whatever critter I have come across on any given day, domesticated or not. If this renovation was something she really wanted, I wasn't going to stand in her way (mostly because I didn't want to be run over!). But I did tell her that these two rooms she wanted, plus the two I had to build underneath them to hold the first two up, would cost more than the entire original house had cost (I had about $100,000 to spare on that prediction). I told her it would take a year of my life (blood, sweat, and tears, oh my!), and it took 1-½ years. But as she pointed out, due to the Great Recession, the price of building materials was down, labor was cheap and plentiful, and interest rates were at an all-time low. And oh yeah, as a real estate agent, I suddenly had some free time on my hands. Thus did Carol Jeanne launch into the construction of her dormitory for future grandbabies.

I began by drawing up a set of building plans. Carol Jeanne began by ignoring them. I pointed out why this thing or that had to be this way or that, but she was pretty easily able to ignore all that... after all, she had a magic finger! She insisted on employing an architect. She said I "didn't have enough imagination," and that I "thought too much in terms of straight lines." When it comes to things like walls and floors, I thought this was a desirable trait, but we took a family vote, and it was one-to-nothing (a consistent election theme throughout our marriage). So we spent a couple of thousand dollars on an architect, and in sincere appreciation of his skills, I have to admit that they were two of the best thousand dollars we spent. His biggest contribution was to nix the idea of constructing the new master bathroom. Instead, he doubled the size of that new space, and created a 15' x 22' new master bedroom, and now Carol Jeanne also has a huge bay window hanging out into the treetops of the hillside in our back yard, which she utilizes as a reading nook. Then the architect reconfigured our old bedroom/bath/closet area into the new master bath and closet, plus he moved the laundry up from the basement into this complex (complete with granite countertops, of course!). And as an added bonus, Carol Jeanne got a *hallway* from the living room into all of this! The hallway, by the way, has a set of doors at either end of it, to assist in separating spaces. Go figure!

As a sidebar, the bonus that I received in this arrangement was a new bath tub. The older I become, the more and more time I spend in the tub. And I had grown pretty weary of having to choose between soaking my legs and hips, or my back and shoulders, because my tub, like yours, would not accommodate both simultaneously. Not so with my new tub. It ain't a garden tub, and it ain't a whirlpool tub. It's a *soaker* tub, and brother can you ever soak in it! It is narrow, so you don't waste a lot of hot water on either side of you. It will cover you from your heel to your neck in hot water. After I'm dead and gone, if I weren't going to be cremated and flushed down a toilet at the funeral home (the heck with that urn and ash-spreading crap), I could easily yank this tub out, and let it double as a casket.

And as a secondary bonus, since I was adding a bathroom and a kitchen downstairs, I yanked out my twenty-two-year-old water heater, and replaced it with two new ones. Can you believe that I lived in a house with a wife and three daughters, from diapers to wedding gowns (the daughters, not the wife), on a single-element, forty-gallon, electric water heater? It's a miracle we didn't kill each other (the wife, not the daughters). I was famous for comments such as, "Once you run the water hard enough to get you wet, you can't get any wetter by running it harder!" or, "You're running a shower, not a jet engine!" These new tanks are fifty-gallon, dual-element heaters, and they're interconnected so that when one starts to cool off, the other one kicks in to pick up the slack. One of them is right under my tub, so hot water is instantaneous! Carol Jeanne can take a shower while I take a bath, and I can listen to both the washing machine and the dishwasher running in the background with never a moment of concern about having enough hot water. Is this a great country, or what?!

We encountered a significant obstacle early on, however, as the Great Hall was to be twenty-one feet deep. This would have put its base on top of the septic line (If you want a fun afternoon, try digging one of those babies up!), and county code required an offset of five feet. Carol Jeanne really wanted that full twenty-one feet, and both she and the architect were stumped. Why not, I asked, pull the basement footing in the required distance, but then, on the upper story, cantilever the floor of the Great Hall over the basement wall, and get the full twenty-one feet back? Carol Jeanne was confused. The architect was amazed. I was vindicated! Score one for engineering!!

I don't want to bore you with every detail. Unlike the original construction, this time I had a builder, but not a general contractor. I did a little carpentry. I did all of the un-wiring of the old house, trying to remember how I had fed the circuits when I wired it twenty-two years ago. Most of the time, I guessed right. When I was wrong, it was the 4th of July, but only for a split-second (in engineering terms, about one hertz, which is one full cycle of the sine wave of the current, or 1/60th of a second)! Then I wired the new additions. The new basement area had morphed into a media center, a game room, walk-in storage, a full bathroom (where the laundry used to be), and a kitchen, so there was plenty to do.

In the fall of 2009, I began painting. My builder didn't want me to do the painting, because he said I would hold him up, and he was used to working with a four-man painting crew. He was a great builder, but he only worked eight hours a day, five days a week. I worked eighteen hours a day, or more, seven days a week. The fall/winter of 2009 was cold and wet. I was cold and wet. I lost track of the number of times after midnight that I crouched out in the woods, often in the rain, sometimes in the sleet, cleaning paint brushes and rollers. I painted everything from the baseboard to the ceiling, but not until I had sanded it all, not until I had puttied and caulked it all. I caulked so much crown molding that I often, literally, left streaks of blood from where the skin of my fingers was just flat out gone. I had no fingernails. Gone. I painted it, all of it, but not before I primed it. In my world, if it ain't primed, it ain't painted. So after I primed it, I painted it with a finish coat, then I painted it with a second finish coat. A few really focal points got yet another coat.

After I finished painting all the new stuff, I started in on the old. Once you start cutting holes through walls, knocking old walls out, building new walls up in old spaces, and replacing hardwood floors, there isn't anything that doesn't have to be repainted (Actually, there was one hall bathroom that didn't have a single wall in it changed, so I won't have to paint it until February... a little time off for good behavior!). When I finished all that, I started painting the exterior, old and new, front porch and back (There are two back porches.), along with two patios and an oversized garage. I painted ten exterior doors (Think about that for a moment. How many exterior doors are on your home...two, maybe three, anyone have four?!), and *seventeen* columns! I painted almost 5,500 square feet of heated space, plus the exterior, a minimum of three coats – and that builder never waited so long as a cup of coffee for me. When it was all done, he admitted that he didn't think someone "my age" could have done it. He even admitted that his own painting crew wouldn't have done as good a job.

There's an old saying that not all alcoholics are painters, but all painters are alcoholics. Well I'm here to tell you that there's a good reason for that. If you had cut my throat, I don't know what would've poured forth: blood, paint, or Scotch! For a year, we lived from one spare room in our house to another, depending on where the least construction was taking place. We lived between stacks of boxes, like glorified bag ladies. We spread furniture and belongings among Carol Jeanne's parents' home, her sister's home, and even among our children's homes. Our clothes were spread in every nook and cranny of our house, most of mine hanging from a pipe in the ceiling of my workshop, and it was far from being a dust-free environment. When the hardwood floors were finally being sanded and finished, we lived in the basement.

I'd like to say that I finally finished the renovation, but that wouldn't be completely true. The concept of finishing something like this is God's little joke on me. However, the parts that have been finished are magnificent, a tribute to my architect and builder, and everyone who laid a hand to it. We had two great tile men. We had a crew of Yugoslavian Jews who could fit granite to micrometer tolerances. I used the same heating and air contractor I used when I first built the house, and the same with the insulation contractor. But I still have a small mountain of red, Georgia clay in the back of the house that I will use to re-landscape the yard, once I have finished replacing all the irrigation lines that had to be ripped out. I have a few spotlights to finish wiring, but I don't particularly want to do it when the high temperature for the day doesn't make it to the freezing mark, and I'd be standing on the top of a twenty-five foot ladder in a twenty-five mile an hour wind. And of course there are a myriad of things you thought you'd finished, but that's before Carol Jeanne changes her mind about it, and says, "Hey, you know what *WE* ought to do... ?" And then she points that magic finger!!!!!!!!

The Back Of Our (New) House, December 26th, 2010

A partial view of the Great Hall!!

The rest of the Great Hall

Part of Carol Jeanne's new kitchen

Half of Carol Jeanne's new bedroom and reading nook

Carol Jeanne's reading nook from the outside
(with my hand built stone planter at the base!)

Carol Jeanne's favorite room... the covered/open tile patio

My favorite room... the screened porch! Carol Jeanne's parents' house is in the background.

Our backyard seen from Carol Jeanne's reading nook. The little path is to her mother's house.

The Full Crew. Note the boys' Christmas shirts from Dad!!
Ben, Rachel (28), Garrett, Megan (23), Rebecca (26), Chris,
first grandchild Will

Looking back, in some respects, 2009 and 2010 were disasters. Personally, from a professional/financial perspective, I did not do very well. I did not contribute to the family checkbook what I should have at this point in life, and that can wear thin on your self-esteem. But it hasn't been all bad. As a matter of fact, other than a lousy real estate market, we have done quite well. The economy, in a perverse sort of way, gave me the opportunity to build the house that Carol Jeanne wanted.

We haven't missed any meals, our children are healthy and happy, and we have become grandparents. Youngest-daughter Megan completed her Bachelor's degree in Early Childhood Education, and passed all four components of her certification examination on the first try! Middle-daughter Rebecca completed her Master's degree in Middle-School Education! She and husband Chris are thriving in Dahlonega, Georgia, which seems to be the perfect place for them to be right now. They have the two wildest dogs (Bella and Haydey) I have ever met. They adore one another, and are a perfect pair (the dogs, I mean). With the arrival of Will, Ben and Rachel are working through schedules (both baby and work), and are sifting through care givers. Luckily, Rachel's sisters are within roughly an hour of either side of her, and both have been making the trek to look after Will on the limited days that Rachel is back working as a neo-natal intensive care nurse.

Carol Jeanne has a great job, and she has retirement in sight. In just a few more years, she will step down from the hospital (This very week marks the beginning of her 29th year at Athens Regional Medical Center.), and devote herself to her children and grandchildren on a full-time basis.

This life – our brief walk upon this earth – holds no guarantees. There is no such thing as security, only the illusion of it. We own the breath that's in us now, and nothing more. So all things considered, we have much to be grateful for. My life is full of blessings, and every now and then, I actually have enough sense to realize it, and to appreciate it. Here's a prayer that the same will be true for you in 2011. Peace and joy!

....

What troubles me is a sense that so many things lovely and precious in our world seem to be dying out. Perhaps poetry will be the canary in the mine-shaft, warning us of what's to come.
Galway Kinnell

....

Last year, everyone who reported back to me loved the poem *Cardinals* (one of my very favorites of all time, by John Stanizzi). Everyone was also touched by the poignant poem of a son caring for his aged, invalid father in *Baptism*, by Ted Thomas, Jr. Several of you, however, asked about the meaning of the final line of the final stanza of *Baptism*:

> I pat him dry,
> he lets me dress him
> in the white
> hospital clothes,
> comb his hair,
> put him to bed,
> and *forgive him.*

The last line is enigmatic. I did not write the poem, so I cannot say what the author had in mind. Perhaps, as is ultimately the case with every poem, its meaning is imputed by each recipient. There is no "Meaning," but there are many "meanings." That caveat duly noted, I wonder if the author of the poem was acquainted with the writings of the theologian Reinhold Niebuhr, who wrote, in a three-step progression:

> Nothing that is worth doing can be achieved in our lifetime; therefore *we must be saved by hope.* Nothing we do, however virtuous, can be accomplished alone; therefore *we must be saved by love.* No virtuous act is quite as virtuous from the standpoint of our friend - or foe - as it is from our standpoint; therefore *we must be saved by the final form of love, which is **forgiveness**.*

We are saved (an undefined term, here) alternately by hope, love, and forgiveness. This is, it seems, a wrinkle on Paul's triumvirate of "faith, hope, and love, but the greatest of these is love." For Niebuhr, forgiveness is the final form of love, the capstone of salvation.

We are acutely aware of our desire to receive forgiveness, which is joined at the hip to our desire for acceptance. Forgiveness, and acceptance, are sacraments that we can bestow upon others, but only if we have first learned to grant them to ourselves.

In the poem, the son offers the father the final form of love – forgiveness – whatever that means and all that it implies. It must mean, at the least, that the son understands that he is, himself, less than perfect, that he is "damaged goods." His recognizes that he has shortcomings, acknowledges (*confesses*) them, and understands that there is, therefore, a latitude that he must grant to other pilgrims in life's journey, even the mistaken, the wrong, and the guilty – as he himself is.

As he forgives himself, he forgives his father for the father's share of the baggage in a lifetime's worth of a father-son relationship. In doing so, a piece of the son's puzzle of salvation falls into place. And in doing so, I would imagine that the son would hope to receive as much from the father... but it's not a requirement. This is the meaning I ascribe to the final line of Thomas' poem.

I am in over my head in expressing these thoughts. Writing these last couple of paragraphs has given me a massive headache, but thank God for Scotch whisky. I am a forester/engineer/real estate agent (as well as a state-certified emergency medical technician, a licensed commercial driver, a licensed private pilot, and a mobile OB/GYN [unlicensed, but I own a van]). I studied physics, not metaphysics, and the only insights I have on existentialism are based on personal experience. Nonetheless, because there is Scotch whisky, I shall share with you this bit of metaphorical philosophy.

You must first plant the seed of forgiveness, which is a *notion*. You must then germinate that seed, and nurture it to full blossom, which is a *desire*. You must bring that seed and blossom to fruition, which is an *action*. The actualization of forgiveness is, I believe, a turning of the mind, a variant of the sacrament called repentance, and which may be experienced from either side of the equation. The completion of this cycle results in a harvest, which is a *consequence*. It is called redemption, a transcendent moment for the mortal soul.

....

Lord, I believe. Help thou my unbelief.
Gospel of Mark 9:24

....

2011

____ ____ ____ ____

Andy Rooney retired from *60 Minutes* this season. Although it was a day he said he dreaded, after thirty years in that role, in his 1,097th broadcast, he was blessed with the opportunity to bestow his own benediction upon his career. One got the poignant sense of a days-gone-by firehorse, retired to the barn, whose ears hear the clanging of the bells, and whose mind still goes where the body no longer can. He professed that he thought of himself, and always would, "as a writer, not a television personality." He said that he became a writer because he "didn't think anyone was paying enough attention to the written word." He concluded by saying, "I've done a lot of complaining here, but of all the things I've complained about, I can't complain about my life." He also confessed that "... there weren't many people in this world that have been as lucky as I have been... a lot of you have sent wonderful letters, and said gracious things to me when you met me in the street. I wasn't always gracious about it...I don't say this often enough, but thank you."

In addition to his final essay that night, Andy was also the subject of one of the traditional, three feature stories. He was interviewed by Morely Safer. Morely questioned Andy about the amount of mail he received. Andy acknowledged that it was "a lot, tons of mail." I'm going to present the rest of their exchange about letters as a quotation, because I taped the episode, and have transcribed it word for word.

Morely: Do you answer any of it [the letters]?

Andy: Not much, no. I mean, who would want to answer an idiot that has the bad sense to write me a letter? I mean, it's a certain kind of person who writes you, and they're not my kind of people, usually.

Morely: But they are your kind of people!

Andy: Well, I suppose. Every once in a while, I'll answer one, but not very often.

Well Andy once did a feature on politicians' ubiquitous use of the phrase, "God bless America." He castigated them for being reflexive and vapid. Guess who wrote him a letter?

February 5, 2001

Mr. Rooney:

Concerning your feature of February 4, "May God Bless The United States of America," I would like to say, "AMEN!" If I were going to make such a blanket request, I might at least want to suggest to the Almighty some reasons for doing so:

• God bless the United States of America… because we're the last chance you have to bring your message of peace to a heathen world. You really need us, God.

• God bless the United States of America… because in the past we've been such good stewards of the many blessings You have already given us. We've made the absolute most of them, and are ready for more.

• God bless the United States of America… because we have more television evangelists per capita than any other nation on the face of the earth. We deserve something extra for having had to listen to them.

On second thought, a more appropriate national benediction might be addressed to our Citizens: "Let each American so live each day that God will want to richly bless every one of us… whether we believe in Him or not."

Respectfully,
Coleman P. Hood

P.S.   I believe.

CBS NEWS

A Division of CBS Inc.
524 West 57 Street
New York, New York 10019
(212) 975-4321

Coleman P. Hood
1351 Overlook Ridge Road
Bishop, Georgia 30621

Dear Mr. Hood,   April 29, 2001

How can you ever forgive me for being pleased and surprised by such a good letter from Bishop, Georgia?

Thanks for writing it.

Sincerely,

Andrew A. Rooney

"Every once in a while, I'll answer one, but not very often."

. . . .

None of us is as smart as all of us.
Kenneth Blanchard

. . . .

253

Well all this talk about *60 Minutes* has brought to mind when it first came on the air. Our family lived at 5143 Beckford Drive, just off Sharonview Road in Charlotte, North Carolina. It was a three-bedroom, two-bathroom, brick ranch. Couldn't have been over 1,100 square feet. Ruth and Chris bought it brand new, with no air conditioning. Rennie had his own bedroom. Timmy and I shared the third bedroom until Amy came along, about the time I was in first grade. Then Chris and his father Cy converted the living room into a bedroom, so Timmy and I moved up the hall into it.

The sound of that *60 Minutes* stopwatch ticking off the seconds will forever in my mind be associated with *3-In-One* oil. You see, Chris had these electric hair cutting shears. When we needed a haircut, on a Sunday night when *60 Minutes* came on (This was after the broadcast had moved from its original Thursday night time slot.), he'd line us up in the kitchen, and we'd take turns sitting on a stool while Chris crew-cut our heads. In between each kid, he'd pull out a little can of *3-In-One* oil, and lubricate those shears. When your haircut was done (It took about *60 Seconds* per kid.), you'd be bald, and smell like *3-in-One* oil! I still remember *60 Minutes* posting graphs of the killed and wounded in Vietnam for the week just past, while I was getting oiled and scalped. By the way, over the course of thirty-two years of marriage, I still get my hair cut on a stool in the middle of the kitchen floor on the first Sunday night of the month while I watch *60 Minutes*, only now Carol Jeanne does the honors. That's 384 haircuts and counting. Am I consistent, or what?!

Well remembering that much has brought to mind a bunch of other childhood memories. It would be way too expensive to tell them to a shrink, so I think I'll tell them to you, instead. These reminiscences will be more for my siblings than for the general audience, although I certainly hope all of you will be inclined to take the journey with us... you might get a laugh. Actually, they will be more for my brothers, Rennie and Timmy, because my sister Amy was the baby of the bunch, and she was too young to remember anything of the time these memories were formed. Actually, these will be more for my older brother Rennie, since my younger brother Timmy neither reads (never did) nor receives (no longer does) *The Newsletter*. He's in the same league as my mother-in-law in that regard, but that's a story for another time. If I'm the one to tell it, it will most likely have to mean that I outlived him. We're only thirteen months apart, so it's not out of the question. In his way, he's as health conscious as I am, but I'm much less neurotic, and I'm not a hypochondriac.

As I told you, we lived on Beckford Drive. It was while living there, about the time I was in kindergarten, that Ruth broke my arm one Sunday evening. She had been in the kitchen making supper... frying chicken as I recall. The rest of us were in the backyard, when Ruth came tearing out of the house, screaming that she had seen a mouse in the kitchen. Daddy and the rest of us ran into the house to investigate. We didn't find the mouse, of course, but Chris got the bright idea to put his ballpoint pen in a paper bag. He handed the bag to me, and told me to run out, and shake it at Ruth, and tell her the mouse was in it. She screamed (again), and lit out across the drive with me hot on her heels. She made it to the family car (It was a 1963 Pontiac Catalina, sea foam green on the bottom with a white top. It became my car when I turned sixteen, in 1972!). Anyway, Ruth jumped into the front seat of that car, and I was in the process of shaking that bag at her when she slammed the door. Chris had to take me to the hospital, and the father of a friend of mine, Dr. Don Kellum, set my arm and put me in a cast.

The name of our little subdivision was Sharonview Acres. Practically speaking, it had four distinct "boroughs" (Centuries before, an aspiring bunch of Yankees modeled the division of New

York City on the borough concept of my neighborhood, but they needed five.). One borough consisted of the houses that faced the main road. The only kid along that stretch who I ever knew was older than me, a kid named Brent McKnight. He was smart, and reserved. He never played snake-in-the-gutter at the bus stop. He went on to become a lawyer, and later, I believe, a judge. He died of cancer a number of years ago. Our subdivision was a big horseshoe. Beckford Drive was the right half of the horseshoe, and it was our borough. The left half was Allison Avenue, another borough. Then there was another road that bisected the horseshoe that was named Chadwick Place. It was a borough unto itself, and I think I remember one kid on that street named Chip who was neat because his house had a garage, and it had a bonus room over it. The rest of the houses had carports or nothing.

We knew some of the kids in the Allison Avenue borough, but we never really hung out with them. There was the Scott family. Their son David was killed on a Friday night in a car wreck, 100 yards from the entrance to the subdivision. His mother, a nurse, was one of the first people on the scene of the wreck, and was the one to discover her son. As I recall, he had walked to the end of the street, then hitched a ride – it lasted about three seconds. Since it was a Friday night, I was at Cy's house, but my brother Rennie called to tell me about it. Also on Allison Avenue, there were the Cooks, who had a pretty daughter named Candy, another family named Hood (They had a daughter named Robin, but they weren't kin.), the Taylors had brother-sister twins, and then there were the Southworths. The Southworths were a great American family. I have no idea what Mr. and Mrs. Southworth did for a living. They weren't rednecks, and they weren't exactly white trash, but boy, were they different. All the kids knew that they slept in the nude. Mr. Southworth had an admirable collection of Playboy magazines, and didn't even try to hide them. Their house wasn't filthy, but it was the messiest trash heap you ever saw. Their oldest child was a daughter named Jane. She was almost as smart as Brent McKnight. Remember Marilyn, the really straight, prim-and-proper daughter on *The Munsters*? Jane stood out from the rest of her family just as starkly. The boys were Rick and Jack. They were both a little older than me, and they were wild as the wind. They both had long hair before anyone ever heard of The Beatles or The Rolling Stones. The last I heard of either of them was a picture my father sent me out of *The Charlotte Observer*, showing Jack sitting on a Harley-Davidson motorcycle, wearing a German army helmet, as a member of Hell's Angels.

Down the right side of Beckford, the families ran Bolton (In their backyard was a separate little brick house that contained the well for the whole neighborhood. In the summer, we would play poker on their back porch with their son, James Glidewell III, while watching Johnny Carson on *The Tonight Show*.), Hood, Gamble (They had a high-strung daughter that no one really liked.), Milliken (They had two adopted children. Rick was Rennie's age, and I think at one time he held the state record for the mile run. The daughter, Carol, was my age. She died several years ago.), Bishop (I shot the middle son, Davey, in the eye with a BB gun, but thank God he did not lose his sight. Their father was a dentist, whose name was Elmo, but everyone called him Bud. Late in life, he suffered from dementia – he wandered away from home one day, fell in a pond, and drowned.), Shockley, Ward, Boyer (Their son Evan had a hearse for a car.), Huntley, Childers (M.D. Childers was the ophthalmologist they took Davey Bishop to, who saved his eyesight.), then a couple of more houses with families we didn't really know. The last one on the right was a kid a couple of years older than me, named Scott Flint. He always had a buildup of spittle in the corners of his mouth, and he walked way up on his tip-toes, like someone had just branded the heels of his feet. No one really hung out with him. Down the left side of the street, the families were Lowery (Their house actually faced the main road, but their driveway was on Beckford, across the street from our yard. Their dad was a Ford car salesman, and they eventually sent their son, John, off to military school. When he returned, he taught me how to spit-shine shoes by shining the right shoe of my pair of cordovan penny-loafers, and then quitting. It probably took me a month, but eventually I shined the left shoe to the equivalent of the right. To this day, I shine my own dress shoes, and you can count your teeth in the reflection.), Powers, Tines (They had a son, Bunky, who was a kleptomaniac.), Seymour (In the summer, their daughter had dances in their driveway, and they would spread rock salt on the pavement so that the kids could do the twist.), Hodgin (I thought that the father looked like Cary Grant. Their oldest son, Bill, remains a close family friend. He drove my older brother and the family's Chevy Mailbu to meet up with the rest of the family at Litchfield Beach in South Carolina when he was just sixteen. Their second son, George, who was my age, died of a drug-overdose.), then there were the Rices and the Bells (All the boys thought Mrs. Bell was hot. She looked like the woman on the TV show, *Sheena, Queen Of The Jungle*.). I could tell you stories about each one of these families, but there just ain't enough time for it here.

There were several great childhood landmarks around the borders of our subdivision. On the Allison Avenue end of the horseshoe was a dirt drive. A big pine tree at its entrance was where David Scott died in the car wreck. At the other end of the drive was a one-room cabin. I kid you not! In the cabin lived Leroy, a very old, very large, very black man. I don't know what Leroy did for a living, if anything. Everywhere he ever went, he got there on a bike. Not a ten-speed, not a mountain bike, but an old Schwinn with big, fat tires and no gears. Leroy had a big basket on the handlebars, and another one behind the seat. He always wore bib-overalls and a hat (a real one, not a baseball cap), and always had the stub of cigar in the corner of his mouth. Leroy was kind and gentle. He enjoyed visiting with you, and you were just naturally respectful of him. You could go in his house, if you were curious enough. It had a sour, sweaty smell. I would dearly love to know what ever became of him, which would pretty much consist of how and when he died, because everything else about him was the same as the day before and the day after.

Across the highway from Allison Avenue was an abandoned house site. The house was long gone, but the stone foundation was still readily identifiable. There was a circular drive and several very large oaks. The place was called Eptings, so I guess that's who must've owned it at some time, but none of us ever knew any of them. The great thing about Eptings was that it was where all the boys took girls to go "parking" once they got their driver's license. I don't think teenagers go parking anymore. But they did back then, and on a Friday evening, we would hide out in the weeds, and in the limbs of those giant oaks, and we would torment those couples to distraction. Every now and then, a boy would jump out of the car to chase after us, which is just what we lived for! And every now and then, one of them would catch one of us. I seem to remember my older brother Rennie taking a pretty good pounding one time.

Another great place was "the sawdust pile." It was on the edge of a large field, through the woods, almost directly behind our house in the subdivision. Years before it must've been where someone had set up a temporary sawmill that logged the forest that became the field. All the kids on Beckford Drive spent countless hours playing on that giant sawdust pile, losing plastic army men by the dozen. Not far from there, another landmark was "the bullet place." It was a small ravine (really, a giant gully) that led to a creek. At some point in time, it must have been a shooting range for someone, because the ground was fairly covered with bullet shells. I think they were all .22 caliber, and we thought it was neat.

At the very back of the subdivision, we had a sewage treatment plant, kind of a giant septic tank. I don't remember that much about it. It was fenced, and drained into a good-sized creek (The creek from the bullet place drained into this creek.). I don't remember it stinking (Off of Park Road, a couple of miles from our house, and very near to Billy Graham's home place, was a municipal sewage plant on Sugar Creek [how ironic!], and that place stunk to high heaven! When you could smell Sugar Creek at our house, you knew it would rain the next day.). Anyway, the thing that made the sewage plant memorable was that there was a pretty good hill leading down to it (They put a sewage plant at the bottom of a hill. There must have been some reason!). In the winter, when it snowed, that hill is where every kid in the neighborhood would take their sleds and trash can lids and cookie sheets. You could get up a pretty good head of steam by the time you reached the bottom. Problem was, if you weren't pretty good at steering your sled, when you reached the bottom, you had two bad choices. You could overshoot the hill, and end up in the creek, or you could bail to the right, and end up in the fence of the sewage plant. Sometimes you would ricochet off the fence, which was an abrupt stop, but otherwise not too bad. Sometimes the front half of you shot through the bottom of the fence, before your coat or pants hauled you to a stop, much like a jet fighter hitting the arresting cable on the deck of an aircraft carrier. Then you had to wait on some other kid to take pity on you, and release you from the frozen agony of the fence. That pity was never quick in developing. When it snowed, the walk to the end of our horseshoe-shaped subdivision, sleds in tow, was filled with excitement and anticipation. The long walk back to our house at its entrance, frostbitten and soggy, was a miserable trek.

. . . .

I want to die like my Grandfather, peacefully and in my sleep...
not crying and screaming like everyone else in the car.
Will Rogers

. . . .

Well I'm obviously very late getting *The Newsletter* out this year. There are two reasons for this. First, I blame it mainly on rocking horses. When my oldest daughter, Rachel, had her first child, Will, I built her a rocking horse (*The Newsletter*, 2010). It turned out pretty well, and was (still is) a solid fellow, having logged many hours of faithful service, first to Will, then to younger sister Caroline. Back around the first of the year (the last one, not this one), my middle daughter, Rebecca, informed us that she, too, would be presenting us with a grandchild that Fall, so I knew that I would be making another rocking horse, which I placed on my mental calendar for the summer. Somewhere along the way, I had the bright idea that I might as well go ahead and make one for my youngest daughter, Megan. I feel certain that her day will also come. Then I had the brilliant idea to make a rocking horse for each of the three girls out of antique, longleaf heart pine. A long time ago, I managed a business that milled reclaimed heart pine beams from old mills into flooring and decorative building materials. I had pretty much fallen in love with the beauty – and history – of that wood. Much of it was a living tree when Columbus arrived. Old Ironsides, the world's oldest ship still in service, is made of longleaf heart pine. The material I was working with was literally centuries old. It is my hope that these three horses will be become treasured family heirlooms, lasting through several generations of children, remaining in loyal service long after I am gone. On a sidebar, this thought put me in mind of Neil Diamond's song *Morningside* (more on that later).

Anyway, this project eventually took on a life of its own. It's all "handmade." You can use power tools, but there aren't any straight lines, just lots of bevels, miters, and curves. You have the occasional straight piece, but it will have a curved piece attached to one side, and a beveled-mitered piece on the other. Trying to match it all up can be quite maddening, and trying to do it an hour here and an hour there can be unspeakably frustrating. Doing it all three times over could drive a man to drink... fortunately, I have a driver's license!! At any rate, it took me until Christmas Eve to finish the lot of them, and to have them ready for Christmas morning. From my perspective, it was all worth it.

Now, back to Neil Diamond's song, *Morningside*, which is the name of a cemetery. On the underside of each rocker, I burned in my name, the date, and "For my children," the refrain from *Morningside*.

Now to the second reason for my tardiness in writing to you this year. This I blame on my daughter Rebecca. She had a baby in September. In October, she announced that she and husband Chris would be running in a 10K in December (which they did), and a half marathon this February. I had seriously injured myself playing tennis on New Year's Eve (2012), partially tearing the adductor muscle in my right thigh. Outside of rupturing my ACL, it was the most painful injury I have ever experienced, and that includes a torn rotator cuff and kidney stones. I refused to go to the doctor, because I knew the only thing they would be able to do was to operate. Every time I coughed, I felt like someone was pulling barbed wire through my groin. I literally could not run the length of my carport – I went 280 days without running a single step. When Rebecca made her announcement, I was just beginning to jog the length of our driveway; I say "jog," because running was no longer an option. Running is something I used to be able to do, and I was pretty good at it. *Quoth the Raven, 'Nevermore.'*

Anyway, I figured that if she could have a baby in September, and then run a half-marathon in February, then I should be able to do that also (the run, not the birth). I overlooked the fact that she had been running in races right up until her delivery, and that she is twenty-eight years younger than I. But I figured that I would train secretly, then show up at the race to run with her (if I could keep up, which wasn't too likely), and give her moral support. I just want it to be a father-daughter bonding moment, not something that I have an overwhelming portfolio of. I hope the fact that there are not that many 57-year old men out there willing to train 300 miles just to run 13 more with their daughter will earn me some extra father-of-the-year points.

The race is this coming Saturday, and who knows how things will turn out? What I do know is that I'm late writing this thing because I picked the coldest, wettest, snowiest, windiest damn winter in more than a century to try to learn how to run again!!! All the things that have usually come and departed by the last week of February – jonquils, forsythia, crocuses, Daphnes, Lenten roses, Quince – have not even put in an appearance, it's been so cold and miserable. I have run in driving rain, single-digit temperatures, winds over thirty miles per hour, and snow. I never made an excuse or missed a training session. The Wednesday morning before the race on Saturday, we had four inches of fresh snow and ice on the ground. So, I trained on the elliptical in the basement instead, but ran ten miles that Friday. I ran on Christmas Day and New Year's Day. As for the delay in writing, it's not just a matter of spending the time to train, it's all the hours of rest, recovery, and thawing that really take it out of you. When you're shivering to death, you have no interest in sitting in front of a computer to write. I have single-handedly managed to double our electric bill the past two months, simply by virtue of all the hot baths I have had to soak myself in!!

Speaking of spending, do you have any idea how expensive it can be to run a half marathon? In addition to paying for hot water and the $35 entry fee, I have spent: Advil $20, two massages $130, one shot of cortisone $60, one heating pad $25, whey protein powder and carbohydrate gel $65, bright "road-crew green" T-shirt to wear when running on the road $20. Average cost per mile for all miles run, about $1.20... for everything else, there's MasterCard.

Well, as it happens, I did not get this edition out before the big race, as I had hoped to do. Therefore, I will fill you in on the details. First, Rebecca was not able to run. She and daughter Reese spent the week at the doctor's office with severe respiratory infections, and she could not even travel to the house for the weekend, so this was a huge disappointment. The race was up to her husband, Chris, and me. As it turned out, this was a "trail run." I had seen that mentioned on the website, and since the race was being held at a nearby state park, I had these mental images of pastoral, idyllic countryside, a run that would be combined with the wonders of nature along park trails that a family might stroll after a Saturday picnic. I could not have been more wrong!!

What I found myself in came straight out of the abyss of Hell itself. Keep in mind that my son-in-law ran this course, and I will have his witness that I am neither making this up nor exaggerating things. There were not ten feet of this race that occurred in a straight line. There were not ten feet of this race that was on level ground. The course was exactly one person wide – if you wanted to pass someone, you had to race by in the woods and underbrush. We ran a pig path covered in pine straw and slick Georgia clay; the ground had been frozen under four inches of snow the week before, but that was all washed away in a three-inch rain the day before the race. There were pine cones and roots galore. You would run/slide down a four-foot embankment into a mud pit, then straight up a six-foot wall on the other side. There were places where you literally used your hands to claw your way up and over. I fell flat on my face FIVE times, and would summersault and roll downhill until my feet came back around, then off I'd go again. Nothing I did in the way of training prepared me for this, and I trained on a pretty tough course. Son-in-law Chris beat me by two minutes and twelve seconds. I finished second in my age group; some guy two years younger than me who competes nationally (whatever that means) edged me by two minutes and thirteen seconds. I've never hurt so badly in my life. I'm so sore that my hair hurts. Never again!!

. . . .

There is a point in the life of every problem
when it is big enough to see, yet small enough to solve.
Mike Leavitt

. . . .

2013

I lost my father on March 14th. Chris Hood was a couple of weeks shy of his 84th birthday when his physical ailments overtook him. As a physician, he understood that his Parkinson's disease and his prostate cancer could never have gotten better. But they could have gotten much worse. Certainly he knew that, and I imagine he was grateful to have passed on when he did. As I said in his eulogy, the last years were cruel to him, but they were only a small part of his life, and they do not ultimately define him. I have not a doubt that if Chris' Creator, at any point in his life, had laid his life out before him from the cradle to the grave, Chris would have gladly taken it – twice if given the chance. In my estimation, that's a pretty good life.

Ten days after I lost my father, I lost my best friend. Mike Guilbeau was a tennis pro, a fitness freak, and his word was his bond. Mike and I were runners. I was never in the same league as Mike, because he was truly gifted, plus I was seven years older than he. But I have this one claim to fame. Mike and I once ran a 5K together over one of his favorite courses. He knew exactly where he was going, and what was coming next (uphill, downhill, intersections). I didn't have a clue, so my only hope was to keep him in sight. Because of where we started, I knew that the last part of the course coming in would be uphill. I was a little better than Mike at running uphill (He would absolutely blister me running downhill.), and I hoped that I might be able to catch up to him in the homestretch. I didn't. Mike beat me that day (as he always did), and he set his personal best time ever on that course. I finished seven seconds behind him. That's my claim to running fame, and I am damn proud of it – I finished seven seconds behind Mike Guilbeau on his best day. Mike was only fifty when he lost his life to cancer. I gave his eulogy, as well.

Even as death diminished our family in 2013, life affirmed its place in the cycle, as Rebecca and Chris presented us with our third grandchild and second granddaughter. Reese Avery Davis made her debut on September 12th. She is amazingly happy and observant. Her favorite thing in the entire word is taking a bath, which she loves doing more than a baby otter! Her granddaddy is teaching her the ABC song, and how to touch her nose.

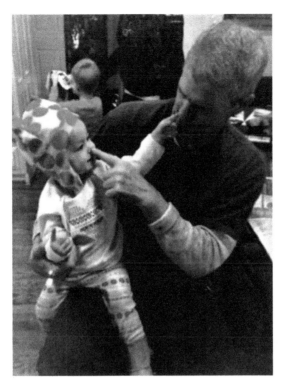

Reese Avery Davis

We added to our family in another capacity in 2013. I am an animal person, and most any animal will do. I even try to accommodate snakes, including venomous ones (They are not poisonous.). To the greatest extent possible, I adopt a "live and let live" policy. I have my limits: anything that feeds on me or mine, anything that spreads disease, anything that destroys my home, is fair game in the struggle for survival. To that end, critters such as ticks, mosquitoes, flies, termites, and fire ants had best take cover. But if I turn over a log, and discover a black widow, I'll put the log back from whence it came, and move on. I figure the spider will stay put, and if it didn't, I figure that I can outrun it. I have no quarrel with bees of any description, as long as I see them before they see me.

But I digress. My preferred pet form is a dog, as close to Heinz 57 as possible. Not that that really matters... dogs adopt me, not the other way 'round. Never been a huge cat person, other than a cat one of my daughters once had (see Nemo, *The Newsletter*, 2004). Nemo succumbed to one of those critters on my bad side... a virus spread by a tick (The usual feline host is the bobcat, who can survive the virus, but a domestic cat cannot.). Anyway, ever since our experience with Nemo, I've had an inclination to give a cat a chance at becoming a family pet. Every Saturday, our local paper runs snapshots of the animal shelter's pets of the week, one dog and one cat. Every Saturday, I would point to the picture of the cat, and tell Carol Jeanne, "That looks like a nice kitty." Every Saturday, she would look me squarely in the eye (sometimes both of them) and say, "You're not getting a cat. No more pets!!" This is mainly because Carol Jeanne is about to retire, and she wants to start traveling, mostly to see her grandchildren, but also overseas where they have bad food and terrorists. She thinks that I should travel with her, but she knows that as long as I have pets to look after, that home is where I'll be. Anyway, one Saturday I showed her the kitty of the week, a really pretty, almost all-black kitty with a white blaze on her chest, and I said, "That looks like a nice kitty." She glanced at the picture, looked me squarely in the eye (possibly both), and said, "You're right, it is a pretty kitty. Maybe we should adopt her." You could have knocked me over with a feather!

Although we live in rural Oconee County, this animal shelter is in the neighboring Clarke County, a hotbed of social engineering and a semi-socialist proving ground for University of Georgia professors and other people that would vote for Obama for a third term if they could. Suffice it to say that it is easier to adopt a Yugoslavian orphan than a Clarke County cat. That is not a joke. I won't bore you with all the details (not even the cuss fight I had with the shelter's femi-Nazi director). But while I was standing there waiting on them to process the thirty-something pages of red tape that I had to complete (They gave you a full page to describe "in your own terms" [as if you could do so in someone else's terms] the nature of the living environment that the pet would be introduced into "IF YOUR ADOPTION IS APPROVED."), I drifted over to the cage in which our kitty was jailed. There were probably two dozen of these cages stacked one on top of the other, floor to ceiling and side by side. None of the cats could actually see any of its neighbors face to face, but the kitty I had come to adopt was sticking her paw out of her cage, and wrapping it around the corner to play with the kitty in the cage beside her. This kitty was also black and white, also female, and the same age. That's when it hit me... why in the world would anybody ever adopt a single kitty? Wouldn't it be just as simple, just as cheap, to adopt two (As it turns out, the answer is "No!")? That way, they could be playmates, and keep each other entertained. I don't suppose that I have to tell you what I did. When I arrived back home, I put my head down, laid my ears back, and took my beating like a man!

Dory (left) and Dilly

We judge ourselves by our ideals. Others judge us by our actions.
Coleman Hood

2009

I have some quotes from Mark Twain that I would like to share with you. All prospects are that five days from now, my family will have a very Merry Christmas. There will be an orgy of materialistic gift giving, and I shall be at the front of that parade. On a more somber note, there will be prayers, and thanksgiving, and commemoration of the birth of Jesus, but all of that will also be celebratory, and rightly so. But not every day is Christmas Day (Las Vegas lays the odds at about 364 to 1.). Life has other dimensions, and I think that the following thoughts from the pen of Mark Twain to be as meaningful, as heartfelt, and as soul searching as any sermon I heard in the past year.

In addition to his weekly show, *A Prairie Home Companion*, Garrison Keillor has a daily radio show, *The Writer's Almanac*. You can hear it on your local public radio station, or you can access it on-line, where you can choose to read it or listen to it. Either way, it takes about five minutes of your time. This show celebrates significant dates in literature and the arts, and every show ends with a poem. Earlier this fall, the show featured this vignette on Mark Twain. It is not *Pollyanna* (December 19th is the birthday of its author, Eleanor Hodgman Porter.). It is not for the faint of heart. It is not for the ostrich. It is for the truly living.

"On this day in 1897, Mark Twain wrote a lyrical, heavy-hearted letter from London to the Reverend Joseph Twichell in

Hartford, Connecticut. He was Twain's closest friend. Twain's 24-year-old daughter, Susy, had died from meningitis the previous summer. He would forever consider it the most devastating loss of his life. He'd been traveling overseas and missed her last days [and funeral]. The following winter, he wrote about the ways in which his daughter's death affected him, and about the gratitude he felt for his pastor friend's uniquely perfect sense of sympathy. His letter is a lament of great grief intertwined with an ode to his friend's great compassion. Twain wrote to his best friend of forty years:

> I do no want most people to write [to me], but I do want you to do it. The others break my heart, but you will not. You have something divine in you that is not in other men. You have the touch that heals, not lacerates. And you know the secret places of our hearts. You know our life – the outside of it – as others do – and the inside of it – which they do not. You have seen our whole voyage. You have seen us go to sea, a cloud of sail – and the flag at the peak; and you see us now, chart-less, adrift – derelicts; battered, water-logged, our sails a ruck of rags, our pride gone. For it is gone. And there is nothing in its place. The vanity of life was all we had, and there is no more vanity left in us. We are even ashamed of that we had; ashamed that we trusted the promises of life and builded high – to come to this!
>
> I knew that Susy was part of us; I did not know that she could go away; I did not know that she could go away, and take our lives with her, yet leave our dull bodies behind. And I did not know what she was. To me she was but treasure in the bank; the amount known, the need to look at it daily, handle it, weigh it, count it, realize it, not necessary; and now that I would do it, it is too late; they tell me it is not there, has vanished away

in a night, the bank is broken, my fortune is gone, I am a pauper. How am I to comprehend this? How am I to have it? Why am I robbed, and who is benefited?

I am working, but it is for the sake of the work – the 'surcease of sorrow' that is found there. I work all the days, and trouble vanishes away when I use that magic... I have many unwritten books to fly to for my preservation.

You must be aware of that history, that tragedy, that suffering. Otherwise, you would never appreciate the depth of Mark Twain's literary legacy. Otherwise, you would think it just the glib – or acerbic – ramblings of a gifted mind. You would not appreciate this:

Sanity and happiness are an impossible combination. No sane man can be happy, for to him life is real, and he sees what a fearful thing it is. Only the mad can be happy, and not many of those. – Mark Twain

Like I said, it's as good as you'll get in any sermon. Nothing against sermons, or the folks who deliver them. Indeed, the Twain vignette is quite the encomium to his sometime-pastor, always-friend, and, I would think, a tip of the hat to all those devoted saints who learn the art and compassion of balancing the two. I have known a handful, myself. Sometimes they are called upon to show us pictures. Other times, they must hold a mirror.

Life is a miracle, a gift. Life is fragile, and fleeting. Life can be a struggle. Life can be so brutal that there are worse things than dying. Life holds only one guarantee of which I am aware. Be conscious of each day. Do the best that you can. Whenever possible, be kind.

....

A productive drunk is the bane of moralists.
Woody Allen

*An alcoholic is someone you don't like
who drinks as much as you do.*
Dylan Thomas

*Everyone should believe in something.
I believe I'll have another drink.*
W. C. Fields

....

2012

Carol Jeanne and I did not pay for a wedding this year, so family news is limited. However, I suppose that the birth of our second grandchild would merit mention. Oldest daughter Rachel and husband Ben presented us with Caroline Elizabeth Elder on October 4th. I really haven't had time to ask, but I assume that she was named after Caroline County, in Virginia, where Carol Jeanne and I first lived (Bowling Green) when we married. Carol Jeanne will gladly, and quite contentedly sit holding her for hours at a time. About a year from now, I will become of some passing interest to her (Caroline, not Carol Jeanne). In the meantime, no, she doesn't look just like Rachel did when she was born, nor does she resemble her father's baby pictures. In my objective estimation, she bears a striking resemblance to a scarlet prune.

Meanwhile, her older brother, Will, and I have become great friends. This is not egotism nor overestimation on my part, as Will is great friends with everyone he meets! After Will was born, Carol Jeanne began saving money for a playscape. When I was a kid, we had "forts." These were haphazard affairs, built by us in the backyard of any neighborhood kid who had either a good, forked tree, or perhaps two or three trees growing close together. The construction of these forts was always facilitated by a new home being built nearby, from which scrap lumber could be appropriated on the weekends, and there were always nails galore just lying around. Well those days are gone! The modern fort is an engineered, factory pre-cut, modular assemblage. It is delivered on a flat-bed truck, with a packing list, a parts list, and an instruction manual. Apparently, these three documents are written by three different parties, as none of the nomenclature carries over from one text to another. I am pretty sure that the instruction manual was written in a foreign language, then translated into mostly English.

Once the truck driver and I unloaded the behemoth, I laid every piece out in the front field (We finally settled on the field as the best place to erect the thing, after I adamantly refused to indulge some of Carol Jeanne's hare-brained ideas about clearing a place in the woods to put it, which would have required the use of a bulldozer and dump truck, at a minimum! She thought that a rake and shovel would suffice. This topic created some marital tension at the very outset of this project, which spared us from having to develop it later on.). Anyway, I laid this thing out in a very orderly, good-engineering fashion. Every piece was supposed to have a bar code/name tag stapled to one end, and the majority of them did. I stuck the unidentified pieces off in a separate pile.

The instruction manual was almost fifty pages long, and gave an estimated time to assemble of *twenty-five hours!!!* I got stuck on "Step One." Some of you will think I'm joking. The joke would be on you! Of the four main pieces called for in Step One, two of them did not exist, or at least they were not tagged by the name called for in the instructions. Carol Jeanne suggested (She sug-

274

gested a lot of stuff over the course of this project. See "marital tension" above. Her favorite thing was to inspect my progress each evening when she arrived home. It was such fun to have busted my hump putting something together by myself that should have taken three men [big ones!] to do, only to have her walk up and say, "Now why did you..., " or "Are you sure that...," or "The picture on the web page makes it look like..."), anyway, Carol Jeanne suggested that, while the instructions didn't say so explicitly in Step One, what they obviously must have meant to say was such-and-such. Well I told her right quick, right there, that I wasn't about to be on the hook for several thousands of dollars to someone who was supposed to have this down to a computer-generated science, to have to interpret something in Step One only to find out in Step Twenty-one that, by golly, no, that wasn't what they meant after all, and having to disassemble all the way back to Step One, and start over. No sir, I shut that project down right then and there.

I had her call and email the "nice man" that was so helpful in picking out the most expensive unit that this outfit makes, and let him know in no uncertain terms that what we had here was "failure to communicate," to quote Captain (Strother Martin's character in *Cool Hand Luke* – he was never given a name)! It took the nice man two days, but after comparing his own company's three documents, as well as the bar-code tags on the individual pieces, he admitted that there was no way for anyone to assemble this playscape based on their directions. His own people couldn't do it! The problem, he said, was that not too many people (as in no one but me) tried to assemble one of these things on their own. Most folks paid the assembly fee, and they would send a crew out (for only a few hundred dollars more). The people in his plant that assembled them did not read the directions, because over time, they had simply learned which piece went where and in which order. They didn't pay me a consulting fee for my engineering services, but after another two days, I had unified all their extraneous crap into a monolithic code. The consequence of which was:

The Modern Playscape

Note the old-fashioned, homemade balance beam at the bottom left corner, courtesy of Granddaddy!

2013

Well, in the interest of winding this thing up before Easter, I have just one more rant to make for 2013. This has to do with television ads. They absolutely get on my last nerve, and I have to set the record straight on a few of them. Let's start with Celebrex, an arthritis medication, whose manufacturer runs a series of ads with the tag line, "A body in motion." They state that a body at rest tends to stay at rest, a foreshadowing of Newton's first law of motion, and so far, so good. It's when they actually get to the first law that they fall flat on their faces. The ads state that, "A body in motion tends to stay in motion." Clearly they want arthritis victims to associate their ability to be in motion with Celebrex. But I'm here to tell you that if they don't have any better a grip on pharmaceuticals than they do on physics, I wouldn't swallow one of their pills any faster than I would swallow their advertising swill. The first law of motion states that, "A body in motion tends to stay in motion *until acted upon by an outside force.*" Does that seem like an insignificant mutation of the law, an innocent (or ignorant) "doctoring" of the facts in order to better suit their advertising story line? Not so! Forget treating the symptoms of arthritis (There is, of course, no cure for either type.). If the folks at Celebrex are right, then gravity and friction are things of the past, and they have discovered the holy grail of engineering... the perpetual motion machine!! Idiots.

"Ozempic is not meant to cause weight loss, but it may help you to do so. Patients taking Ozempic experienced a weight loss on average of up to twelve pounds." That's a statistically incorrect statement. The terms "on average" and "up to" do not belong in the same sentence. Possibly weight loss averaged twelve pounds, or, alternatively, possibly people experienced weight loss up to twelve pounds, but in no way did they do both. I believe that the manufacturer of Ozempic does not understand the definition of "average." If they cannot handle that little slice of science, I'm not trusting them to control my blood sugar level. And by the way, why the hell do pharmaceutical companies spend billions of dollars each year advertising their drugs to me? I can't prescribe them to myself. Talk to my doctor. I'm too busy reading the fine print that details all the ways this stuff can kill me.

Or how about this offering from the car manufacturer Infiniti (Infiniti is a brand of car for people who like Nissans, but insist on paying more than Nissans cost. The same is true for the Toyota/ Lexus crowd, and the Honda/Acura folks. Everything about these tandem models is made by the same company in the same factories; the single biggest difference between any of them is the price.). Anyway, this Nissan ad shows someone driving down a twisting road, behind a large truck, as the announcers intones, "What if you owned a car that could predict an accident *before it happened?*" Now I ask you, is there any other way to *predict* an accident, or anything else for that matter? If you want to simply stand around until after the accident has happened, then I am sufficiently omniscient to say, "I coulda told you that was going to happen." But then our friends at Infiniti go one step farther, stating that their car, "... helps you avoid accidents that you don't see coming." Is there any other kind?! If you have an "accident" that you did see coming, then that is not an accident; that is simply Darwin's theory at work! This type of "accident" is usually preceded by the victim saying, "Hey, watch this!" If he didn't see what was coming, everybody else did, right down to the video feed on their cell phones.

Do you get the DealDash.com commercials on your TV? They feature a variety of women who are all pathetic losers. Please don't think that I'm being superficial or judgmental. The people that wrote these ads picked these women just as intentionally as any Victoria's Secret ad model that you will ever see. They begin with some overweight, slightly hunchbacked woman who talks with a swishy lisp (again, all intentional) gushing that, "I won this camera for only $95.00!" What she calls "winning," most of the rest of us would call "buying," but that's a distinction that's readily glossed over. She goes on to gush that in her first four months on DealDash, she "won" 104 items. Do you get it? She has no life, she shops non-stop on cable TV, she thinks that her compulsive spending is leading her into becoming a winner... it's just what the advertisers want all the other pathetic losers that buy into this tripe to believe and mimic. So sad.

American Family Insurance irritates me. Their slogan is, "Your dream is out there. Go find it, and we'll protect it." Let me promise you that they have no intention of "protecting" anything. If they did so, your house would never be burglarized, flooded, burned to the ground, or destroyed in a tornado. What this company does do, hopefully, is to *insure* your property, wherein they would reimburse you for your loss up to the limit of your policy (minus your deductible, of course). If they don't understand the difference between those two words, how much might they not understand about the business they're supposed to be in? I think I'll protect myself, and be insured by another company.

Centrum Silver has an ad with a man saying, "I've been on the fence about a daily multivitamin. My wife recommended Centrum Silver. Now there's a new study out about multivitamins, and they used Centrum Silver... so I guess she was right." About what?! The "study" was probably underwritten by Centrum Silver – they don't bother to disclose who did it– and this comment says nothing about the study's premise or conclusions. Go ahead and let your wife "recommend" (yeah, right) how you ought to take responsibility for your health. He probably plays golf with her... on

Saturday mornings for crying out loud!

How about the Binder & Binder ads for "America's most successful social security advocates" (and they actually might be at the top of this sleazy heap, according to a feature on *60 Minutes*). The part that cracks me up is the idiot at the end of the commercial, with a sloppily knotted tie, pushing a damn cowboy hat onto his head as he assures you, "We'll deal with the government... you have enough to worry about!" Like the fact that you're contending with the United States Government's Internal Revenue Service, and you're being represented by somebody wearing a cowboy hat!

Cold-eeze guarantees to "shorten the length of your cold or your money back." How the hell would they – or you – know?! How long would your cold have lasted if you hadn't taken their product? Exactly when, clinically speaking, did your cold begin? Exactly when did it end? How do you know that your cold didn't last longer because you were busy choking down Cold-eeze instead of knocking back a little Jack Daniels? Anyone that has ever purchased this product, regardless of the results, should take them up on their claim to refund your purchase price.

Christian Mingle irritates me on so many levels. Where to start? How about "finding God's match for you?" This somehow seems to suggest that God is finished working on stuff like world peace and hunger, and is taking the afternoon off to help you shop for entertainment. There are roughly nine billion people on the face of this planet at this moment. I'm guessing a little over half of them are women (If God is matching me up with someone, it should be a woman; if your tastes incline you towards men, regardless of your own sex, more power to you.). That means there are about 4.5 billion women out there for God to weed through to find "the one" for me. A quick glance at the babes on the covers of the magazines in my Kroger check-out line suggests that God is facing quite a task in narrowing my choice down to only one. The notion that there is only one true love in this world for anyone is nonsense, but let's get past that. One of the couples in one of the ads advises, "Christian Mingle is the incredible vehicle that God used to bring my wife and I together." I guess that God and Christian Mingle were so busy sorting through those 4.5 billion possibilities that they both forgot to run that quote through a grammar check before airing the ad. I'm pretty sure that God brought "my wife and *me* together" would have been the proper way to state it. That's no worse, though, than eHarmony's statement that they will find you a match that is "truly unique." Here is a great rule of thumb: if you're thinking about modifying the word "unique," think about something else! Nothing is very unique, truly unique, or extremely unique. Such phrases simply reveal your total lack of understanding of the definition of the word unique. It's kinda like being pregnant... either you is, or you ain't.

Well I could go on and on, and yes, perhaps I already have. Suffice it to say that Geico Insurance doesn't understand the difference between "computer animated" and "computer generated." A doctor (!) for the American Cancer Institute advertises that the greatest benefits in their approach to treating cancer "is our ancillary services." I'm glad I'm not a doctor, because I would have said "*are* our ancillary services." The American Cancer Institute also boasts about its gene-based protocol for tailoring individualized care. The doctor in this ad says, "Genomic testing is the future of cancer in every way." Probably she meant to say that genomic testing is the future of cancer *treatment* in every way! In an attempt to compete with cable TV networks, AT&T U-Verse ads for their wireless service always talk about not being tied to a "TV outlet." What is a TV outlet? I have never used that term, nor have I ever heard anyone outside of this ad use that term. They twist themselves into a pretzel to avoid saying a "cable outlet," because we all know that that's the 800-pound gorilla in their room. I absolutely roar with laughter whenever I see the Ally Bank ad that shows some total stranger shoving a briefcase filled with $10,000 on some black man, asking him to "watch it for me," and assuring him that he "will be right back." That African-American gentleman is surrounded by a sea of white faces in a downtown business district while he sits and squirms on that briefcase, looking more nervous than a whore in church! The possibilities are limitless... and too easy. Would you join me in supporting a ban on ads for catheters, final expense insurance, reverse mortgages, gold and silver ("What's in your safe?"), secret Biblical codes for amassing wealth, and wounded warriors? I don't have anything against wounded warriors, but I'm pretty sure that those expenses should be up to the federal government that caused them to become wounded in the first place, and if finding those funds is a problem, let's hold that government accountable, rather than casting their future on the hopes of handouts and charity. My cynical suspicion is that there are some folks making some serious money off of "administering" the donations intended for the wounded, but maybe I'm wrong. And speaking of wounded warriors, let me make one more distinction; serving in our country's armed forces makes you a veteran, not a hero. If you were a clerk in the supply room at Fort Benning, you were a soldier, you served your nation, you became a veteran... but it don't make you a hero. If you're that soldier, I'm betting you already know that, and could probably tell the rest of this nation which soldiers are the true heroes. Oh well.

. . . .

There are only two ways to tell the truth.
Anonymously and posthumously.
Thomas Sowell

Tell the truth and run.
George Seldes

If you'll stop telling lies about me,
I'll stop telling the truth about you.
Mitchell Tenpenny

As scarce as truth is,
the supply has always exceeded the demand.
Josh Billings

. . . .

2012

I've told Carol Jeanne that when I die, I want to be cremated. She's asked me what I want done with my ashes. "Tell the funeral home to flush 'em down a toilet," I've told her. "Oh, but don't you want us (she's assuming she'll still be around) to spread them on your land so that you'll always be a part of it?" she asks. She doesn't seem to have any problem with the thought of my body being turned to toast, but for some reason the thought of a quick flume ride for the residue leaves her unsettled, and she thinks it will leave me detached from my land. Let me tell you, this land already commands a sizable account of my blood, sweat, and tears, literally. And, to date, I've run up a three-decade-and-counting bar tab with my septic tank. I'm here to tell you, if that don't marry me to this land for as long as a man can manage it, a little barbeque ain't gonna help matters!

On a sidebar, I have a very conservative friend who wonders if cremation is morally acceptable. "Why wouldn't it be?" I've asked him. He wonders how you'll get into heaven, and what'll you "look" like if you've been cremated. When addressed logically and scientifically, of course, this is nonsense. Just what body are we talking about? The one you were born with? The one you took on your first date? The one you died in? Of course, folks that were buried at sea, or a lot of the folks living in the vicinity of Krakatoa in August of 1883, or Hiroshima in August of 1945, are going to have a hard time pulling their acts together as well. What this causes me to wonder about is just how much of our bodies are "ours."

The last I heard, the earth has approximately the same number of atoms that it has always had. We've gained a few, of course, courtesy of meteorites and the occasional cosmic dust bunny. And we've shipped a few out of the system, courtesy of our various space programs. Overall, though, we're pretty much stuck with our original equipment. I was taught that matter cannot be created or destroyed. In engineering school they were so adamant about this principle that they elevated it to the status of a law... not just any law, but the very first law of thermodynamics (There are three of these laws. The second deals with entropy, and the third deals with the cessation of molecular motion at absolute zero [-460 degrees F], the lowest temperature possible.). If you analyze this just a little bit, you will come to realize that no atom in you is unique to your corpus; they've all been recycled, predominantly from previous organic substances, which would include dinosaurs, Moses, Joan of Arc, you name it! For my perplexed friend, this means that if we attempt to enter heaven with a physical body in any way related to the one we worked through here on earth, there's gonna be one hell of a tug of war for spare parts!!

. . . .

Any idiot can face a crisis.
It's this day-to-day living that wears you out.
Anton Chekov

. . . .

2020

I retired my hairbrush this past year. Have any of you ever done that? Have any of you even given a thought as to where your current hairbrush came from, or how long you've had it? I have had this brush for fifty-five years. It has a tortoise-shell handle, with nylon bristles, at least to the extent that it still has bristles. Since I brush my hair from left to right (because I'm right-handed), the bristles are all slanted from right to left. I received this brush as a Christmas present from my sister, Amy. My brothers received one as well. Our mother is the one who actually purchased these brushes, then gave them to Amy to give to us, so Ruth was able to kill two birds with one stone (The boys needed hairbrushes, and she felt she needed something for Amy to give us.). Neither my brothers, nor my sister, have any recollection of these brushes, but I, obviously, have held onto mine. It was a good brush, I'm utilitarian, and I'm cheap. If my replacement brush lasts as long as its predecessor, it could possibly be my last one!

....

Don't be humble. You're not that good.
Mae West

....

2011

When I was a kid, my parents bought a little plot of land, seventeen acres, in the neighboring county (Union County). At the time, it was just outside of the town of Weddington. As soon as we bought it, my father's father, Cy, set my two brothers and me to work fencing it. We cut all of the cedar posts that we used to fence it (If my life depended on it, I couldn't tell you where they all came from, but it took hundreds of them to fence in all seventeen acres.). We dug the post holes, toted the posts, tamped them in with our shovels, then strung the barbed wire, and hammered the staples into place. We bought some cows to graze it. We had Black Angus steers, while my father's aunt and uncle (the ones whose backyard backed up to ours), who owned the farm next to ours, grazed white-faced Herefords. I remember that they had a mean cow, a cow who would chase you if she saw you crossing her pasture, and I have no doubt she would have killed me if she could have. I had to cross that pasture if I wanted to fish in their pond, and running for my life may be one of the things that made me an exceptional runner. The thing that saved me every time was my dog Kobuk (named after the town in Alaska), who would attack her at the risk of his own life.

Our cows needed water, but the little creek on our farm wasn't reliable in the summer. Our grandfather solved that with a few sticks of dynamite. We went to a wet, seepy spot at the creek's springhead, and dug a hole in the heavy clay with our post-hole diggers. Cy attached some primer cord to a blasting cap, and used his pocket knife to pierce the side of one of the sticks of dynamite, and shoved the blasting cap into it. He wrapped the dynamite into a little bundle with the primer cord, then lowered it into the hole, which by this time was beginning to fill with water. Then he used his foot to scrape the muck back into the hole, and took the post-hole diggers to tamp it down. I remember being scared to death that he would set the dynamite off with all that tamping, but of course that didn't happen. He reeled off several feet of the primer cord, which was manufactured to burn at a rate of one foot per minute, and we climbed the hillside to settle down in the woods and await the action. Being little kids, we quickly became bored waiting on the explosion. I can't remember exactly what distraction I was occupied with when that dynamite let loose, but I clearly remember being shocked back to the matter at hand, and being covered in a storm of swampy water and mud. When the air cleared, our cows had a good watering hole! Eventually, Cy oversaw the construction of a small pond, maybe half an acre, and set the three of us to building a one-room cabin overlooking the pond. He died before he could finish the chimney. In later years, I know my older brother, then myself, would take dates to "the farm." My father dubbed the cabin "Hood's Whorehouse."

In those long-ago days, that farm was in the middle of nowhere. Now, it is inside the town limits of Weddington, surrounded by subdivisions and million-dollar homes, within a stone's throw of Lowe's, shopping centers, and yuppie restaurants. After our mother died in February of 2017, we put the land on the market. It should have jumped off the shelf within a week. But there's a snag. The North Carolina DOT, for the past twenty years or so, has periodically announced its intention to extend Rae Road through that neck of the woods, and through the back of our farm. They have surveyed it, and held public hearings on it. They have not, however, ever built it. Never bought any right-of-way. Never funded the project. Nothing. Their own terminology/classification of this project is "inactive." But with the rumors about it out there, and your property covered in survey ribbons and stakes, who would ever buy it? No one would buy the land where the highway will (possibly) one day run. But after four years of agony, and paying taxes, we finally have found a developer who will buy everything outside of the proposed DOT boundaries – about 12.5 acres. They plan to develop a single-street, ten-lot subdivision, to be called Belle Mar. They will give us an easement through the cul-de-sac of Belle Mar to the remaining land, which Union County and the Township of Weddington will continue to tax us on, while waiting on the DOT to pull the trigger, or for Hell to freeze over, whichever comes first. Weddington will have a public hearing on rezoning the land the first week of January, and then, please Lord, they will vote to approve the subdivision at their February meeting, after which we will close on the sale of the farm in February. [Editor's Note: The sale of the front portion of the farm did take place, but not until August. That land sold for something a little north of $65,000 per acre. Then, in October, the same developer bought the remaining 4.5 acres, the land beyond the DOT road extension. That land sold for only about $15,000 per acre, but at least we were out from under the burden of paying taxes on it for eternity. My CPA turned that into a nice financial loss for tax purposes, saving me and my siblings a significant amount of money.]

. . . .

I have the heart of a child. I keep it in a jar on a shelf.
Robert Bloch

. . . .

2012

The day after our youngest daughter's wedding, which in my Scotch-addled memory was somewhere around the Fourth of July, at a brunch at Carol Jeanne's brother's house, just after I became the oldest person that Rabun had ever pulled to a skiing position behind his pretty-damn-fast boat, my daughter Rebecca started telling her sisters about an upcoming triathlon. Since Rebecca and her husband Chris are young, and because they are both jocks, and because he is a youth minister (and so is she when she's not

288

teaching school, or going to school), she told brothers-in-law Ben and Garrett that they should enter this triathlon. For whatever reasons (It didn't appear to involve Scotch insofar as they were concerned.), the two of them agreed. It was to be held about twelve weeks away, on September 30th, at Lake Lanier Islands Resort. That being settled, they turned as one to look at me, and ask, "How 'bout it Dad, are you in?" You have to realize that, given the magnitude of boat traffic on Lake Oconee on the Fourth of July weekend, trying to ski on it is like trying to soothe hemorrhoids by sliding down a corncob. That water was rough, and I was suffering from post-traumatic-stress-disorder. I guess I said yes to something, but to what I had no idea.

As it turned out, what I had agreed to do was to swim a quarter-mile, ride a bicycle for thirteen miles, then run 3.2 miles. I told my kids that the last time I had been on a bike or gone swimming, NONE OF THEM HAD BEEN BORN! This was a FACT! To be honest, once I was sober, I wasn't particularly intimidated at the prospect of this. I knew I could run, just not fast. I figured that I could learn to ride a bike again. I knew, based on my twice-weekly routine of jumping rope, that the swimming would be a bitch. Swimming and jumping rope have this in common – either you're doing it, or you ain't. When you run, you can find ways to coast. When you bike, you don't have to pedal downhill. When you jump rope, you better keep it going, and if you stop swimming, you sink!

The kids are young, and in reasonably good shape without doing anything special. I figured they would be slow in starting their training, and probably a little haphazard about pursuing it. I figured I better start the next morning. I did. I laid out a training regimen from that day to race day, and I stuck to it. If anything, I increased it, once I convinced myself I wasn't going to die. The biggest adjustment was getting my bun-bones used to the shape and size (or lack thereof) of a modern bicycle seat. And as I researched this triathlon business (and it is a business… an industry, really), I quickly came to the realization that the biking was the key. If you swim fifty-percent faster than I (and you wouldn't), over the course of a quarter mile, that gains you about four minutes. If you run a 5K one minute per mile faster than me, that gains you about three minutes. But if I ride a bike one minute a mile faster than you, that gains me THIRTEEN minutes. It doesn't take Einstein to figure this puppy out.

But, as my research revealed, here's the rub. Your time on the bike doesn't have nearly so much to do with you, as it does with your bike. Rebecca loaned me a mountain bike, and two friends loaned me "hybrids." What Rebecca and sons-in-law Ben and Chris were riding were "road bikes." You don't buy these at Wal-mart. These bikes go for over a grand; the mid-grade versions can easily hit five grand, and the prices for a premium bike get a little on the expensive side. Some of these bikes have insurance policies!! As the burned-out, ex-hippie at my local bike shop said, he could put Lance Armstrong on my mountain bike, and put me on Lance Armstrong's bike, and I would beat Lance Armstrong (Dude!). I started calling around, dropping heavy hints to biking friends, and begging strangers, but I was coming up with zilch. Then one day I happened to be talking to a guy up the street (my dead-end, out in the country, red-neck street), and I tell my neighbor about entering this triathlon. Would you believe he had just completed one the weekend before?! What were the odds? He has one of these five-thousand-dollar bikes, something he lucked into on the used-bike market with the same ex-hippie at our local bike shop. This bike has virtually no metal in/on it. It is mostly carbon composite. No, he didn't offer to loan it to me, but what he did say was that he would lend me his old bike, an old road bike. It might have been old, but so was I! Now I was in the race.

As race day drew closer, I had an inspiration. I decided that I would wear the same shirt, the same shorts, and the same socks that I wore when I ran my marathon thirteen years ago. Possibly some of you can believe a man would own a T-shirt or shorts for over a decade, but no one would believe that you could own the same pair of socks thirteen years later. Even if you did, how could you possibly identify them?! Well, at the time I ran my marathon, my girls were all involved in athletics, and they all liked to steal my socks (Thorlo rolltops!). In order to thwart them, I marked all of my socks in Sharpie indelible ink with my initials. And for the marathon, I bought a brand-new pair that I marked with a large "M" across the toes. And yes, I still have them thirteen years later, and yes, even though they've been washed a few times, you can still see the "M."

In 1999, in the marathon, I ran at 8:08 per mile. In 2012, in the triathlon, I ran 8:08 a mile. It wasn't as far, but in 1999 I wasn't hopping off of a bicycle after a thirteen-mile sprint. I'm here to tell you that when you try to run after a serious bike ride, you think you're going to fall face-first into the pavement. Your legs, especially the proximal end in which the permanent vertical smile is housed, have no intention of performing that particular task! Well the big day came. At 7:30 AM, on September 30th, with the sun breaking the horizon in the east, and under a shining full moon about to set in the west, we plunged into Lake Lanier. The five of us (three sons-in-law, daughter Rebecca, and myself), finished within twelve minutes of one another. I was the middle of the pack, about six minutes out of first place, and six minutes ahead of last place. I finished fourth in my age group, but the three guys ahead of me are all retired, and now triathlons are what they do for a living (on very expensive bikes!). After it was over, the kids were asking me if I had thought I could do it, did I think I would whip them (I resisted the urge to point out that I just had whipped two of them!)? I told them that they were asking the wrong questions. The *real* question is, twenty-eight years from now – when they are my age – will they be able to post the same time they did this past September?!!!

In some ways, twenty-eight years is not such a long time. It's about how long I might reasonably expect to have left to walk the face of this earth, and I'm pretty sure that it's gonna go by pretty fast. On the other hand, when I think about the mileage I've put on my body in the past twenty-eight years, it seems like a long time.

Built three houses, rebuilt both knees, torn rotator cuff, carpal tunnel syndrome in both wrists, too many nicks to remember. As for this triathlon business, I'd like to have tackled it on a more level playing field. Give me the body I had twenty-eight years ago – the body that I had when I was their age, and we wouldn't be talking about no stinking six minutes outta first place!!

. . . .

I like long walks, especially when
they are taken by people who annoy me.

Noel Coward

I have never killed a man, but I have read
many obituaries with great pleasure.

Clarence Darrow

. . . .

2017

Let's take a few minutes to talk about stuff on TV that drives me crazy. For everything that is sold on TV, the ad will tell you that, "For a limited time, you can double your order, just pay a separate fee." That separate fee is the purchase price of the first item you bought. Who can be dumb enough to fall for that? I don't understand pharmaceutical companies that advertise their drugs, then tell you, "Do not take this drug if you're allergic to it." Well how the hell should I know that? I only know one way to find that out on my own, and by then it would be a little too late. Shouldn't the doctor that's prescribing it to me handle that issue? Also, remember not to take their drugs if you have been to an area where certain fungal infections are common. Again, how the hell should I know? They certainly aren't giving you a list of them. I'm pretty sure that I haven't been to one of those areas, unless one of them exists within sixty miles of my house, because that's about as far as I go, but still, you'd hate to take a chance on it. Finally – for now – some of these ads also tell you to "contact your doctor if you begin to experience gall bladder problems." All together now: How the hell should I know? Why don't they tell me what the symptoms of gall bladder problems are?

While we're talking about medical commercials, I've noticed many ads touting their medical products as "FDA cleared." That is not the same thing as "FDA approved," a certification that should not be of any great comfort itself, if you understand the process. In 1976, the Medical Device Amendments were added to the Food, Drug, And Cosmetics Act. Thereafter, new medical devices (e.g., MRI, PET, and CAT scanners) have to go through a premarket approval process; that sounds good, but the reality is that these devices slip from "premarket" to "market" status about as easily as an illegal alien at our southern border. After a medical device enters the premarket phase, it is seldom heard from again. Now if that isn't scary enough for you, consider the value of being "FDA cleared." This means that the manufacturer of the device in question has given the FDA a warm pat on the back, and told them not to worry, that their new device is "substantially equivalent" to some other medical device that existed before the 1976 amendment was added, and therefore all that pesky testing isn't necessary, no, not at all. This is how we end up with messes like wire mesh implants and vagus nerve stimulators (which stimulate your vagus nerve, but can also simultaneously stop your heart, which can be problematic, and which I'd tell you to ask someone who experienced this affliction if you wanted to find out more about it, but that, too, is problematic). Finally, a number of the ads state that their product has been "clinically proven." That's it, that's all, just "clinically proven." Clinically proven to do what? They never say. Perhaps this product was "clinically proven to be totally ineffective and pose significant health risks." But, based on their ads, we'll never know.

Some woman who has a show called *Shark Tank* (I've never seen it.) is peddling a dual-traction device to relieve lower back pain. It's totally bogus, but the main reason that I would never buy it is because the pitchman begins by saying, "Just lay on your back...". If the dual traction team doesn't understand English grammar, I'm not going to trust my lower back to their grasp of medicine and physics.

Domino's Pizza has some kind of rewards program that they claim "makes it easy for you to earn free pizza." Am I the only one that sees the incongruity between "free" and "earn?" Of course, Christians have struggled with that dichotomy with regard to grace for the past two thousand years and counting.

If I never hear another commercial for My Pillow, it will be too soon. Just how much science can go into a pillow? I'll concede that we've come a long way from using a rock, but enough's enough! If you refer to yourself as having "invented" a pillow, you're pretty much swimming in the shallow end of the pool.

Watch this guy's ads closely. The first thing that you should notice is that he makes sure that his giant crucifix, which he wears around his neck, is hanging outside of his shirt, rather than tucked inside of it. That's a warning flag in my book. Then he goes back to the "early days" of his company's research and development, showing these cheesy, sepia-style photos in black-and-white, and there that crucifix is again! Next, as you watch his ads, notice how much of the time he is holding his pillow in his lap. I don't want to be salacious (just suggestive), but watch that pillow closely. Just what is the nature of the relationship between this guy and his pillow? Is it legal? Then he gets in a subtle dig of xenophobia, telling you that his pillows are manufactured "right here, in my home state of Minnesota." Finally, these commercials feature various people using his product (You can tell he truly is from Minnesota, because all of the people in his ads are white as snow. Guess he hasn't gotten the PC bulletin on accepted ratios of diversity in advertisements.). Anyway, the featured couple in his ads are shown sleeping blissfully on their pillows. The lady, a cute blonde, wearing a lavender sleep top, is lying on the right side of the bed as you look at it. Later, toward the end of the commercial, they flash back to this couple, and she is sleeping on the left side of the bed. Is there a couple anywhere out there that spontaneously swaps sides of the bed in the middle of the night? And speaking of nighttime, if Mike really wants his customers to get a better night's sleep, tell them to try sleeping *at night!* Look closely at his ads – everyone in every one of them is sleeping in broad daylight!

This past year, he introduced his newest product, the My Mattress Topper. His ads for the mattress topper (this is a mattress topper, not the mattress itself) trumpet the following three claims:

Layer 1 - MyPillow® patented foam, in a solid piece, provides superior support and durability

Layer 2 - Transitional foam provides optimal comfort, evenly distributes body weight and helps relieve pressure points

Layer 3 - Cover made from Phase Change Material to keep your body temperature regulated throughout the night

I have a Master's degree in engineering (just like Howard Wolowitz on *The Big Bang Theory*). I have authored articles on my engineering research that have been published in scientific journals, and which have been cited – literally – around the world (I probably should have told most of you to sit down before reading that, so that you would not have had as far to fall, but it is true.). My major professor, whose career was advanced, in part, through my research (which is the way academia necessarily works), reads much of my writing, and has told me I wasted my time in engineering. He says that I should have been a journalist. But back to the point at hand, I have completed courses in strength of materials, heat transfer, thermodynamics, and more. I'm guessing that Mike Lindell has studied none of it. Not one of his claims is supported by scientific fact. In fact, the facts contradict his claims as patently false. His claims are as baseless as his claim that any of his products will be the best of its type that you will EVER experience (He personally guarantees it.). In addition to My Pillow and My Mattress Topper, he manufactures My Sheets (Egyptian Giza cotton), and My Towel (American cotton). He's invented everything short of the actual mattress. I'm betting that next he'll invent My Toilet Paper, and he's going to guarantee it will be the greatest toilet paper that you will ever use!

Nowadays he's expanded his product line to include slippers, bed sheets, mattresses, mattress toppers, and towels. Every ad for every product includes the same lie. He "personally guarantees that these [slippers/sheets/towels/pillows] will be the best [slippers/sheets/towels/pillows] that you will ever own." *Ever?!* That's a pretty long time. How can he possibly know that no one else will ever make a better slipper/sheet/towel/pillow? The fact is, of course, that he cannot make that guarantee.

NEWS FLASH

This just in. Mike Lindell has just announced the "invention" of MyPillow 2.0, a new and improved MyPillow. Well if that's true, what happened to all those claims he made about the original MyPillow being the most comfortable pillow that you'll ever own? He personally guaranteed it! Did he not just prove himself to be a liar? What about all the people who bought the original MyPillow? Shouldn't he refund their money, or at least send them a MyPillow 2.0 replacement?

Finally, Mike Lindell routinely announces "sales" on his various product lines. He states that they have to move some item out to "make room" (whatever that means) for a new product line. Apparently there is an upper limit, some maximum, total number of his products that can exist. My Slippers that originally sold for $150 a pair can now be had for a paltry $29.95 – and he's still making a profit on them at that price. In his ad for whichever clearance item he's hawking, he always says the same thing: "Quantities are limited, and won't last long. When they're gone, they're gone for good (his good), so please order now." And he plays that same damn ad for month after month after month. My Pillow, my ass.

I wish there were some way to compare the average number of cars that pass through a green light today, as opposed to the same light twenty years ago. When I leave the Kroger shopping center on Sunday afternoon, I have to wait on a green arrow to make the necessary left-hand turn toward home. That green arrow is there for exactly fifteen seconds. Miss this light, and you have to wait two minutes and forty-five seconds (Please don't doubt me.) for it to turn green again. I have exactly zero interest in doing that, so once the light turns green, I wish eagerly for every idiot that is in line in front of me to get going. But none of them can, because the biggest idiot is the idiot at the front of the line, and they are too busy texting to notice that they have burned five of their fifteen seconds of green looking at their device! Eventually, of course, they happen to look up and move on. And here's the amazing thing, the idiot behind the first idiot isn't blowing his horn, or even right on the first idiot's bumper, because they're still staring into their own lap! You should be able to get at least twelve cars through a fifteen-second light (That's the vehicle-equivalent length of the turn lane that the DOT invested many of my tax dollars to determine.), but of course their studies were based on how people drove twenty years ago. There were idiots around then, too, but they weren't texting. So what happens is that you get three or four cars through the intersection on the green arrow, then another half dozen on the yellow light, and on into the red, at which time the last car to run the light is occasionally picked off by a driver who was paying attention when his light turned green, and drove off when it did. I've told you this before, but the difference between genius and stupidity is that genius has its limits!

Do any of you recall when Monday was laundry day? That was it, the whole deal for the whole week. Sheets on the line like sailboats throughout the neighborhood.

I read a fair bit, and usually two or three books at a time (I keep one at the kitchen table, one by my chair in the den, and one in the meditation center.). This past year I tried to read William Faulkner's *As I Lay Dying*. I'm here to tell you that it cannot be done. He had to be on drugs to write it, and you'd have to be on drugs to read it, and *think* that you understood any of it. You didn't.

Linguistics is "the study of human speech, including the units, nature, structure, and modification of language." I would like to assign a linguist to study the composition of interviews as narrative in modern, American culture. Specifically, I would like them to analyze the evolution of a person's inability to answer a direct question directly. By which I refer to the ubiquitous use of meaningless word salad by the respondent before getting around to making any meaningful point that they may have to make (which probably they do not have). Pay close attention to any interview on television or radio. We have come to the point that the answer to a question will almost invariably begin with one of the following expressions: "Well," or "So," or "Look," or my personal favorite, "Well, so look..." As soon as I hear you say that, I write you off. I have no interest in hearing what else you say. It is my personal prerogative as a sentient being.

And tell those damn kids to get off my lawn!!

. . . .

War is the unfolding of miscalculations.
Barbara Tuchman

. . . .

2012

In February, it fell my lot to once again make that long, sad trek to the vet. This time, I was taking my oldest dog, Ginny. When Carol Jeanne and I first married, we moved to Virginia, and adopted a puppy from the Richmond SPCA. As a reminder of "back home," we named this dog Georgia. So, a few years later, after we had moved back to Georgia, and this stray hound came along to adopt us, we named her in honor of our time in Virginia, to wit, Ginny. Since she was a stray, I don't know just how old she was, but she lived with us a little over seventeen years. She wasn't pure-bred, but she had a lot of Walker hound in her. She was tan and black, and in her younger days I called her my honey-faced hound. She was deathly afraid of thunder, and knew when a storm was coming hours before it would arrive. You didn't need *The Weather Channel* when you had Ginny around! She would claw a hole through the bottom of Stone Mountain to escape thunder if a storm arose while we were away from home, and she had been left outside. I eventually discovered that she had dug a storm shelter under the girls' playhouse, in a space less than a foot high. To make her escape easier, I cut a little "door" into the back of the playhouse, which she seemed to greatly appreciate.

When Ginny first appeared on the scene, we had just acquired a Jack Russell Terrier puppy. MacKenzie was a gift to me from my parents, following the death of Georgia. Ginny started dropping by in the mornings, out in the front field, to make MacKenzie's acquaintance. I didn't figure there was much future in that, because MacKenzie, being a Jack Russell Terrorist, was pretty territorial, and very much the alpha dog of either sex on our street. At any rate, Ginny belonged to the people across the street, so I didn't give it much thought (Though I do remember thinking they didn't seem to feed her very well, as she was thin as a rail.). To my surprise, however, Ginny found favor with MacKenzie, and they were quickly spending ever-longer parts of the day with one another, playing wildly in the field. Ginny was incredibly shy; she didn't want anything to do with me, and would trot off if I got too close to her. I can still remember quite vividly the first time she ever took a dog biscuit from my hand. But again, she belonged to our neighbors, so I didn't dwell on it.

Then one day I came home to find a Mayflower moving van in the driveway across the street. I walked over to speak, and see where they were off to. We talked awhile, and eventually I said good-bye. As I was leaving, I turned around, and jokingly told my neighbor to be sure to remember to take his dog with him. "What dog?" he asked. "We don't have a dog." I honestly thought he was kidding! He wasn't. That was the day I knew I had a new dog, and thus I had to come up with her name.

Megan had just started first grade when Ginny arrived. Now she's graduated college, and is married, and teaching school. Ginny was here through all of it, through all of the girls. Through all of the girls' middle schools and sports, high schools and proms, learners' permits and drivers' licenses, colleges and graduations, weddings, and even grandchildren. She outlived another four dogs and two cats along the way. She was the most humble, unassuming animal I have ever known. She never in her life begged a table scrap; she never in her life jumped up on a piece of furniture; she never in her life ate out of a bowl other than the one I set before her; she never in her life scratched on a door to go in or out. She greatly preferred to stay in the background, and it was easy for most folks to forget that she was even a part of the landscape. But not me.

Ginny had a way of running that we labeled "fanny-loping." She could outrun all of the other dogs – and there were a couple of fast ones through the years – without looking like she was even trying. That would drive the other dogs crazy, and as she let them catch up to her, she would turn her rear flank into them to keep them at "arm's length," while teasing them on. I swear she was dog-laughing at them! When I would go for my run, Ginny and the rest of the pack would go with me. She would hit the edge of the spillway along the lake at a full run, and lap water as she went, never breaking stride. After we would cross the bridge, the other dogs always took off straight-up the hill, looking for squirrels and rabbits and deer. But not Ginny. She always took the flank, following the path around the far side of the lake. Whatever the other dogs flushed, whatever ran past them or through them, Ginny was going to be there to gather up!

Eventually, of course, all of my dogs have come to the end of their running days. Then they "retire" to walking around the lake. It's about three-quarters of a mile for the loop, and when they can no longer run, they walk to get their exercise. Ginny finally fell into this group, and was later joined by others. Now, when Ginny would run, it was only in her sleep, legs pumping furiously, paws twitching wildly as she pursued her phantom game. In the last year or so, she had to shorten her walks to just the quarter-mile loop between our house and Carol Jeanne's parents' house. When this began to be too much of a challenge, I knew a dreaded time was quickly approaching.

When I arise in the morning, I dress, then head for the living room. By the time I reach it, whatever dogs aren't already between my feet are arriving from whatever spot they slept in the night before... they all tend to shift about, even from upstairs to the basement. Except for Ginny. When I arrive in the living room, I know that she will be fast asleep on her LL Bean deluxe dog bed. She was the first dog I would speak to, the first one whose ear I would scratch, and tummy I would rub, and the rest of them knew it. The rest would stand by, sometimes joining me in greeting Ginny by licking her face, and giving her a few cordial sniffs. But they knew to wait. No one was going out the front door for that first morning romp until I had greeted Ginny (Ginny herself would not arise until after my breakfast, when we would all trek down to fetch the newspaper.). Even to this day, first thing in the morning, my dog Bailey stops dead in front of me on our way to the front door, and pauses for me to say good morning to a comrade who is no longer there.

Ginny had gotten slow. She was slow to rise, slow to move, sure to stop and sniff anything that wasn't in the same place it was the day before as she made her way to the back door. Lord, it took forever to get her out of the house in the morning. Standing there holding the door wide-open for her, I swear the furnace or the air conditioner would cycle twice before she made it out! She acted like she couldn't hear, so we communicated with hand signals and arm-waving, but out of a sound sleep in the living room on her LL Bean deluxe dog bed, she damn-well knew whenever the can opener was running, or if a plate was being scraped at the sink. To her last day she was healthy, had a great appetite, could see like a hawk, and could follow any scent trail that she wanted to. She could blissfully sleep twenty-three-and-a-half hours a day. She was content. She may have been stiff and sore, but hellfire, so was I!! She was not in pain. That was my assessment, and I was very conscious about monitoring that.

None of which made that last week any easier. The judgment of extending to one of God's creatures another day of life is an awesome responsibility. Perhaps it is even presumptuous. If I were to be honest, I suppose that deep in my heart I hoped that one morning I would walk into that living room to scratch her head, and find that she had crossed over in the night. But that just wasn't going to happen. All those years of running and walking (along with blueberry-pomegranate juice and soy milk every morning, followed at night by a bowl of Jack Mackerel canned fish and a baby-aspirin) meant that her heart, lungs, and brain would long outlast her rear legs, which finally failed her.

The distinction between benevolence and selfishness can be a fine one, a line that easily blurs in the face of the eternal consequence. And so we took that last, sad drive. Once again, I have washed and dried a stainless-steel bowl, and tucked it away upon the pantry shelf. It rests now in hopeful expectation of that time when God might once again call me into the sacrament of stewardship, tending to another stray until the day when its Creator returns to fetch them home. Since it was MacKenzie who really adopted her, I buried Ginny just below MacKenzie, in a little hollow between two mounds on the edge of the front field. It was her favorite spot, where she loved to sun bathe, and await my return whenever I left the house. Like MacKenzie, I laid her to rest facing the end of the drive, so they'll always know when I've come back.

Ginny
? – February 21, 2012

The art of Management is to keep the five guys who hate you away from the five who haven't made up their minds.
Casey Stengel

A team effort is a lot of people doing what I say.
Michael Winner

A team takes on the personality of its coach. Mine were always obnoxious.
Al McGuire

2012

Twice a year at my church, I serve in a position that they call "worship leader." This is a lay person who takes care of announcements and housekeeping details during the service so that the preacher can focus on the heavy lifting. One of my duties is to deliver the "Prayer For Understanding," a regular feature in our order of worship. As a means of heading this thing to a close, I thought I'd share this with you. It's in all-capital letters because, while I still do not wear reading glasses at the age of 56, the light in the pulpit is poor, and this made it easier to read the darn thing without losing my place! Anyway, even if you're not a Presbyterian, I hope it will be meaningful to you.

Prayer For Understanding
July 15, 2012

GRACIOUS GOD, WE GATHER THIS MORNING TO DO
THE IMPOSSIBLE. WE SEEK TO KNOW YOU, BUT WE CAN
ONLY KNOW ABOUT YOU. WE SEEK TO DEFINE YOU, BUT
WE MUST USE THOUGHTS AND WORDS, AND YOU WILL
FOREVER BE BEYOND THESE THINGS. THE FINITE CANNOT
POSSESS THE INFINITE. NO SET OF HUMAN BELIEFS CAN
FULLY POSSESS YOU. NO CREED CAN FULLY EXPRESS YOU.
NO RELIGION – NOT EVEN OUR OWN – CAN FULLY CLAIM
YOU. DELIVER US FROM THAT ARROGANCE.

BUT FEEBLE THOUGH THEY BE, OUR THOUGHTS AND
OUR WORDS ARE THE BEST THAT WE CAN DO. HONESTY
COMPELS ME THIS MORNING TO CONFESS THAT I DO NOT
PERCEIVE YOU TO BE A PERSON-LIKE BEING, DISCRETE,
LIKE US, ONLY BIGGER AND BETTER. WE SPEAK OF YOU
METAPHORICALLY BECAUSE IT IS THE BEST OUR INADE-
QUATE WORDS CAN DO. BUT I REALIZE THAT NO ONE SITS
ON YOUR RIGHT HAND, BECAUSE YOU HAVE NO HANDS.
YOU DO NOT SIT ON A THRONE, BECAUSE YOU DO NOT
HAVE THAT WITH WHICH ONE SITS UPON A THRONE. WE
CALL YOU HEAVENLY FATHER, BUT YOU ARE NOT AN
ANATOMICALLY GENDERED BEING, AND WE MIGHT JUST
AS APPROPRIATELY – AND JUST AS METAPHORICALLY –
NAME YOU MOTHER OF LIFE.

AND SO WE USE OUR INADEQUATE, FINITE WORDS TO
PONDER THE INFINITE. WE DO THIS IN THE TRADITION OF
OUR FOREFATHERS IN FAITH, IN THE TRADITION OF THE
ONE WE NAME THE CHRIST, THE ONE WHO CALLS US TO
NEWNESS OF LIFE, TO ACTIVE MEMBERSHIP IN YOUR

KINGDOM, HERE AND NOW. YOU ARE OUR CREATOR. I AM PART OF YOUR CREATION, AND PART OF YOU IS IN ME. I AM PART OF YOU. TEACH US THIS MORNING, CREATOR GOD, HOW THE GOD IN US CAN SEE THE GOD IN OTHERS. WE SEARCH FOR YOU AS A FISH SEARCHES FOR THE WATER. TEACH US OF THAT THIS MORNING. AMEN

....

We search for God as a fish searches for the sea.
Rumi

There are people in the world so hungry that God cannot appear to them except in the form of bread.
Mahatma Gandhi

....

2001

—————————

Prayer For Understanding
September 23, 2001

Almighty God, we live in perilous times... but what era of human history has not been perilous? From hunting mastodons with sticks, to Egyptian bondage, to Babylonian exile, to Roman imperialism, from Mongol hordes to the Black Death to the Great Depression to the Holocaust to Hiroshima to the Cold War to terrorism, we have always been a threat to ourselves. In the words of the cartoon philosopher Pogo, *We have met the enemy, and he is us.*

What is different today is our ability to *know* how perilous our times are. We *all* know. We know *instantaneously*. We know as *eyewitnesses*. We know *repetitively*, from the "film at 11:00" that is played over and over on our televisions and eventually in our minds and even in our sleep – until our dreams turn into nightmares.

Father, already cries for justice have reached Your throne. Do not count my voice among them, Lord. I want no part of justice... I am guilty. I want mercy, not justice. Help us, Lord, in fulfilling our Christian duty to forgive those who have persecuted us, to pray for the lost, to love the unlovely... because we have been all of these things ourselves. And before we protest that while we may have sinned, we haven't murdered anyone, much less innocent women and children, let us be reminded that the bombs of the American government have done exactly that. Perhaps it wasn't our government's intention, perhaps it was done without my consent or even my awareness. But this is of no consolation to the mothers and widows who have filled their own body bags and their own cemeteries with the carnage of American bombs... such as a pharmaceutical plant where their husbands and children worked making aspirin. Their pain, too, is real, their indignation, righteous. We can no longer dismiss their deaths as "acceptable collateral damage." Lord teach us that such national indifference and arrogance only worsens our dilemma.

I realize that sanity, economic stability, and civilized society – and yes, justice, too – will demand that something be done. We cannot go through life in fear of death. We don't want to be afraid every time we get in an airplane, or go to Sanford Stadium, or to Georgia Square Mall, or to Disney World. We should not have to think twice before we breathe the air or drink a glass of water.

Father, in the days to come, difficult decisions will of necessity be made. Help us to understand that these decisions will also be violent, fatal decisions. They will not be without consequence. Lord, we pray for our national leaders and our military personnel, for intelligence officers, security officers, and rescue personnel, for pilots and air marshals, in the face of these decisions. Give them wisdom. Show them how to hold the guilty accountable while sparing the innocent. Guide them that they may eradicate this cancer with the deft touch of a surgeon and not the lumbering swipes of a butcher. Give us the resolve, before the blood flows, to stay the course. As we recall that for every action there is an equal and opposite reaction, let us consider the appropriate course to chart. And once we embark upon this mission, keep our hand to the plow, that those who we will ask to die for us will not have died in vain.

Father, for those who are hurt and bewildered and who do not know You, for those who live apart from Your forgiveness and love, please let them know that this was in no way a part of Your will. This was not part of any plan of a loving God. This was the doing of man in a sinful world where man is permitted, for a season, to exercise his will and judgment, no matter how terrible it may be. God be with those who are so consumed with hate. God be with those who will die in the days to come. Impart Your grace to them. Reveal Your love to them. Remind us all, dear Lord, that love wins. Love always wins. Only love wins. In the name of Christ, amen.

. . . .

Every formula that expresses a law of nature
is a hymn of praise to God.
Maria Mitchell
(the first female astronomer in America,
and the first American astronomer to discover a comet)

. . . .

Prayer For Understanding
Blessed Assurance (Of A Creek)
Sunday, September 27, 2015

There's a creek below my house. It must have been there for a mighty long time, because the creek bed is about fifty feet below the ridge along my backyard; it had to have taken a long time to carve a creek bed that deep. If I took you down there and showed it to you, you'd say, "Yep, that's a creek alright." If I took you down there a year later, you'd say, "Yep, that's still a creek. No doubt about it." If I asked you if it was the same creek that you'd seen the year before, you'd say it was. I would too.

But I see the creek every day. It looks different at different times, but it's the same creek. In Spring, it's clear and gushing. In Summer, it might slow to a trickle, tinged green with algae. In Fall, it's full of red and golden floats. After a big Winter rain, it can be a raging torrent, stained red by Georgia clay. It's always the same creek, but it is never the same water. The water that makes up my creek is there for the second that you see it – or don't – then it's gone, forever lost in its journey to the sea. It's always the same creek, but it's never the same. Its only constant is change.

The Church is like that. Worship is like that. Things change. The liturgies, the creeds, the hymns – even the beliefs – change. They are not permanent; they were never intended to be. Not even the worshipers are permanent. All of them – all of us – are there for the second that you see them, then they are gone – we are gone – forever lost in the journey into our Creator.

I like that. I like the fact that after I'm gone, that creek will continue to flow, discernment will continue to evolve, and humanity will continue to seek to fulfill their intended relationship, one to another, as we strive to attain, in God, our ultimate potential. There is, in that, a *Blessed Assurance*.

I have sometimes thought that, in order to be a good minister, it was necessary to leave the ministry. The profession is antiquated. In an altered age, we worship in the dead forms of our forefathers.

Ralph Waldo Emerson
(upon leaving his position as Senior Pastor
of Boston's Second Church)

2012
———————————

Well, since we've come this close to the precipice of religion, and since this publication is, at least marginally, a Christmas missive, I'll polish this year's effort off by sharing one more church-related item. Each year in our church, the members produce an Advent Devotional. I generally participate in this endeavor, and this year I was assigned the lead-off position. Might as well inflict you with it, too.

December 2, 2012
Genesis 1:1-4

In the beginning God created the heaven and the earth. And the earth was without form, and void; and darkness was upon the face of the deep. And the Spirit of God moved upon the face of the waters. And God said, Let there be light: and there was light. And God saw the light, that it was good: and God divided the light from the darkness.

310

Becky Galvin asked me if I would write for the Advent Devotional. I said I would. She asked me what Bible passage I wanted to write about. I told her, "Oh, just pick one, it doesn't matter." I'll never make that mistake again!! At first glance, creation is a long ways from Christmas – it's a long poke from Genesis 1 to Matthew 1 or Luke 1 (Mark, writing before Matthew and Luke, didn't "do" Christmas, nor did John, who wrote afterwards.). More on the connection between Genesis and Christmas in a moment.

Before we get started, I have to share a Bible lesson I learned a long time ago. The first verse of Genesis is more properly interpreted as, "In beginning." Not "In *the* beginning." I find that to be much more elegant. For Almighty God, there was no "in *the* beginning," which would suggest that there was a time when God was not. The timeline on an eternal God extends infinitely in two directions!

The creation stories in Genesis (both of them) are, of course, metaphorical narratives. They are Israel's story of the birth of the human race, followed eleven chapters later by the birth of their own nation. Almighty God calls both into existence through the exercise of divine volition, through a creative act of holy will.

In the creation legend, the Spirit moves upon the face of the waters. In the Christmas legend, the Spirit moves upon a young woman named Mary. In Genesis, God creates light for the world. In Christmas, God creates the Light of the world. Both give people a means of seeing. Without either, there is darkness and death, both are a source of life.

The Light of the Christ, when invited to do so, can banish the darkness in our lives. The Light of the Christ has transformative powers. It can make new creations out of damaged lives and hardened hearts. Although the author of the gospel we call John did not write a Christmas story, more than any other Gospel writer – more than the other three combined – he employed the imagery of light. He has Jesus saying that he is "the light of the world: he that followeth me shall not walk in darkness, but shall have the light of life." In John we hear that the Light of the world came that we might have life, and that we might have it more abundantly.

Gracious God, I pray that you would move upon the waters of my life. Help me to trade my darkness for Your Light. Peace to all. Amen.

. . . .

Dear God, I cannot love Thee the way I want to. You are the slim crescent of a moon that I see, and my self is the earth's shadow that keeps me from seeing all the moon.
Flannery O'Connor

The Buddha is like a finger pointing to the moon.
Shurangama Sutra

Dear sun, who gives the vision but is not the vision.
K.A. Hays

. . . .

2019

Prayer For Understanding
October 20, 2019

This morning, for our Prayer For Understanding, I want to share a few thoughts with you about prayer. We pray a lot in this church. Our order of worship this morning includes a half-dozen prayers. Before we have the children's story, we always tell them that "first we must pray." Last week I participated in the workday at the University Presbyterian Center, and we had to pray before we spread mulch. Thankfully, Andy did not make us hold hands, and we did not have to sing Kumbaya. So we pray a lot, but we don't really talk a lot about prayer.

I want especially to address these thoughts to our senior youth (Is that an oxymoron?). I am sixty-years old, and I want to say something in church that I wish I had heard in church when I was your age, but I did not. And I hope that if you have questions or interests in these thoughts, that you will take them up with your ministers.

Prayer might be something that is spoken. Prayer might be something that you think (I would say "something you think that you think to yourself," but who else would you think something to?). These forms of prayer fall into different categories: praise, confession, intercession, supplication, and thanksgiving. These types of prayer, in my opinion, always boil down to one thing, the same thing – professing the truth at the center of your soul.

The great liability in these forms of prayer is that they tend to make us think of God in supernatural, Theistic terms. God is "out there" somewhere, and we seek to entice God to come back into God's creation, often to serve our purpose (even when that purpose seems noble). I think that most of us are willing to acknowledge that prayer is not a conduit to victory in a football game, or a winning ticket in the lottery. But we are less willing to let go of the false hope that prayer protects us when travelling, or that it protects us from cancer. If this is the first time that you have ever considered that possibility, it may sound frightening, but it is actually quite liberating.

That notion of prayer envisions God into a rabbit-in-the-hat, a Ouija-board God. Does God cure our cancer because we prayed the right prayer, or because we prayed it enough times to wear God down? Or did we just get lucky, and catch God in a good mood? You understand that there are many more people who die of their cancer than are cured of it. And even those whose cancer is cured die of something. Perhaps they are hit by a bus... guess they should have prayed the "bus prayer." Of course, the real problem with that type of prayer is the type of God that it creates. The God that cures your cancer is either the same God that gave you cancer, or who was looking the other way when it struck you. And if there is a God that cures cancer in response to prayer, that God is much better at it if you happen to live in the United States of America rather than, say, Sudan or Zambia. And that God is much better at curing kidney cancer, or even lung cancer, than pancreatic cancer.

Please note that I have NOT said that I do not believe in prayer, nor that I do not practice prayer. There is much that we can't cover in this brief moment, but I want my prayer life to be informed and intellectually honest. And trust me, I don't know what Donald Trump or Hillary Clinton would do if their phones rang at three o'clock in the morning, but if MY phone rings at 3:00 AM, the first thought to pass through my heart and my mind is going to be, "Oh Jesus, please God!"

But ultimately, "prayer" is not something that you think or say. Prayer is something that you do, something that you live. Paul spoke about prayer in the oldest book of the New Testament, in his first letter to the Thessalonians (He probably didn't write the second one.). Paul exhorted followers of The Way to "pray without ceasing." Obviously, Paul did not mean to pray instead of doing your homework, or getting a good night's sleep, or going out on a date. What Paul meant has been lost to us in our scientific, literalistic, non-Jewish culture. I think that Paul meant for us to so live that our entire life would become A Prayer. Prayer is ultimately a way of being, prayer is a lifestyle. Prayer should become an aspect of our humanity, and our humanity should increasingly become not a set of rules and beliefs, but a life – a prayer – of gratitude and praise. Amen.

Cultivate your vices. You never know when you might
need moral ballast to bargain with the Almighty.
Mark Twain

2016

——————————

This year, I turned sixty years old. I don't have a problem
with that... as a matter of fact, I take a measure of pride in it. Once
you turn fifty-nine, sixty becomes a worthy goal. I only wish I had
a nickel for everyone who ever bet that I wouldn't make it this far.
But turning sixty can make you reflect on things. One of the things
I thought about was that I was once six years old. I told you last
year how I came to my affection for the name Sharon, it being the
part of Charlotte in which I grew up, and where I attended Sharon
Elementary School on Sharon Road and lived in Sharonview
Acres. I remember my first-grade teacher, Mrs. Williams, who was
some distant kin. She kept a jar of malted milk tablets in her desk
drawer, which probably led to my life-long affection for chocolate-
covered, malted-milk balls (Whoppers!). One Friday, when she
learned that I was going to walk home with Bobby Schotz for a
spend-the-night, she gave me one of her malted milk tablets for
extra energy (Fitness freaks know malted milk as "whey," an
excellent source of protein.). We had to walk past the giant pasture
where Southpark Mall now stands, down Fairview Road by the
Celanese chemical plant, all the way out to Park Road. Anyway,
remembering Mrs. Williams caused me to think of each of my
elementary school teachers. All of them were women. In my time,
we had two male teachers in the entire school (but not at the same

time), and both of them were gym teachers (What we now call physical education specialists, only now they don't fund P.E. in the school budget). Anyway, first we had Mr. Coulter, a tall, lanky fellow whose wife was a patient of my father, then after him another man, then finally a woman P.E. teacher. Our music teacher for all six grades for the whole time that I was there was Mrs. Archer, and she liked to play the autoharp. She understood that I could not sing on key, so I was always an usher at school recitals. After first grade, my teachers, were: Mrs. Baldwin (huge jowls, like a bulldog), Mrs. Hunter (also some distant kin), then Mrs. Ison (She was probably the only teacher in the whole school who didn't have gray hair, and fourth grade boys thought that she was hot, even though we didn't fully comprehend what "hot" meant. Actually, we probably felt it more than thought it, but we all knew that she was better than Mrs. Autry, the alternative of the two fourth grade teachers. Mrs. Ison is the only one of my elementary teachers that might possibly still be alive. The others are all long dead.).

For fifth grade, it was Mrs. Cochran, and I capped off my elementary career with Mrs. Hood, who wasn't kin. What I do recall is that she was huge, well north of 300 pounds, with flabby triceps that flapped back and forth when she wrote on the blackboard. I don't know where the idea came to me from, but I do remember that one day I came to class early, and put the all chalk on the floor, at the base of the blackboard (which was actually green). When she waddled to the board to write something up there, she glanced around for the missing chalk, spied it on the floor, and when she leaned over to retrieve it, I took a piece of paper and sharply ripped it in two. She instinctively grabbed the back of her dress, fearing that she had just ripped the seam out of the back of it. She didn't say anything, and didn't launch an investigation to apprehend the culprit, but simply continued with her lesson. I always felt a little bad about having done that. But the point is this – at the age of sixty (or more), how many of you can name your first six school teachers?!

I also remember my first day of school at Sharon Elementary.

My classroom had these giant, casement windows that looked like they came out of an automotive factory in Detroit, and that overlooked the bus driveway that dead ended at the gymnasium. It had rained that morning, but by then the sun was out, and things were glistening. I remember watching a mocking bird singing in the hedge across the drive, and I was so homesick that I thought I would cry (Hank Williams had a similar thought about a whip-poorwill.). Actually, I probably did cry, and more than once. I was not ready to begin school, and I didn't understand kids who were excited about it. There is, in that, a personality divide that endures to this day. I remember that across the bus drive, on the other side of the hedge, lived one of my classmates in a little cottage that sat back from the road. His name was Van Sullivan, and he was prone to getting into trouble. In front of his house, on the main road, there was a little yellow shack that served as a dry-cleaning store that I think Van's parents operated. It survived for decades, but, like the school itself, is now gone. There was another drive at the school, a circular one, with a sidewalk running along the length of it. This is where mothers (in those days, it was not fathers) would pick up children after school, if they had a doctor's appointment or some such thing. Otherwise, you rode the bus or walked. I remember specifically that I was standing on that sidewalk, under a massive oak tree, waiting on a neighbor's mom, Katie Bishop, to pick me up on November 22, 1963, when we learned that President Kennedy had been assassinated.

Here's a random observation. This Fall, I went up to Charlotte to visit my mother for a day. The next morning, as I was preparing to leave, I stood at the bathroom window brushing my teeth. I looked up and down the short, dead-end street that we moved to almost fifty years ago (1127 Crestbrook Drive in 1968). I could see every house on it. On the opposite side of the street, at the end closest to Randolph Road, was the Davidson's house. Their oldest son, Win, was my best friend growing up. His father, Shannon, who I called "Daddy D," is dead (heart attack). Next door, the father was Harold Farris, also dead (suicide with termi-

317

nal cancer). Next to him was Mr. Reynolds, whom I never really knew, but he is also dead (Alzheimer's). At the end of the street, on one side of the cul-de-sac, was Hugh Altvater, a pathologist who died of cancer. Across the cul-de-sac, two different families lived. The first was Mr. Nance, the second was Dr. Grant, both dead. Next door to us were the Levines. The father, Al, founded Pic 'N Pay shoe stores (His little brother, Leon, founded Family Dollar stores.). He died of cancer. Our neighbor to the other side was a couple that was elderly the day that they moved in, the Williams. Mr. Williams was the first to die. My father was the last of all the dads on my street to die. Some of the mothers are gone as well, but all of the men are, and they all went first, before their own wives, or any of the wives (except for Mrs. Williams, who was the first of all to die). Like I said, turning sixty makes you reflect on things.

. . . .

One of the main goals of my living is to know and possess the obdurate truths before which fear and anxiety are powerless.
John Cheever

. . . .

2011

Well, as I sit here writing this, I am as hungry as a bitch wolf in heat (That was a favorite expression of my granddaddy Cy!). I have not had anything to eat in the past twenty-three hours – won't have anything to eat until tomorrow afternoon, a total of forty-two hours. Because I am fifty-five years old, and because my father has a history of colon polyps, in the morning, Carol Jeanne will drive me to the hospital, and I will have a colonoscopy. I am half-way through drowning myself with this miserable syrup they make you drink by the bucketful. At first, you think it's not too bad. Oh sure, it tastes terrible; it probably tasted bad to begin with, but they tried to flavor it so that it wouldn't taste like it really does taste, and now it tastes even worse. But that's bearable. The tricky part is the delayed fuse. You drink this slop, and for a little while you figure it's not doing anything. You figure maybe you can stroll down to the mailbox, or maybe take the dogs for a walk around the lake. Let me assure you that this constitutes an egregious error in judgment!! I'm here to tell you that it ain't even safe to walk to the living room. When the notion tickles the back of your brain that it might be a good idea to start moseying in the direction of some plumbing, let me tell you that you want to run, not walk! I can't wait for tomorrow afternoon to get here. I'm leaving that hospital, and I'm heading straight to Arby's for an order of curly fries! But alas, the hour is upon us, and I must leave you now. The die is cast. Come, let us cross the Rubicon.

....

Well, I'm back. Don't have the official report yet, but the gastroenterologist said things looked fine. He is an Indian (the imported kind, not the domestic variety). His name is Ranjit Mathew. He's a long-time tennis companion of mine. When he entered the room, he told the nurse, "Mr. Hood is my very good friend. Give me him the very best sedation we have – top shelf, single malt!" He knows me well. What he didn't know was that, just before we left the house, I handed Carol Jeanne a Sharpie permanent marker. I leaned over the kitchen counter, dropped my drawers, and had her inscribe my cheeks with, "Merry Christmas Ranjit!" Even under the sedation, when they flipped that gown up, I could hear the nurses howl!

2017

I adopted a new pet this year. Down the street there's a buzzard (actually, a turkey vulture). He (I'm calling it a "he," and I'm not asking "his" input on the matter.) has had an accident of some sort, because his right wing is broken. It will never heal, at least not to an extent that will allow him to ever fly again. He is an immature specimen, because his head is still black (It will change to red as he ages.). He showed up on our street, and hung around for a number of days. Several of the neighbors noticed him, and we would comment about him.

I was concerned about his starving to death. Since buzzards have a keen sense of smell, and since I feed all of my critters canned Jack Mackerel fish as a part of their diet, I figured if I could place some of that in his vicinity, he'd be able to track it down (i.e., it stinks!). It took several attempts before we came to an understanding about one another. First, I made the mistake of trying to catch him. He can't fly, but by God he can hop (I named him "Cassidy," as in Hopalong.)!! He's faster than a rabbit, and if he happens to be hopping downhill, he can actually glide a bit. He can go from the ground to the top of fence post in a single hop, and I've seen him in trees (if the first limbs are low enough), and even on the roof of the house in his favorite yard (He uses the deck rail as a stair step.).

One day, as I was driving down our street, I noticed that someone had run over a squirrel. About a hundred yards down the road, I hit the brakes when the notion hit me... what do buzzards eat?! Carrion, of course, so that day I took him some road kill. Now I keep a bucket and box of vinyl gloves in the car, and if I pass a fairly intact victim on the road (I'm not picking up anything that requires a mop!), I'll toss it in the bucket to take home. Of course, that's not a daily occurrence, but it got me to thinking that canned fish might not be the steady diet that he needed. Then one day as I was cooking my cats' weekly ration of chicken livers (I don't do commercial pet food.), I had the bright idea to feed some of those to the buzzard. Not cooked, but raw and bloody, just like he'd find them in the wild. I take these to him in an empty tuna fish can, and place them almost at his feet (He knows who I am, and lets me get almost to him, but still requires an arm's length protocol.), and he walks over, and starts right in. Then the question crossed my mind whether buzzards need to drink water. Seems they might, because I bought him a little water bowl in the pet department at Walmart (This one's actually for cats... they didn't have any buzzard water bowls.), and I fill it up each day from a bottle, and the next day it's gone, or at least down considerably.

Now this is where this story gets a little strange. It turns out that it may be that none of this is necessary. My buzzard has friends, as in other buzzards. It's the damnedest thing. Every day, one or two other buzzards come to visit him, and they stay for quite a while. They'll sit on the ground next to him, just visiting, and sometimes you'll see them grooming his feathers. Since he is immature, I figure maybe these are his parents. In addition to keeping him company and well-groomed, they also feed him. They will sit next to him, and regurgitate whatever they've eaten. This is how the parents feed their young in the nest, so it's not as farfetched as you might think! I know that you'll think it's farfetched anyway, but like they say, a picture is worth a thousand meals. So "feast" your eyes on this!

While I gained a buzzard, I lost a dog this year. Our oldest dog, Zoe, passed away. Over the many years, her adventures have been well chronicled in *The Newsletter*. From entering the family campground (and thus, the family) on a weekend mountain retreat, to whelping a litter of puppies under Megan's bed (a litter that had already been conceived when she arrived in camp), to fighting otters in the creek, Zoe was a part of my life for over sixteen years. Since I don't know how old she was when she adopted us (other than that she was old enough to have conceived), I don't know how old she was when she left me, but I do know that it was the only time she left me. She had a lot of border collie in her, and as I have written before, I think she saw me as her one-man flock. She didn't let me out of her sight, and she didn't let others between herself and me, not even Carol Jeanne. Most people thought she was unfriendly (mostly the people who brought her from the mountains into our home), but I knew she was simply focused on me, and loyal to me, and intent on protecting me, and I refuse to judge against her for that... damned if I couldn't use a little more of it in this world!

....

We all have the strength to endure the misfortunes of others.
Francois de La Rochefoucauld

A truly free society is one that allows people to live with the consequences of their decisions.
Coleman Hood

....

2017

Finally, and not to dwell on it since most of you already know it, I lost my mother this year. Ruth Marshall Porter Hood was one of the toughest people you could ever meet, and in more ways than one. I gave her eulogy, and through the miracle of modern technology, one of my daughters recorded it on her phone, and posted it to YouTube (search "Ruth eulogy" if you care to watch it). I and my siblings are now orphans, but I am grateful that we have become so only in the fullness of time. I think that I've already told you about the time Ruth broke my arm by slamming it in a car door while I was shaking a paper sack that she thought contained a mouse that she had seen in the kitchen, but actually only held my father's ball-point pen. I also remember the summer I went to Lefty Driesell's basketball camp at Davidson College. Ruth packed me a week's worth of gym socks... all solid wool. Never say that she didn't have a sense of humor!

Since our father died in 2013, it meant that it was now time sell my mother's house, which had been our family homeplace for the past forty-nine years. As executor of the estate (along with my sister, Amy), and as a real estate broker, that task fell to me. Before we could put it on the market, however, we'd first have to empty it out. My father was a pack rat (along with my sister, Amy), a genetic trait that evidenced itself more and more as he grew older. I knew that he had never thrown anything away, but I sort of thought that my mother and her care givers were working on that in the years since he passed away. I was mistaken. He had turned my old bedroom into a shrine of newspaper clippings, family genealogy research, and every book, video tape, cassette tape, vinyl album, CD, or DVD series that Time-Life had ever pro-duced. When it came to World War II, he had it covered! Many of these things were still in their original cellophane wrappers, never opened. He had turned my old shower into a giant filing cabinet, full of calendars, stationery, and, for whatever reason, shoe horns. You read that correctly, shoe horns! He had cornered the world-wide market on shoe horns, along with hundreds – no, thousands! – of red, plastic rulers that were promotional giveaways from some pharmacy at Pecan Avenue and Seventh Street that had long ago gone out of business.

Dreading the inevitable, I set the better part of a week aside, and drove to Charlotte. Prior to leaving, I made arrangements for the delivery of a construction dumpster that could contain thirty cubic yards of volume and four tons (8,000 pounds) of weight. On my way out of Athens, I stopped at Walmart and bought a giant, plastic tub with big handles. Actually, I bought two of them, because my older brother, Ren, would be joining me later in the week, and I figured he could use one, too. When Ren arrived, I assigned him my parents' study to empty. I did not want him doing any hauling of junk beyond the first floor, because – as I told him – I did not have time to carry him to either an emergency room or a morgue. I told Amy that she had one week to empty our parents' bedroom (which by now was nearly empty anyway, since they had not been upstairs in at least five years), and her own bedroom (which she was still living in, even though she owns her own home, because she lived with my parents the last fifteen years of their lives, giving them around-the-clock nursing care). Anyway, she had one week to empty two rooms, and by the end of the week, she was about halfway done. My younger brother Tim, who lives about ten minutes from my parents' house, never put in an appearance – no one in the family has seen or heard from him since the day of my mother's funeral. I believe that the rest of us are comfortable with that. The rest of the house, which was three stories and a cellar, was up to me.

If that sounds bossy or presumptuous, it was. I told everyone that if they wanted anything, they had better come get it. This was actually my third time going to Charlotte for this purpose, the first two being scouting trips to meet with antique dealers and collectors. Funny thing about antiques and artwork, both of which my mother owned in abundance, they're expensive as rip on the buying end, but nearly worthless when it comes to selling. Anyone that would haul off anything was doing me a favor, and they were welcome to it. I also told everyone in advance that I was not going to have any sympathy, empathy, mercy, or nostalgia of any kind, that I would be an SOB if necessary – as it occasionally was! I was going to empty fifty years of living out of a three-story house in one week and be done. I would pass brother Ren with my Walmart tub full of medical records, and he would try to stop me. "You can't throw those records in a dumpster; those are Daddy's patients' records!" Really? What were they going to do, sue him? He'd been dead for four years, and the vast majority of those patients had been dead for decades longer. Those records went right around Ren, and into the dumpster. I would pass sister Amy with my Walmart tub full of banking files, and she would try to stop me. "You can't throw those files in a dumpster. They have Momma's and Daddy's personal information in them!" What was someone going to do with it? Most of those accounts had been closed, literally, for decades. For that matter, most of those banks no longer even existed. Those files went straight past Amy and into the dumpster. Anything on the third floor that would fit through the window found its way into the yard below by way of same. I'll tell you straight-up that I was making a round trip from the third floor, to the dumpster, and back up two flights of stairs every eight minutes, and I was proud of it. It could have killed a younger man. That dumpster had everything: hundreds of feet of garden hose, mattresses and box springs, books by the hundreds, unlabeled photographs by the thousands (*"Portraits hung in empty halls, frameless heads on nameless walls, with eyes that watch the world and can't forget, like the strangers that you've met."*), and also a few shoe horns and red, plastic rulers. I knew I would be cutting it close on exceeding the volume limit of the dumpster, but I had no doubt that I had long ago passed the four-ton weight limit (I was right about that, and paid the penalty for it!).

Along the way, our Porter cousins showed up to pitch in. They did this first by arriving with a cooler that could have doubled as a coffin, and it held every beer and spirit that you could imagine (which didn't necessarily increase productivity, but made me tend not to worry about it so much). They brought platters of food to an empty kitchen and refrigerator, more than an army could eat. And they toted stuff. We packed moving vans of stuff to go to their various houses, and a couple more to carry stuff to Amy's self-storage clinic for bag ladies. Nephew Andrew, along with nephews Chris and Chris (We have a plethora of Chrises in our family, due in large part to the influence of my father, Chris. We have Chris Hood, Chris Hood, Chris Porter, and Chris Davis.

Pick a Chris. You can't sling a dead cat in our family without hitting one.), pitched in as well. I left a stack of wheelchairs, walkers, and canes on the front porch the size of a small mountain for the Salvation Army to collect. I loved my father, but if he had been there just then, I would have killed him. Late on a Sunday afternoon, I crawled into my truck to head back to Georgia. Ren had left a few hours earlier, and I figured the odds were 50:50 that I would catch him in the biggest U-Haul truck that he could legally drive before we made it back home. I gave 1127 Crestbrook Drive one last look, then moved on, as life is wont to do. But not before I privately granted myself just a few moments of nostalgia... and a lifetime of gratitude.

> *Sing out your songs,*
> *and ring out your stories and rhymes.*
> *Weave from your dreams*
> *the mystical dances that lead us to*
> *bind in heart and mind.*

Home And The Heartland, from *Riverdance*

The Things That Lives Are Made Of – or so we sometimes think

There is one thing to be said for country clubs. They drain off
a lot of people you wouldn't want to associate with anyway.
Mark Twain

I wouldn't belong to any club
that would have me as a member.
Groucho Marx

. . . .

Eulogy for Ruth Marshall Porter Hood
March 2017
———————————————————

Edna St. Vincent Millay wrote these words:

> Thou famished grave, I will not fill thee yet.
> Roar though thou dost, I am too happy here.
> Gnaw thine own sides, fast on. I have no fear
> Of thy dark project, but my heart is set
> On living – I have heroes to beget
> Before I die. I will not walk anear
> Thy dismal jaws for many a splendid year.
>
> 'Til I be old, I aim not to be eaten.
> I cannot starve thee out; I am thy prey
> And thou shalt have me. But I dare defend
> That I can stave thee off. And I dare say,
> What with the life I lead, the force I spend,

> I'll be but bones and jewels on that day,
> And leave thee hungry even in the end.

Those lines sum up so much of my mother. She grabbed onto life, and clutched it with the tenacity of a snapping turtle. It wasn't always joyful. It was often painful and arduous, but it was her life and she wasn't going to let circumstances circumvent her taking a deep, long drink of it. Her life circumstances were her circumstances, they were not her life. Even as her body failed her, her mind was sharp. She wanted each new tomorrow, and never lost her will to live. She was a stubborn woman when it came to getting her way, and she granted no exemption to death. Like a dandelion growing through a crack in a sidewalk in the midst of drought during an August heat wave, Ruth persevered and survived.

I am Coleman Porter Hood, the second son of Christopher Kennedy and Ruth Marshall Porter Hood. On behalf of my sister Amy and brothers Ren and Tim, we thank you for your gift of presence here today, and for taking the time to be with our family as we remember the life of our mother. Reverend Fobel, thank you for your ministry to us in our mother's passing. It is good to be home, here at Sardis Presbyterian, once again.

It occurs to me as we gather together, that my father's father's funeral service was held in this sanctuary. His mother's funeral was in this sanctuary, as was his own. I cannot count the number of Sunday mornings that I sat in these pews in a stiff, white shirt, with a clip-on bow tie, wearing itchy, wool pants, which, if it had not been for peppermint lifesavers and Juicy Fruit gum, I doubt that I would be standing before you today.

There is no cause for sorrow here today. Our mother has died, but her life is not over. I confess that I do not know for a fact what lies beyond the pale of this life and this world, but I do have hope. I have hope that Ruth is in a better place. I hope that Ruth is with Chris – but given the wonderfully tempestuous nature of their love, I'm not certain what effect Ruth's presence might be having on the better place that Chris has been in these past four years. Ruth and Chris married on June 24th, 1950. The next day, the Korean War broke out, but that conflict lasted only three years. Ruth and Chris didn't declare a truce until Chris' death in 2013. I hope that their armistice remains in place as Chris learns once again how to cope with a Porter personality. Chris was fond of saying that the Porter family motto is: "If it doesn't fit, force it, and if you can't force it then..." Well, we're in church, so I guess I won't be able to tell you the Porter family motto. My hope is that they are once again together, and that their love is now complete.

Although both our father and mother have died, their lives on this earth are not over, even as they also rest in the eternal presence of God. At the very least, our parents live on in this life for as long as any of their four children walk the face of this earth. They have left an indelible imprint on our lives, and it is an honorable imprint. Whatever our shortcomings may be – and God knows that the Hood clan has our share of them – we seek to be an honorable people, to fulfill the legacy bequeathed to us by our mother and our father.

On December 28th, 1966, Ruth was horribly injured in a car wreck. My younger brother Tim and my sister Amy were in the car with her. While they fortunately remained in the car, our mother was ejected from it – this was years before the advent of seat belts – and Ruth struck a pine tree. She broke her back. She broke her right leg. She broke just about everything in between. Her leg was so mangled that the doctors wanted to amputate it, but were more afraid that the operation would kill her than would the useless leg. Either way, the doctors said that she would never walk again.

Thus began a fifty-year tradition of our mother defying medical science and common mortality. Some women collect jewelry or fine clothes. Some women travel around the globe to destination vacations. They play tennis or bridge. Our mother had surgeries – dozens and dozens of them. There were many times that our father – having to stay home to earn a living and look after four children – would put her on a plane to fly to Philadelphia to undergo operations at Thomas Jefferson Medical School. And she would do that by herself, including the flight home after surgery, making her way through two airports in a wheel chair, wearing a leg-length cast. Over the course of her life, she endured and absorbed unspeakable pain, yet she never complained about that. There was no self-pity. She was tougher than any Navy Seal.

But again, her life circumstances were her circumstances, they were not her life. She was a voracious reader, a gourmet cook, she had Hollywood beauty, and she was a true and full partner in life with Chris. She was a private person; she did not have vast numbers of friends, but she was loyal and devoted to those whom she allowed into her inner sanctum.

Ruth Hood was an eclectic collection of contradictions. She did not suffer fools gladly. When you were a kid, you needed to know what kind of mood Ruth was in before asking her to help you comb your hair or brush your teeth. She was quick to let you know if you threatened to fall short of meeting her expectations, or when you began to wear thin on her very limited patience. By the way, rumor has it that she passed this genetic code to at least one of her offspring. With Ruth's passing, I have now inherited the mantle of "world's most impatient person."

At the same time, Ruth was one of the most generous people you could ever meet, giving freely of her earthly treasure. For someone who was a near cripple, she was maniacally hyperactive. Watching her try to spend a spare moment sitting on a couch to thumb through a magazine was to witness an act of violence as she tore through the pages as if practicing some bizarre martial art. She had an obsessive sensitivity to the Emily Post views of etiquette, comportment, and protocol. When Carol Jeanne and I became engaged, and sent out our wedding invitations, Ruth was mortified to find that we had used a print style other than traditional engraving, so she had her own set of invitations done "the proper way" for her side of the family. Yet even into the twenty-first century, she gave no thought to hopping into Chris' 1963, stick shift, no radio, no air conditioning, Plymouth Valiant – which Chris had inherited from his father in 1972 – and driving up to Harris Teeter in sweat pants and an Army fatigue jacket (She and Chris had a matching set!).

And she was our mother. She was not a warm and fuzzy June Cleaver. Like her mother before her, Ruth believed that a handshake was as good as a hug. She was a mother, our mother, and a fiercely good one. The mother-child relationship is special. You can eulogize a person, you can memorialize a life, but how do you stand up here and capture the essence of that special bond between mother and child? For my part, I will defer to the words of America's former poet laureate, Billy Collins, who wrote this poem entitled *The Lanyard*.

> The other day I was ricocheting slowly
> off the blue walls of this room,
> moving as if underwater from typewriter to piano,
> from bookshelf to an envelope lying on the floor,
> when I found myself in the L section of the dictionary
> where my eyes fell upon the word *lanyard*.
> No cookie nibbled by a French novelist
> could send one into the past more suddenly—
> a past where I sat at a workbench at a camp
> by a deep Adirondack lake
> learning how to braid long thin plastic strips
> into a lanyard, a gift for my mother.
> I had never seen anyone use a lanyard
> or wear one, if that's what you did with them,
> but that did not keep me from crossing
> strand over strand again and again

until I had made a boxy
red and white lanyard for my mother.
She gave me life and milk from her breasts,
and I gave her a lanyard.
She nursed me in many a sick room,
lifted spoons of medicine to my lips,
laid cold wash-cloths on my forehead,
and then led me out into the airy light
and taught me to walk and swim,
and I, in turn, presented her with a lanyard.
Here are thousands of meals, she said,
and here is clothing and a good education.
And I replied, here is your lanyard,
which I made with a little help from a counselor.
Here is a breathing body and a beating heart,
strong legs, bones, and teeth,
and two clear eyes to read the world, she whispered,
and here, I said, is the lanyard I made at camp.
And here, I wish to say to her now,
is a smaller gift—not the worn truth
that you can never repay your mother,
but the rueful admission that when she took
the two-tone lanyard from my hand,
I was as sure as a boy could be
that this useless, worthless thing I wove
out of boredom would be enough to make us even.

Ruth cooked for us, cleaned for us, partnered with Chris to put a roof over our heads, clothes on our backs, and send us to top-notch schools. She did what all good mothers do, but we were blessed to have had an excellent one. I am grateful that she was my mother. I am sorry that so much of her life was hampered by suffering, but I celebrate her courage and tenacity. I am glad that her suffering has ended. There are worse things in life than dying.

She rests now in her faith in her God, this God of the book of The Revelation, this God Who has wiped away all tears from her eyes, and banished her pain. She now rests in this God of the Epistle to the Corinthians, this God Who has dissolved her earthly tabernacle, and given her a new house, not made with hands. She now rests eternal in the heavens. Praise be to God.

....

Women and cats will do as they please.
Men and dogs should relax and get used to it.
Robert A. Heinlein

Women who seek to be equal with men lack ambition.
Timothy Leary

....

2018

I'm afraid that this year's *Newsletter* is going to be a bit scattered, lacking focus (You're probably thinking that this is the case every year!). My problem is that this year I have too much time on my hands. Carol Jeanne retired four years ago, and this year, I have finally begun to slow down. The last vestige of employment benefits that Carol Jeanne received from thirty-two years at the local hospital was access to a financial planner. The hospital cancelled her retiree health coverage this year, pulling the plug on the agreement that we had operated under these past three decades (Thank you, Barack Obama!). Then they abandoned ship on administering her retirement accounts (She has three "hospital" retirement accounts, and we have always contributed the maximum allowable amount to each.). The money, of course, was ours, and the hospital couldn't mess with that, but we had to meet extensively with the financial planner to move the three retirement accounts into six new investment accounts. Transferring these funds was not a linear exercise, as each fund was first transferred to a holding account, then divided up into the new accounts. This created an avalanche of emails and snail mails that leaves you bewildered, to say the least. Now the hospital is terminating the access to the financial planner, but we will continue our relationship with him at our expense.

We've always met with this fellow at least once a year, usually around my birthday. Since I am a year older than Carol Jeanne, we always assumed that I would retire a year before her, which reminds me of the Yiddish proverb, *If you want to make God laugh, tell him your plans.* At any rate, when we met with him (the financial planner, not God) back in April, knowing that I was ready to slow down, I asked him what the consequence would be to our finances if I never earned another paycheck. He looked at me and said, "Based on the retirement goals and assumptions that you have given me, you passed the point of needing to earn income several years ago. In addition to your other retirement accounts, you both have Roth IRAs, and unless you live to be 100, you should think of them as inheritance for your grandchildren, not as retirement accounts. *I assumed that you have continued working because you wanted to.*" At that point I embarrassed myself somewhat by asking him if he was out of his damn mind?!

I left that conference, and started my slow slide into retirement. However, I must confess that it has not been as simple as merely walking away. All of my working life, I have worked towards the goal of early retirement. I have sold tens of thousands of dollars of sick leave back to my employer, whenever I had the option to do so (I think that I missed about three days of work in my entire career, and two of those were when I had reconstructive knee surgery for a ruptured ACL.). I have never in my adult life taken a week of vacation to spend in a hotel room. My goal was to be able to quit completely, as quickly as possible, and to then do just as I pleased. Play golf once a week – at least – as opposed to once a year. Stay home to work on my land, spend a day (or a week) without getting into an automobile. Now that I am years past the point of having to earn a living, it has been incredibly hard to accept it, to embrace and live it. Let me be clear, we still have to have income. We are nowhere close to being able to simply make monthly withdrawals of our assets from now until the age of 100 – far from it. But now it is time for our money to work for us, rather than the other way around. Our money, our savings and investments, now earn more than I possibly could in real estate. Some of the difficulty in accepting this is a matter of habit and discipline, two of my strongpoints. Some of it, I suspect, is insecurity. All of it is maddening!

The point of all of this being that when you're working full time, and you're really busy all the time, and there is typically too much to do, it tends to focus your attention, and sharpen your time management skills. I am discovering that having too much time has the opposite effect. These days, it seems I can't keep a steady thought in mind for ten minutes without my attention straying to God knows where. I go to my shop or office to begin some project, and two hours later, I'm deeply immersed in something, but I don't think it's what I set out to do... I'm not really certain that it is not, however, because for the life of me, I can't remember what that project was!

I used to be the most focused person I knew. Whether I was keeping track of multiple tasks for various clients at differing stages of real estate transactions (with pretty serious implications regarding doing those things correctly), or as an engineer planning and designing a project, or – once upon a time – flying an airplane, I was a pretty intense fellow.

My father often said that you did not need to be a genius to be an OB/GYN, that it was "procedure, procedure, procedure – sponges out better equal sponges in." A clinician would take offense if I said that I suffered from obsessive/compulsive disorder, because, very technically, I do not meet the clinical definition. But make no mistake, my entire life I have been obsessive and compulsive, living daily by scratching off the line items of my to-do list. Dylan Thomas admonished us, *Do not go gentle into that good night, Old age should burn and rave at close of day; Rage, rage against the dying of the light!* I embrace the sentiment, but I am not waiting until "the dying of the light" to engage in that combat – it begins for me each morning at 5:15. But these days, I am becoming obsessed with the hereafter. I stand in the middle of a room, asking myself, "What did I come in here after?" So be forewarned that whatever it was that I sat down here to write to you about, from time to time, I might follow the path of a line that intersects a circle at a single point, to wit, a tangent.

We began the year with a full moon on January 1st. We finished that month with a blue moon (i.e., the second, full moon in the same month) on January 31st. The next full moon was March 1st. There was no full moon in February, none, although there would have been had this been a leap year. After the full moon on March 1st, there was another blue moon on March 31st. You'll have to wait until 2037 before this happens again. I'm looking forward to it.

Here's a thought. It doesn't matter how deep the water is if you can't keep your head above water and still touch the bottom. If you are in over your head, you can measure the depth in inches, feet, or fathoms, and it doesn't matter at all. Under these circumstances, there is no such thing as shallow water. You can drown at any depth, if you're in over your head.

Here's another thought. When the label on a package of Pampers says "up to 15 pounds," it is not referring to the load capacity. You might want to keep that in mind!

I am discovering that old age seems to consist largely of moving piles of crap around. I pick up a pile of crap on the kitchen table, and move it to my desk. The next day, I move a pile of crap from my desk to the kitchen table, and yep, it's the same pile. I can spend an entire Sunday afternoon in my shop, doing nothing more than moving crap around. I'm turning into my father!

I always marvel when an obituary in the paper states that so-and-so died at the age of 92, and they follow this fact with the statement that so-and-so "was preceded in death by her parents." No kidding!! Unless her parents were either eight years old when so-and-so was born, or they are in the Guinness World Book Of Records as the oldest people alive, I reckon they did precede their child in death! I hereby decree that henceforth, if the parents are named in an obituary, but are not specifically cited as survivors of the deceased, the protocol shall be that they have previously kicked the oxygen habit.

. . . .

One good thing about being a man
is that men don't have to talk to each other.
Anonymous

A man does not mature until
he has exhausted all other possibilities.
Wilfrid Sheed

There is so little difference between husbands
you might as well keep the first.
Adela Rogers St. Johns

If they can put one man on the moon, why not all of them?
Anonymous

. . . .

2018
————————

In other news, my world is daily populated by Idiots. Perhaps you have met some of them. They are the people that wait until the cashier has tallied up the last item in their shopping cart before they start rummaging through their purse to look for their check book – on second thought, they are the people that even write a check at the grocery store, instead of using a credit card. Idiots sit texting at traffic signals after the light has turned green, and they drive in the left-hand lane a half-car ahead of the driver in the right lane, never passing anyone. They sit behind the white stop-line at an intersection, refusing to enter it, so that they and about two more cars could make it through on the yellow light. Not having spent enough of their limited life at the intersection, they choose to sit through another cycle of the lights... you never know when something interesting might happen! Idiots compose the peculiar clans at Walmart, pierced and tattooed, that position their shopping cart in the center of the aisle, then stand on either side of it, in total oblivion to the folks before and behind them that wish to pass by (Evolution has seen to it that the fewer the number of members in the clan, the greater their girth, thus assuring the successful obstruction of commerce.). And speaking of the girth of Walmart Idiots, you can bet that the greater the girth of the female specimens, the greater the likelihood that they will be wearing yoga pants, even though they probably do not practice yoga. They just like providing you with way too much information!! The IQ of an Idiot is in inverse proportion to the number of times they say "like," "you know," "dude," and "totally" in a sentence. I have wanted to comment on Idiots for some time, but I did not wish to offend them unnecessarily. I set my reservations aside, however, when I realized that, because they are Idiots, they will not take offense, as they will not perceive that I am referring to them. They will glance at the fellow to their left, or the one to their right – probably both – and nod knowingly.

Scientists around the world will vote later this year on changing the definition of the kilogram (Not just "a" kilogram, but "THE" kilogram, as in "Le Grand K," kept under guard 24/7 in an airtight vault outside of Paris. Le Grand K has two, exact duplicates that are under similar guard in the United States. They are routinely transported from America to France [but never at the same time, and none of them is ever touched by a human hand, not even a gloved one] to document their ongoing conformity.). They changed the definition of a kilometer several years ago, and now, rather than being based on the length of a standardized bar of platinum, it is based on the speed of light (i.e., the distance that light can travel in a vacuum in 299,752,498 millionths of a second).

The International Bureau Of Weights And Measures is the steward of standards for matters concerning the essentials of physics: magnetism, mass, distance, luminosity, electric current, temperature, chemical concentration, and time. I'm here to tell you that they have abandoned their post. There is another inviolate standard of measure in our universe, or at least there used to be. I refer, of course, to the size of a roll of toilet paper. Whether the roll in question was single-ply or two-ply, the circumference of "a" roll was consistently the circumference of "THE" roll, a universal standard (Which in the case of two-ply paper should be 14.67 square feet in area, and 132 sheets – each sheet four inches wide and four inches long – for a total length of 528 inches [44 feet].). The hardware in your bathroom was strategically developed to accommodate this standard, dispensing in unfaltering fashion the number of sheets requested (and the standard for *that* request, FYI, should be three).

But then some Idiot (see above) came up with the bright idea of marketing "mega rolls." Suddenly, the labelling on a package of toilet paper proclaimed "One mega roll equals *two* regular rolls!" This concept spread like a virus in an airplane, and shortly there developed a virtual arms war in toilet paper. Now, 26 regular rolls – which would have translated into 13 mega rolls – inched ever larger, delivering an equivalent warhead in a mere dozen rolls. Obviously, the next iteration delivered a 30 regular-roll payload in only ten nuclear rolls. The toilet paper industry now required a new lexicon, and so we have "mega rolls," "economy rolls," and "family rolls," to name a few.

The obvious question (It is obvious to me, but apparently of no concern to anyone else.) is, "Why?" Why was any of this necessary? Did making the roll larger somehow make the paper more efficient in performing it's intended task? I think not. Did making the roll larger somehow make the cost of the roll less expensive? You could argue that, by placing more and more sheets of toilet paper on the same size cardboard core, you were lowering the unit cost of the product, but just how many extra sheets would have to be added in order to realize any meaningful reduction in cost to the individual roll? And besides that, do you really think that the toilet paper manufacturers of America have lowered their retail price to the consumer as a consequence of making the size of a roll bigger? No, no they have not!

Today's toilet paper rolls are so large that they will no longer rotate on the traditional toilet paper dispensing hardware. The rolls are wedged so tightly up against the wall or cabinet that you need a winch to turn the dispenser, butt – by design – toilet paper has a very limited tensile strength, and thus the consumer still comes up short. Not to be foiled, the toilet paper hardware industry responded by developing dispensers that are anchored to the wall at only a single point, not two points as are found in the traditional dispenser. The new design allows for the dispenser to hang in a hinged fashion, thus automatically adapting itself to the size of the roll placed upon it. But rest assured that this increase in accommodated capacity will soon be outstripped in the reckless drive to deliver ever larger loads. If you were to place one of these monstrous rolls on the wall of an old-fashioned out house, the thing would tip over. When the day comes that replacing a roll of toilet paper requires the use of a forklift, remember that I warned you!

. . . .

If you see a bandwagon, it's too late.
James Goldsmith

. . . .

2021

———————

Let me preface the following diatribe by noting that I was born at the epicenter of the Baby Boomer generation, in 1956. It was also the epicenter of the good life – Andy and Mayberry, Ward and June. I had a great childhood, and grew up in a golden time. I, and my peers, could leave the house in the morning, and possibly not return until supper. If you didn't come home for lunch, it meant that you were eating it at a friend's house. We could – and did – ride our bikes anywhere we wished. We would ride them down the shoulder of the main highway, without bike lanes or sidewalks, to go to the 7-Eleven and buy Icees. When we couldn't get an Icee, we would drink water – out of a hose, not a plastic bottle. We didn't have store-bought water. Our parents did not know where we were, and they weren't concerned about it. No stranger was going to harm us. In the summer time, after supper, it was back out the door, playing tag, hide-and-seek, dodge ball, and kick-the-can (For some reason, snake-in-the-gutter was reserved for when we were waiting for the school bus.). We played until dark, or even shortly thereafter if we were catching fireflies. Also in the summer, we would listen for the broadcast of "the ice cream man," who announced his arrival with music played over a loudspeaker. He drove a refrigerated truck from neighborhood to neighborhood (We didn't call them subdivisions back then.). He sold ice cream in little cardboard cups with wooden spoons, and popsicles. He wore a change-maker on his belt, blindly dispensing pennies, nickels, dimes, and quarters. Once, lacking any other source of funds to buy my popsicle, I paid for it with a silver dollar! One other fixture of summer was "the smoke man," who made his monthly rounds through the neighborhoods, dispensing "smoke." We would run wildly through the fog bank created by his smoke. This smoke was intended to control the mosquito population, and grownups called his smoke "DDT." No one worried about it. Now, the diatribe.

Typically, I make a very conscious effort to avoid politics in The Newsletter. This year is an exception.

Democracy never lasts long. It soon wastes, exhausts, and murders itself. There was never a democracy that did not commit suicide. – **John Adams**

Up until now, it seemed that America would be the exception to President Adams' observation on democracies. I'm not so sure about that now. The past year or so has convinced me that America is NOT going to hell. We left hell in the rear-view mirror a long time ago. Our society daily abandons common sense in pursuit of nonsense. "People" (savages) burn down their own communities, where they used to be able to buy food, where their neighbors worked to be able to pay their rent, and they are called "peaceful protestors." Criminals are arrested for their crimes, and are put back on the streets as soon as they have been processed, because bail is racist. A thug can literally commit three crimes in a day, be arrested three times, and be put back on the street all three times, all in the same day. So why not defund the police? Nobody is going to jail, so what do you need police for? Look at all the new funds that you could "invest" in equity programs in your community. Oh, right, there's no community left.

I am not a big traveler (big surprise!), but San Francisco is the most fascinating place I have ever been, or at least it used to be. I once lay on my side, and rolled the entire length of Lombard Street (top to bottom, not bottom to top). Today, I would rather camp out in a porta-john at my local Home Depot. It would be more sanitary, and safer. Smash-and-grab parasites block the streets while they loot up-scale stores (i.e., greedy capitalists). Now they have killed an off-duty policeman who was hired to protect a news crew filming the carnage. In San Francisco, you can walk out of a CVS drug store with anything you want. As long as the value of the goods is less than $950, the cops won't even show up to arrest you for a misdemeanor, thanks to the dictums of the Idiot Mayor and DA. I would solve this behavior by posting guards outside the exits of these stores, armed with shotguns loaded with rock salt, with orders to blow the legs out from under looters. Theft would cease in a day. Addicts shoot-up on the street. The homeless and mentally ill no longer search out public restrooms. They drop their pants in the middle of a sidewalk in broad day-light, and answer nature's call. Think about that; you could be fined if you didn't scoop up behind your dog. Who are these people?! Where do they come up with this insanity? If you are letting Cortez and the "squad" do your deep thinking for you, then global warming (It is not climate change – climate has never been static. It is always changing.) is the least of your problems.

I want to be clear from the outset. I had high hopes for the Biden administration. I looked forward to an era of peace in the absence of the angry, orange man. But this administration has been an absolute failure. Candidate Biden was going be a moderate. He was going to reunite our fractured society. He has done neither. He has allowed the far-left wing of his party to hijack his agenda. He is a puppet on a string. My question is, who is pulling the string? He doesn't take questions from the press. If they shout out a question too difficult for him to answer, he gets testy, turns his back, and dodders off the stage (The White House physician, who just gave Uncle Joe a physical – which did not include any cognitive testing – addressed Biden's "doddering gait." That was his term, so I can use it, too.). He castigates the American public in a sanctimonious tone that further divides us, rather than uniting us. Please allow me to explain my disappointment.

First, let's clear up President Biden's confusion over Georgia voting laws. There should be no confusion about this, because Biden has no business in Georgia voting laws, either as President, or as a citizen of the state. I don't care what he said about other states' voting laws, because I live in Georgia, not in other states. Joe Biden referred to Georgia's voting laws as "Jim Crow 2.0." I seriously doubt that Joe Biden could define the meaning of "Jim Crow." His very comment is proof that he does not know what it means, and I very much resent his comment. Let's compare Georgia voting laws with Joe's home state of Delaware. Do any of you remember when we had election DAY, the first Tuesday in November? Polls might have opened around 7:00 AM and closed at the end of the business day, say maybe 5:00 PM. Not anymore, not in Georgia, home of Joe Biden's Jim Crow 2.0.

In Georgia, you can cast an absentee ballot, by mail or in person, no excuse necessary. You can request your ballot up to seventy-eight (78!!) days before an election, and no later than eleven days prior to an election. Georgia law allows early, in-person voting beginning on the fourth Monday prior to an election, including Saturday and Sunday. Delaware, Uncle Joe's home state, does not allow early voting (But that's not Jim Crow.). Georgia does not allow you to give out water to voters within a certain distance of the polling place. Poll workers are allowed to set up self-serve watering stations. If you're voting, you're over eighteen – act like it. Plan ahead, and bring your own water. You also are not allowed to give to people standing in line to vote alcoholic beverages, or twenty-dollar bills. You cannot "harvest" votes (i.e., go door-to-door to collect ballots). If you vote early, you can drop your ballot in a drop-box (an accommodation instituted for Covid). Every one of Georgia's 159 counties must have at least one drop-box. It must be monitored, and its hours of access are business hours – it's not 24/7, like Waffle House. If you can get to the grocery store, a doctor's office, the bank, or the liquor store, you can get to a drop-box to cast your ballot. Georgia requires a photo ID to vote. You have to be able to prove that you are who you say you are, and that you are registered to vote. You have to have a photo ID to drive a car or purchase alcohol. You have to have a photo ID to cash a check, or to apply for credit, to receive food stamps, or to board a plane. Every time I go to a doctor's office, they scan my insurance card, and my photo ID, my driver's license. In Georgia, if you do not have a photo ID, the state will issue you one – for free. It is easier to vote in Georgia today than it has ever been in my lifetime. In Delaware, not so much. Joe Biden needs to get his nose out of our business, and start tending to his own.

Next, let's toss the Constitution in the trash, and mandate Covid vaccinations, mask wearing, social distancing, ad nauseum, for the governed – but not, of course, for those who govern. They might have to go to their hairdresser, a wedding, a concert, or a party at a fancy restaurant. Are you a young, healthy, responsible, no co-morbidity, no Covid infection after two years of exposure person who does not desire to receive a Covid vaccine? You're a racist, homophobic, xenophobe (Unless you're Kamala Harris, who stated that she would never take Donald Trump's word on a Covid vaccine.).

Dr. Fauci is a farce. He originally said that masks were not necessary or effective in halting the spread of Covid (Which, as it happens, is true.). Then he confessed to telling us the "good lie." He lied to us in order to protect the availability of personal protective equipment for health care workers, thereby leaving the world of "science." He was imposing his values on a hierarchy of importance among groups of people. So after telling the good lie, he determined that wearing masks was important – for everyone. Then he said we should wear two of the things! He said that we should wear them in our own homes, among family members that were fully vaccinated, during the holidays, and that we should consider making guests in our homes show proof of vaccination. He said we would acquire "herd immunity" when two-thirds of Americans had been vaccinated. Then he raised it to 70%, then 80%, and now estimates that it will take a 90% vaccination rate to acquire herd immunity. The Centers for Disease Control statistics estimate that over 70% of Americans are vaccinated. It also estimates that 50% of the population has natural immunity (The sum of the two percentages can exceed 100% because there are many people with natural immunity who have also been vaccinated, such as my wife.).

Clearly, based on the concept of herd immunity, there is no scientific or medical basis for vaccine mandates, much less mask mandates for useless paper or cotton masks that are not N-95 grade masks. Your mask is a psychological crutch, a placebo. You might as well wear a clove of garlic around your neck. "Following the science," apparently, means follow me over here, and roll up your sleeve. What a joke. My question is, after two years of hyper-virility, with all the people who have been vaccinated, plus all the people who have survived infection – or died from it – who the hell is left to catch Covid? If you have already had Covid, and have natural immunity that exceeds that of the "fully" vaccinated (As of today, the count for that status is three shots, but it will change by the time you read this.), do not resist, you still must inject the government's vaccine into your body – do as I say (but not as I do). Let me ask you this, if you are, indeed fully vaccinated, what do you care about the vaccination status of anyone else? Anyone can transmit Covid, vaccinated or not. Why are you walking around in the Walmart parking lot wearing two useless masks and Nitrile gloves? Why did you get vaccinated?!

In a speech on February 1, 2020, then-candidate Biden said (And this is exactly what he said. You can Google it for yourself.), "We are in the midst of a crisis with the Corona virus. We need to lead the way with science – not Donald Trump's record of hysteria, xenophobia, and fear-mongering. He is the worst possible person to lead our country through a global health emergency." Donald Trump, through Operation Warp Speed, created multiple vaccines for Covid. He handed the keys to the cure to President Biden, and Uncle Joe promptly drove our nation off a cliff. In the last presidential debate, Candidate Biden said, "We need to shut down the virus, not the country." Guess what he did? Biden said that under President Trump, 220,000 people had died of Covid, stating that their blood was on Trump's hands. He said – and, again, I quote him – "Anyone responsible for that many deaths should not remain as President of the United States." Data from the Centers For Disease Control show that more people have died of Covid under the leadership of Uncle Joe than did under the angry, orange man (at this moment, 350,000 versus 220,000). I guess that Uncle Joe will be stepping down any day now. After being inaugurated in January, Uncle Joe said that he would defeat the virus by the Fourth of July... he just didn't say which year.

Following the "science," Uncle Joe, fully vaccinated, wore a mask on an international Zoom call, sitting at a desk by himself. Google "idiot," and see if his picture turns up. He told us that he would – and I quote – "never mandate masks or vaccinations," until, of course, he did just that. Now, Uncle Joe says get vaccinated, or lose your job, and many people have (Think "supply chain" shortages.). Meanwhile, he lets illegal immigrants, who have an active Covid infection rate estimated to be around 17%, stream across the Mexican border, literally by the hundreds of thousands (soon to be millions, plural), to be resettled without notification in communities all across America (except for Delaware), dumping them into your communities, your emergency rooms, and your school systems (Where, by the way, since they cannot speak English, you will have to hire specialists to deal with them.).

They have better health insurance than I do, at no cost to them, but at great cost to the American tax payer. They have no jobs, or special job skills. Uncle Joe halted the effective "remain in Mexico" policy that the angry, orange man instituted, simply because it was effective and instituted by the angry, orange man (The Supreme Court has told him to reinstate that policy. Of course, the Supreme Court told Uncle Joe, and his snide flack, Jen Psaki, that they couldn't impose vaccine mandates on companies with over one-hundred employees, whereupon the two of them went on national television, and openly encouraged employers to ignore the Court.). And, Uncle Joe halted construction of "The Wall" (see angry, orange man above). Walls are racist and ineffective, but that doesn't stop elected officials from living behind them at home – just try walking up to Nancy Pelosi's front door to ring the bell. Apparently, walls are nowhere nearly as effective in preventing illegal immigration as is the practice of closing your eyes and turning your back.

Uncle Joe will risk armed conflict with Russia over the sanctity of the Ukrainian border, while our "border" with Mexico exists only on maps. Oh wait, I forgot, Kamala Harris is in charge of that problem, so there is no problem! Democrats want illegals here so that they can eventually get them to vote for Democrats. Republicans want them here so they can exploit their labor at slave wages with no benefits, not even worker's compensation. And know this, every single member of Congress (as well as the ones that are married), is culpable. None of them – I don't care which party they belong to – is lifting a finger to resolve this disaster. And that's not just today. It goes back decades. You want to know the dirty little secret about the "Dreamers?" Our government, our laws, our policies, and our practices are just as responsible – or guilty – for the presence of any Dreamer in our country as are the Dreamer's parents. We could have recognized and admitted that – and resolved the problem – but instead, today, we worsen it at an exponential rate.

How much are you paying for gas these days? A year ago, America was energy independent, and was the world's leading exporter of oil. Uncle Joe shut down construction on the Keystone pipeline, and his administration is evaluating whether – or how – to also shut down the existing Line 5 pipeline, the main petroleum pipeline between Canada and Michigan (It flows *from* Canada into the US, not the other way around.). At the same time, he removed sanctions on Russia that allowed them to complete the Nord Stream 2 pipeline to Germany. Russia-Germany-oil pipeline... what could go wrong? Uncle Joe seeks to prohibit new leases for drilling on federal land, and to raise prices for existing leases (Another term for those leases is "contracts," a legal term that is based on their sanctity, which, under the law, is inviolate.). Fortunately, Uncle Joe has excellent relations with Russia and Saudi Arabia, so we can count on them to honor his pleas to increase exports of oil to America. Apparently, American oil contributes to global warming, but foreign oil does not.

Meanwhile, he has requested that the Federal Trade Commission investigate why leading producers in the American petroleum industry have sharply increased gas prices (The retail price for a gallon of gas has risen an average of 57% in the past year. Inflation is at a forty year high, and does NOT include food and energy costs.). Clearly, it is due to corporate greed, not market economics. I guess that if you drive the price of gas high enough, you can eventually make electric cars economically feasible. Then you can virtue signal to the rest of the world by powering your car – with its plethora of environmentally toxic batteries – by charging it with electricity that is generated in a coal-powered electric plant. Or maybe you'll drive a solar-powered car... but not at night. I wonder, when was the last time that Uncle Joe filled a gas tank, or, for that matter, drove himself anywhere. I seriously doubt that he is licensed to drive.

The only thing that Uncle Joe has gotten right was the withdrawal from Afghanistan. Oh wait, my bad. I totally supported withdrawing from Afghanistan, and the sooner, the better. I think that most Americans did, but I haven't spoken to all of them. The angry, orange man was going to withdraw from Afghanistan in 2021. His plan was to withdraw in the following order: first, get the American civilians out; second, get your supplies and materiel out; third, withdraw your military from their bases. Uncle Joe had a different plan. First, abandon your military bases. Second, screw the equipment; just leave billions of dollars of weapons for the Taliban to recycle. Third, withdraw your military personnel. Finally, ask the civilians if any of them can find a way to the airport if they want to return to America. That last phase of his plan had the direct consequence of loss of life for thirteen military members. He did, however, feel bad enough about that gaff to go to Dover Air Force Base to pay his respects to the caskets of the fallen. Problem there was that he kept checking his watch. Why would the President of the United States even feel the need to own a watch? When you are POTUS, let me tell you that the "time" is whatever you say it is. Then, just to make sure that his Afghanistan withdrawal ended on a high note, Uncle Joe approved a drone strike that killed ten women and children, including an American aide-worker. But make no mistake, I pray for Uncle Joe every day. If anything should happen to him, look at who is in the on-deck circle.

Why Uncle Joe kept looking at his watch.

Today, in an effort to delay the spread of the Omicron variant of Covid, Uncle Joe banned travel to the United States from eight countries in southern Africa. When the angry, orange man did the same thing to several countries in the Middle East, Uncle Joe called it a "Muslim ban" (Religion had nothing to do with it.), and he called Trump a xenophobe. Get a napkin, Joe, and start wiping that hypocritical egg off your face.

One more thing. Candidate Biden had great plans for addressing the opioid crisis (Deaths are up about 54% in the past year.). Here's a line copied directly from his campaign website. He said that he would, "... stem the flow of illicit drugs, like fentanyl and heroin, into the United States – especially from China and Mexico." Again, that's a quote. Apparently, the only pipeline that Uncle Joe approves of is the drug pipeline that he daily enables at the border with Mexico. They make the fentanyl in China, ship it to Mexico – literally by the thousands of tons – and then, while Americans die in record numbers from overdoses, Uncle Joe does that thing about closing his eyes and turning his back. Those people "mattered" during the campaign. Now, not so much. Thus far this year, for the first time, over 100,000 Americans have died of overdoses. That's more than all deaths due to car accidents and homicides combined.

CNN reporter Anderson Cooper asked Uncle Joe if he had any plans to visit the Southern border. Again, you can Google this, and hear it for yourself. Uncle Joe said the following: "I've been there before and I haven't – I mean, I know it well. I guess I should go down. But the whole point of it is I haven't had a whole hell of a lot of time to get down." He hasn't had time?! Really?! In a year, he hasn't had time to go to the border? He's had plenty of time to go home to Delaware every weekend. And he says that after one trip to the border, he knows it well. The record shows that in 2008, Biden once (once!) flew into El Paso, Texas, then rode in a motorcade to a campaign rally. El Paso is nine miles from the Mexican border. So there you have it – he's been to the border and knows it well. Probably even better than Kamala!

I am so disappointed. This should have gone so much better, but it is a national disaster, and a national disgrace. Let's Go Brandon!

....

*Man will never be free until the last politician
is strangled with the entrails of the last priest.*
Diderot

If voting changed anything, they'd make it illegal.
Emma Goldman

....

2018

I hit the jackpot on ducks this year. My original flock had dwindled down over the years to just six ducks, but five were drakes, which is not a good thing among ducks. Drakes are about the most violent of suitors on Mother Nature's dance card. When I got down to five drakes and only one hen, she was baldheaded and half drowned from all the attention she was receiving. There is no #MeToo movement in the world of ducks!

For some time, I had been checking with local suppliers in the Farm Market Bulletin, but they didn't have any ducklings available. It occurred to me to check online. You can buy anything online, from a car to a wife, so why not ducks? The first outfit that I found was in Pennsylvania. Their website said they ship the ducks the same day that they hatch. They just put them in the mail. That seemed incredible to me, so I called our local post office. "Yep, we get 'em all the time," I was told. Apparently, ducklings can go the first two or three days without eating or drinking. Long story short, I ordered eighteen ducklings (six Pekins, six Khaki Campbells, and six Muscovies).

Pekins are the solid white ducks with yellow-orange bills that you see in every public park with a pond. Khaki Campbells are about the same size as a Mallard (I don't want Mallards, because every Fall, when the weather changes, they fly off to Louisiana!), but they are dusky brown. Muscovies are every color under the rainbow, sometimes all in just one duck. They get big, red, warty growths called caruncles between their eyes and the tops of their beaks, and I think that they are beautiful. They're big, kinda the aircraft carrier of the duck fleet. Muscovy ducks cannot quack, but, like geese, can graze on grass. But this outfit in Pennsylvania didn't have any Cayuga ducks (a French duck that is generally black, but iridescent, and can go anywhere from green to purple, depending on the sunlight). But I found an outfit in California that sold them, so I bought ten of them. This outfit sold their ducklings by sex, so I ordered seven hens, and three drakes. That oughta make somebody happy!

About the time that the Cayugas arrived, I got a call from my local supplier. He said that some of his hens had been holding out on him. He found three nests in a pasture (I don't know how the foxes, and coyotes, and fire ants missed them!), and he said he had Pekins, Khakis, and Muscovies. I didn't dare turn him down, so I travelled an hour north, and returned with a mixture of fourteen more ducklings. Three times a day I feed them a gallon jug of dry dogfood. They go through a fifty-pound bag every six days ($18 a bag, about $1,100 a year). When Carol Jeanne realized this, she questioned me about it (In addition to the ducks, I also daily feed one horse [not mine], one rabbit [wild], two dogs, two cats, and whatever deer, squirrels, chipmunks, birds, raccoons, opossums, armadillos, and whatever else cares to show up at my corn/sun-flower seed/salt feeders.). She asked, "Isn't that a lot of money to spend on feeding ducks?" My reply was also a question, "What else am I going to spend my money on?"

I need no more "Things." Not golf clubs, tennis racquets, fancy cars, guns, clothes, or tools. As it happens, I have begun divesting myself of some of this. The only thing that I need more of is time. I'm pretty sure that you can't acquire it; it is not a commodity. The best that you can do is to make the most of what time you do have. And by the way, the only "thing" you really own in this world, the only "thing" guaranteed to you, is the last breath you took. The next one is a roll of the dice, and a gift, a loan from your Creator. Fortunately, one thing I don't need much of is more money.

We give a lot of money away... always have. We give to our children and grandchildren. We give to our church. We give to Cousin Chris and Amber's ministry to college athletes. We give to The Athens Neighborhood Health Center, Mercy Health Center, and Athens Urban Ministries. Carol Jeanne donates to United Way (I abstain on that one.), to both the University Of Georgia and Furman University, to Goodwill, The Potter's House, and occasionally The Samaritan's Purse. My greatest charitable delight – without equal – comes from our support of the Thornwell Home For Children in Clinton, South Carolina. So now I spend more than twice as much money feeding critters than I do on Scotch. I don't think that's a bad thing, but if I keep it up, about the age of 95, I might have to start drawing down at least one of those Roth IRAs!

. . . .

Don't mistake endurance for hospitality.
Anonymous

. . . .

2019

As I begin writing this year's missive, Christmas is a little more than two weeks away. Yesterday, while Carol Jeanne was off visiting our children and grandchildren, I began the annual emptying of my closet of Christmas gifts. I do most of my Christmas shopping in January, when the deals are really good (not like the prices for amateur shoppers on Black Friday or Cyber Monday). The true deals are in January. Since I am buying on the cheap, I buy LOTS of stuff, mostly for my sons-in-law. I've been told that I'm not very good at shopping for my daughters, and I haven't given Carol Jeanne anything other than cash in forty years (I never gave her a real gift that she didn't return.). Consequently, my closet resembles a Sam's Club warehouse for the next twelve months. I usually forget half the stuff I've bought, but since most of it's for my three sons-in-law, I buy most everything in threes, unless I see a great price later in the year on something that I forgot that I've already purchased, in which case I'm storing six of that item for the year! So, about this time of year I rent a forklift and start unloading my closet, and the spillover inventory stored in my shop. By this time, I've collected a bunch of big boxes, which is not difficult to do, thanks to the steady stream of boxes delivered daily at this time of year to Carol Jeanne by FedEx, USPS, and UPS. Plus, our kids forward most of their Christmas gifts for their kids to our address for the big day. Anyway, I set up boxes for each daughter and son-in-law in my bedroom, and start stocking them with the contents of my closet. By this time, some of the gifts are as big of a surprise to me as they will be to the recipient. I don't gift wrap anything. Instead, I make my girls sit on the couch in the living room (The boys' shift comes next.), while I sit behind them. I tell this daughter or that, "Close your eyes," and I plop their gift in their lap. With the boys, since I'm buying in threes, it's usually "Ok, all the boys close your eyes." They're more likely to roll them than to close them, but they generally like what they see! Whether they do or not, it's my big day, and I get a huge kick out of it. The day after Christmas, when all the kids are gone, and the house is once again silent, my closet stands empty. It's a bittersweet moment. The expectation – the journey – is always more rewarding than the mere destination. It almost makes me sad... but then I remember, January is only a week away!!!

. . . .

A sermon should be like a woman's skirt. Short enough to attract your attention, but long enough to cover the essentials.
Winston Churchill

. . . .

Here are some things that I have never paid for: someone to haul my trash, someone to change the oil in my vehicles, someone to cut my hair, anyone to cut my grass or clean my gutters, someone to wash my vehicles (I am probably the last person you know who still waxes his vehicles [every three months]), someone to rotate my tires, paint anything. I have never paid interest on a monthly credit card bill.

Here are some ads that should be banned from television. The "Capillus" hair restoring laser hat. A foot stimulator (this one allows you to dance with your granddaughter). Anything that treats toenail fungus. The sinus flusher/vacuum. Tac glasses. Diapers for grown women. Pills for grown men that are not having a hard time of it. Hoses that shrink after use. Cleaning crystals for your windows. The patio awning that lowers the outdoor temperature by twenty degrees (It doesn't.). They start their ad by telling you that the awning costs less than $700 (that means $699), but if you order right away, you can get a special discount of $200, so that you only pay $600... I'm not kidding. Whoever developed that awning did not major in math. For over a decade, advertisers have been telling you that if silver returns to its all-time high, you stand to profit by over 200%. Isn't that telling you that the bottom has dropped out of the commodity market for silver? The silver you bought a decade ago is worth 25% of what you paid for it.

At Thanksgiving, as middle-daughter Rebecca was headed out the door for Dollywood, she texted me a photo of a "dollhouse" bookcase that her oldest daughter, Reese, was asking Santa to bring her. She said that it was the one thing that she had been asking for, and she wouldn't let it go. She said that Chris didn't have time to build it out of Reese's sight before Christmas, and asked if

I would do it. Who could resist a challenge like that, even if it didn't include Maureen O'Hara and Natalie Wood?

....

Denial empties everything of meaning. If our failures have no meaning, then there are no victories. When you fail, pick up the pieces, take them home, and see what you can make of what is left. This is God's gift of next time!

Anonymous

....

This year, the evening before my high school classmates and I gathered for our forty-fifth reunion, I gave a eulogy, my fifth. That seems to be a large number of eulogies for someone who is only sixty-three. This one was for my best friend in my adolescent years. I grew up across the street from Shannon Winslow Davidson. He was one of the most complicated persons that I have ever known – truly a walking contradiction. At any rate, I want to share that eulogy with you now. You may find him to be as interesting, and as complex, as I did. There's a good story or two along the way, and, I think, two valuable thoughts for all of us.

Shannon Winslow Davidson, Jr.
January 31, 1956 – July 23, 2019

The words that we speak here this evening will be of happy memories, friendship, adventure, kindness, and love. Win's life mattered. Win's life made a difference in our lives. That is what we are here to share with one another. But if the words we speak here tonight are to be truly meaningful, if these words are to have integrity, these words must also be honest.

In too many ways, Shannon Winslow Davidson was a tortured soul, a tragic figure. He could vex you beyond exasperation. I cannot begin to imagine the agony of his family – first, his parents, and later, especially his brother George Gray – as they watched Win make bad decision after bad decision, powerless to alter his course. Win thought that the best way to get past a temptation was to give in to it. When faced with the choice between two temptations, he always picked the one he hadn't tried yet. Throughout his life, Win wrestled with his demons, and we will not have joined him in exorcising them from his life story unless we acknowledge their existence here tonight.

360

Do any of you remember the standardized aptitude tests that we took in tenth grade? The tests were broken down into a half-dozen or so categories (things like language skills, math skills, spatial recognition – I didn't even know what spatial recognition meant, so I knew I wouldn't do well on that category). Your results were reported as a percentage of the test-taking population that you outscored. Win scored in the 99th percentile of every category. The genetic code that made him intellectually brilliant, in some ways made this world trivial and boring to him; he was often lazy and prone to taking shortcuts. And of course, another part of his genetic code predisposed him to addiction. Win was addicted to everything except good judgment. Like you, like me, Win was damaged goods. But he was not only that. He was more – much more – than that, as is witnessed by this gathering of his peers.

Win was a bon vivant, with an easy style. He had a golden tongue; I know that it is cliché to say it, but he could have sold ice to an Eskimo, or screen doors on a submarine. He was a gifted artist. He was a gentle person. He was a generous person. Win never met a dollar that he didn't like, but their friendship never lasted long. With Win, it was always easy come, easy go. But in the going, he did not care on whom the dollar was spent – himself, a friend, a stranger in need, or a stray dog that looked hungry – even if the dollar in question was his last, and the source of his next one was unknown.

We knew him as Win. In our latter years, I called him Winslow, because that was how he identified himself to me when he would call. "Coleman, this is Winslow," he would say in his slow drawl. Indeed, we were bound together as members of the Winslow Gang, and we were referred to as such by his parents, by our parents, and occasionally by the Charlotte-Mecklenburg police department.

If the truth be told, among a very close band of boys, Win was my best friend. It is a testament to his magnetic personality and charisma, that he would not have said that I was his best friend. Everyone was Win's best friend, especially whoever hap-

361

pened to be standing in front of him at any given moment.

In 1968, my parents built a home across the street from the Davidson's on Crestbrook Drive. It was the summer between our sixth and seventh grades, the transitional summer from elementary and junior high school. I can remember as clearly as I am standing here at this moment the first time I encountered Win – I did not "meet" him, I encountered him, much as one encounters a force of Nature. I was in the driveway of our neighbors to the other side of our house, the Levines, that first evening after sup-per. Win came pedaling up the street on some sort of bike that I had never seen. It had multiple gears, hand brakes, cables running everywhere, and it could be folded in half. Win rode up on this bike, and made some kind of snarky, challenging remark to me. As I am inclined to do, I replied in a way that might generally be classified as being somewhat of a smartass. As the saying goes, it was a perfect storm.

Win didn't threaten, he didn't hesitate. He simply stepped off that weird-ass bike, and began to deliver the first of many beatings that he would administer over the course of our adolescence. Win was much bigger than me then, and I don't know how far he would have gone in thrashing me that night, had it not been for Kobuk. Kobuk was my dog, a mixed breed of some sort, but about 90% German Shepard. About the time that Win jumped on top of me, Kobuk jumped on top of Win. Never again did Win lay a finger on me if Kobuk was within the sound of my voice. Welcome to Win's world!

In our adolescent years, the Davidson's house became the center of our universe – a sanctuary, really. Mama D took us in, tolerated us, counseled us, and fed us. Daddy D gave most of us our first cigarettes, assuming that you could smoke a Lucky Strike. Win's bedroom, in the basement of their home, next to their ga-rage, was our headquarters. In that room, we held countless bull sessions, most of them centered around the women in this room tonight. We hatched nefarious schemes, snuck out at night, and even made pipe bombs.

There are certain words with which I have an uneasy relationship. Damnation would be one of them. Another would be salvation. However, redemption is a word that I treasure. The thought of regaining something of value, the thought of being restored to wholeness over the course of our lives and in the fulness of time, holds great appeal for me. Redemption is a concept that has as its two bookends deliverance and liberation. Redemption envisions a new way of being. I know without doubt, through all of the complexities that constituted Shannon Winslow Davidson, that he was redeemed. That he IS redeemed.

Finally, I would like to say that over the course of the fifty-one years that Win and I were friends, I kept up with him about as closely as anyone did. I always called him on his birthday, and he would usually call me on mine. He would call me when he was feeling low, or in a crisis, or in need of money. I earnestly tried to be there for him, whenever and however he needed me.

That being said, I am aware of one of us who did vastly more for Win than I did, one who probably did more for him than all of the rest of us combined. I think it is entirely appropriate this evening to acknowledge the walk and witness of Steven Jaynes. Win himself often spoke to me of the many – but by no means all – acts of charity that Steven extended to him. It is not my place to go into the details, but it is my place – indeed it is **our** place – to note Steven's friendship, and his acts of brotherly love, for Win. If I could take only one thing with me from this gathering, it would be to aspire to the example that Steven has quietly followed, which is, of course, nothing less than following the path of Jesus, the path that Win ultimately claimed as his own.

So now, a toast to Win!

. . . .

If life were logical, it would be men who rode sidesaddle.
"Cowboy" Perk Carlson

. . . .

Carol Jeanne and I celebrated (or at least observed) our fortieth wedding anniversary this year. Some of you were present at our wedding. I distinctly remember walking down the aisle of the Milledge Avenue Baptist Church sanctuary, and having a panic attack. I wondered what in the world had I gotten myself into. What in the world had I gotten HER into?! Well, the simple answer is that you don't know, you haven't a clue. It's something you're going to have to figure out on the fly, as it were. In five or ten years, you will have probably begun to put some of the pieces of the puzzle together, but perhaps not. There are no guarantees regarding such matters. The only certainty ten years out is that you will not have amassed ALL of the answers, nor will you ever do so. No one does.

"Honey, wake up! I just remembered something
you did that annoyed the hell out of me!"

CartoonCollections.com

2019

_____

    I get up every morning at 5:15. I've never used an alarm clock for this. It is the optimum time for me to arise and get through all of my rituals and routines (I have a lot of them!) before 9:00 AM, when my "normal" day begins. I accomplish more by 9:00 than most people do in a day. At 6:15 I plug in the coffee pot (the old, percolator type), then the dogs, the cats, and I head out the door to feed two carrots to the horse that lives across the street (Babes is thirty-five years old, and all of my three children and seven grandchildren have grown up feeding him.). Then we snag the newspaper, and head back to the house (except for Mondays, when our embarrassing excuse for a newspaper does not publish a paper, and for Tuesdays, when they do not publish a paper paper, only an electronic paper that you have to read online, which is awful). Anyway, one of my favorite things about walking down to get the paper during the Fall is seeing Orion The Hunter reappear in the Southern sky. He's been around the whole time, of course, but it's been too light to see him (Think Wendell Berry and "day-blind stars."). I love watching him move across the morning sky. You lose sight of him for a couple of weeks when we rescind the lunacy of daylight savings time, and it's suddenly again too light to see him in the morning. But since we lose about three minutes of light each day this time of the year, eventually he comes back around. Orion is a constellation, of course, but not a zodiacal constellation. His belt, made up of three stars, is one of the sky's most recognizable asterisms (along with the Big Dipper). Orion has the bright, blue star Rigel for his left foot, and the red giant Betelgeuse for his right shoulder. As he traverses the sky, he is followed by his two faithful hunting dogs, Canis Major and Canis Minor. Canis Major includes the star Sirius, the brightest object in our sky outside of our solar system. By this time of the year, at 6:15 AM, he has slipped over the horizon in the western sky, and has bid us good-bye on our morning stroll. He'll return in the middle of next August, and I hope to be here to greet him!

. . . .

Success is getting what you wanted.
Happiness is wanting what you got.
Dale Carnegie

To spend your time complaining about what
you don't have is to waste what you do have.
...
You may pass contentment in your search for success.
Anonymous

A man is rich in proportion to the
things with which he can do without.
Henry David Thoreau

. . . .

2019

I lost track of my buzzard this past year. He didn't fly off, since his injured wing would never allow him to fly again. But he was great at hopping, and could find his way to the roof of a house if we wanted to. If he built up a head of steam, he could glide for a good distance. About the only thing that would have posed a threat to him was a coyote, but I don't think one of them got ahold of him. My guess is that late last Winter or early this Spring, he hopped off looking for love. I hope he found it!!!

I made up for the loss of my buzzard by acquiring foster-parent status over some of Nature's other little ones. One morning last Spring, I heard some squeaking in the woods on the edge of my yard. I walked over to investigate, and saw a ball of down flopping around. It took me a while to catch it, and a while longer to figure out that it was a baby woodpecker, more specifically, a Northern Flicker. I could tell that he had fallen from his nest (or, more likely, was pushed out of it by a sibling competing for food).

I assumed the nest was somewhere in the giant oak tree whose base he was huddled about. I wasn't sure just where the nest was (It would have been a hollow somewhere up the tree.), but I was sure that I would never be able to return him to it. So I found a Tupperware dish, drilled some holes in the side (and a few in the bottom for drainage), ran some wire through the holes, filled the dish with leaves, wired it into a dogwood tree next to the oak, and tucked him into it. Before I made it back to the house, his mother was in the Tupperware with him, and fed him right along with the others, until they all finally fledged. As he grew, he got to where he could hop out of the Tupperware, so occasionally I would have to scoop him up before the cats could find him, and return him to his dish!

Lost and Found!

First flight!

My next discovery was in the woods between my house and the pond. I was heading down to feed my ducks, and I thought that I had stumbled across a newly hatched duckling in the leaves. I was wrong. It was a new hatchling, but it wasn't a duck. It was a baby owl, also probably pushed out of its nest by a sibling competing for food! This time I could clearly see where the nest was, a large hollow about sixty feet up in giant beech tree. Since there was no way that I would ever get that bird back where it had come from, I carried it up to the house while I studied on the matter. While I was doing that, I offered the little fellow some raw chicken liver (I buy a pint of chicken livers every week at Walmart, then cook them on the stove to feed my cats, who love them.). Turns out that this owl loved them too!! He could eat his bodyweight in chicken liver in about five minutes. I gave some thought to raising him that way, but I knew it was going to be a lot of work. Then I thought about the woodpecker and the Tupperware, and had an epiphany. I went to my shop, took some scrap lumber, and built a large "box." I left the front of it open, with just a little base on it to keep him hemmed in. I drilled some holes in the top, and ran some wire through them. I took an extension ladder and that box, and found a nice oak tree that faced directly at the beech tree where the owls' nest was. I toted the box up the tree, and wired it into place. Returning to the ground, I picked up the baby owl, and started back up the ladder, glancing back over my shoulder to make sure that the mother wasn't about to swoop down and tear my eyes out!! The baby was pitching a fit, and the mother was watching every move I made. I dropped the baby in the box, scurried back to the ground, and looked up to see the mother glide silently from the beech to the box. The parents raised that owl right there in that box. On the day that it fledged, I was fortunate enough to see his first flight, as he settled on a limb in the tree next to his box. I took it as Nature's way of saying "Thank you!"

I'm little, but check out my talons! And pass me more liver!!

Suspicious Mom!

Growing Boy!

Heading off on my own... thanks for your help!

Finally, I used to fill up my bucket of duck feed each night before going to bed (The duck feed is actually Ol' Roy dry dogfood kibbles from Walmart. It floats, and the ducks can go through a full bucket in less than two minutes.). But then something started getting into the feed. One night, just before bedtime, the dogs went ballistic. I flipped on the carport light, and found my culprit. Rather than engage him in an endless land war in Southeast Asia, I decided to just add him to the shopping list. Now he has his own bowl, and each night he wanders into the carport for a big handful of kibbles, and the leftover pear core from my lunch.

Turns out that I'm not the only critter whisperer in the family. This summer, granddaughter Sadie discovered the wonderful world of toads!!

Sadie Ray Davis and her newest friend (She has lots of them!!).

. . . .

There is no right way to do a wrong thing.

Harold S. Kushner

. . . .

I had another interesting encounter with owls this Spring. After my first experience as an owl foster parent, I moved the owl nest box that I had built to a tree behind my barn. Bingo, they nested in it the very next season. One evening, I'm walking by the barn, and here's what I saw:

This little fellow had tried to fledge too soon. Momma owl was peering down at her chick, and at me. I picked the owlet up, set him in a white pine tree, and went about my business. First thing next morning, I checked on him, and he was still there. I figured putting him back in the nest box would be the best thing to do. I put my ladder up, retrieved the chick, and headed for the ladder. Mom came along as well, keeping a close eye on me. I didn't make it as far as the second step on the ladder before she dusted me off of it. I gathered myself and the chick, and gave Mom a stern lecture. Back up the ladder I went, backwards this time, keeping my gaze on her. When I got within reach of the nest box, I turned to lob the chick in it, and in the split-second that I had my back turned, she nailed me!

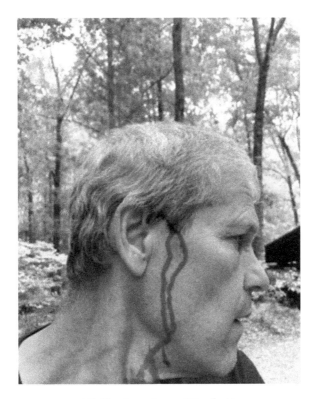

Talk about gratitude!!

. . . .

We are each of us angels with only one wing,
and we can only fly by embracing one another.
Luciano deCrescenzo

. . . .

2018

I want to say that I've missed my parents this year, in some ways for the first time. That is not to say that I didn't mourn their passing at the time, or in the intervening years. But mourning and missing are two different things. At the time of a loved one's passing, you learn about – and are overwhelmed by – the industry of death. Immediately, there are arrangements to be coordinated with a funeral home and a church, and there is an obituary to write. Then there are death certificates to be processed and acquired (Get at least one dozen "originals" of the death certificate, because you're gonna need them.), insurance policies to process, final bills to be paid (something that doesn't happen in thirty days), lawyers and accountants to consult, bank accounts and credit cards to be closed out, utilities to be turned off, tax returns to be filed, personal property to be distributed among family members, estate inventories to filed with the state (and a fee to be paid on the value of the inventory... leeches!), Social Security to be notified, property to be sold...the list is seemingly endless. All of it occupies so much of your time, and all the while the rest of life rolls right along. It can become overwhelming, so much so that it occupies all of the time and energy you have available regarding the departed. There isn't a lot of time or energy left to actually think about them, or time to spend simply remembering.

My father died in 2013, and my mother passed away in 2017. And while I was sad to lose them, there were also aspects of their deaths that were blessings for them, and the realization of that truth buffers the sorrow. There is sorrow, and there is a sense of loss, but you simply have to delay dealing with much of it because of everything else that you have no choice about dealing with. But in the past year, I have found myself meaning to pick up the phone to call them, before you realize that that will never happen again. Perhaps there is some news story of the day that you would have discussed with them in times past, but then you realize that times are, indeed, passed. Something comes up in the way of family news, and you realize that there will be great-grandchildren that they will never know, at least not in this life. And all of it has finally, I suppose, begun to settle in with me, and it makes me miss them. I would love to have just one more Thanksgiving meal with them, one more Christmas morning, or just a Saturday evening.

In the past year, I have thought a number of times about my mother's last year of life, most of which was spent in an assisted living facility. Two memories burn bright for me, two dishes that I prepared for her, and carried to her from Georgia. One was a cheesecake that I made from a recipe that she had given me, and which I have become fairly adept in preparing. She was delighted to receive it, and to stow it away in the little refrigerator in her room. The other dish was her recipe for Manhattan clam chowder. She sat up in her hospital bed, and wolfed that soup down in sheer ecstasy! She was truly thrilled with these treats, and I will always cherish her joy in receiving them. Being a gourmet cook herself, I think that she was proud to see one of her offspring inherit some of her recipes.

And I have thought about my father, as well. The memory of his last year or so that comes most frequently to me is from one of my final visits to Charlotte and their home on Crestbrook Drive. Most of the daylight hours of my trips home at this point in life were spent doing chores around the house, things that they could no longer do for themselves. It was impossible to get everything that needed doing done, but you did what you could. On this particular trip, there was some minor thing that needed to be repaired – I honestly cannot recall what it was. What I do recall is that the repair in question necessitated a trip to Home Depot (My sister Amy works for Lowe's, and Lowe's is my preferred destination back home, but there is no Lowe's close to my parents' home, and Home Depot is two miles from the house.).

As I was preparing to leave, Chris announced that he was going with me. It was cold and rainy outside, so this meant getting him bundled up appropriately, and that took a little while. I didn't mind that, and we had a good visit in the ten minutes required to travel to the store. Once we arrived at the store, I had to get him out of the car, and help him navigate his stroller through the puddles in the parking lot. I didn't mind that either. Once inside, I set off to accomplish my mission in the shopping tradition of men: know what you need, know where to find it, get it, check out, leave. I excel at that.

Christopher Kennedy Hood had something else in mind. Once inside the store, he abandoned his stroller for one of the handicapped scooters that one may employ in big-box stores. He knew exactly where to find it, and he knew how to operate it. It crossed my mind that this was not his first rodeo. He seemed content with this arrangement, so I left him on his own, while I set about to get whatever it was that I was there to get. This took about two minutes, and then I started looking up and down the aisles to find Chris.

I can't recall exactly when we had to take the car keys away from Chris, but as a physician, he knew why it was necessary to do so (He had advanced Parkinson's disease.), and he didn't fight it too much. It wasn't this way when Chris had had to take the keys away from his own mother. As a widow, she saw driving as her last link of independence to the outside world, and she fought it tooth-and-nail. After Chris took her keys from her, she did clandestine driving using back-up keys that she had stashed away when she saw the handwriting on the wall. She racked up a number of fender benders. Eventually, Chris wised up, and took not just her keys, but her car from her. He took his mother's car back to Crestbrook, and drove it for many years after his mother's death, until his time came to give it up and let Ruth do the driving for both of them.

The point of this is that Chris might have lost his driving privileges on Charlotte's public streets, but in a Home Depot handicapped scooter, he was untouchable! He would cruise down every aisle – slowly – savoring the freedom, although I did not understand at the time what was taking place. If he passed whatever he was looking for, rather than just backing up a few feet, he would motor all the way to the end of the aisle, travel the full length of the next one, then drive back down the aisle he had just been on, stopping maybe five feet from his original point of departure. This did begin to bother me. "Daddy, why don't you just back up?" I would ask him. He claimed that, in reverse, the scooter made a beeping noise to warn everyone that it was backing up, and that the noise hurt his ears. It was true that the scooter beeped in reverse, but his objection was an abject lie, because he was stone deaf.

But I could see that it was pointless to argue. The Porter side of our family can erupt like a volcano, and two minutes later have no recollection of anything having happened. The Hood side says nothing, but they file transgressions against them away in the Book Of Life, and you better by God know that there will eventually be a Judgment Day. Chris liked to say, "The wheels of justice grind slowly, but exceedingly fine." It was with this grim resolve that he lowered his head, blocked out the rest of the world, and motored on. In oblivion. Slowly.

Despairing that I would ever escape the Home Depot, I begged him to tell me what he was looking for. "I need some #8 wood screws," he said. What in the world could he possibly need with #8 wood screws?! There was no point in asking him, so I simply reached over his head, grabbed a little bag of a half-dozen #8 wood screws, and thrust them in his hand. "Here are your screws, and now we're leaving! I have to get back to the house." I pretty impatiently, and probably roughly, got him out of the store, into the car, and back home.

I told you in last year's *Newsletter* about how, after Ruth died, we emptied out the house, and I discovered all of the many things that my father had hoarded like a bag lady: shoe horns, rulers, stationery... there was no rhyme or reason to it. In the kitchen, in a drawer that most every family has – a drawer where you keep a screwdriver, a tape measure, a flashlight and some extra batteries, those types of things – Chris had a drawer full of little bags of #8 wood screws! That's when I realized what our trip was truly about for him, and that I wasn't the first person to have endured his brief sabbatical from the prison that his home in some ways had become. The remembrance of my impatience that day shames me. When I think of my father now, when I think back on that day, I would give a month off my own life to have a do-over on that trip to Home Depot.

. . . .

Adversity introduces a man to himself.
Albert Einstein

. . . .

2022
———————

If the year 2022 was a fish, I'd have thrown it back. In the span of twelve months, I had both of my knees replaced, and I had both of my rotator cuffs reconstructed (complete ruptures of all four muscles/tendons in both shoulders). I had enough MRIs and X-rays to make me glow in the dark! Getting an artificial knee is painful, but not as painful as NOT getting one (or two). Getting a rotator cuff reconstructed is doubly painful, but again, not as painful as the pre-surgical joint. Move a torn rotator cuff the wrong way, and the pain will – literally – drop you to your knees. I went through some pain in 2022. I ground my teeth to the gums, sucking air through my clenched teeth, trying to cope with the pain, both before and after surgery. Then there's the rehab. About three months for a knee, about six months for a rotator cuff. After that, you're on your own, and it's up to you as to how full a recovery – and how long a rehab – you want to go through. It's up to you as to how hard you work. I still rehab all four parts three times a day, five days a week. Replacing a knee is analogous to rebuilding a car's transmission (For the record, the time required for my second knee replacement, from the time I limped in the door to the time I hobbled out, was two hours and thirty minutes!). Rebuilding a rotator cuff is like building a Rolls Royce, from the ground up.

Then there was the prostate cancer. Have I mentioned the prostate cancer? My PSA had been rising gradually over the years. My primary care doctor left his practice, and I was assigned a new one. He looked at my PSA, and said it was time to have a urologist look into it (He did a lot more than just "look" into it!). He gave me the finger – not the middle one – and told me that the upper left quadrant of my prostate was "hard and irregular." What he meant was that I had prostate cancer, and he damn sure knew it. But he went by the book. He sent me for an MRI of my prostate, which further highlighted irregularities. From the outset, he said that he intended to do a biopsy, but he wanted the MRI to use as a road map for the parts of the prostate that he wanted to get tissue samples from.

Women know the agony of childbirth, but since they do not have prostates, they will never know the agony of having one biopsied. I know something about pain (See the paragraph above.). Nothing compares to the experience of a prostate biopsy (And I have had kidney stones, the male version of giving birth.). No anesthesia, no sedation. Forget the humiliation – just get me down off the ceiling! The doctor told me, "I know this is easy for me to say, but you've got to relax. You're fighting me on this." Well you're damned right I was! Like the *USS Enterprise*, this guy was trying to boldly go where no man has gone before. After the urologist had left the room so that I could "get cleaned up," I sat up, exhausted, on the exam table. I was surprised to find that there was a nurse standing behind me. I looked her straight in the eye, and told her, quite seriously, that there was no way that I was ever going to prison! She laughed out loud!

So I received a definite diagnosis of cancer. I had my prostate removed (a prostatectomy for those of you are keeping score), but that was just medicine's first little joke on me. One thing led to another, and they began to peel me like the proverbial onion. First, I had to travel to Gainesville, Georgia, to undergo a prostate-specific PET scan. You can't get one at the local 7-11 (The bill for this one was $17,000.). They loaded me up with a syringe the size of a can of Coke, only this can was filled with radioactive dye. The technician carried it into the room in a lead box. This scan would show the oncologist where to target my thirty-eight rounds of radiation. The prostate MRI had the added bonus of revealing that my iliac arteries – basically the arteries in my thighs – were abnormally large. That didn't particularly concern me, as most everything in that area of my anatomy is abnormally large! But off to a vascular surgeon I was sent for further evaluation. This guy is someone Carol Jeanne and her family grew up with. I remember him when he was the diameter of a broomstick. He was very thorough, very professional, very reassuring. He ordered a CT scan. After reviewing the scan, he didn't really think that the iliac issue was anything to be overly concerned about, and said we would just revisit the matter in six months to make sure that nothing had changed. *BUT*, he said – and in the words of Tony Kornheiser, "There's always a 'but'" – the CT scan had revealed something that did concern him. It seems that I had a lesion on my pancreas. To say the least, he had my full attention. Forget knee replacements. Forget rotator cuff reconstructions. Hell, forget prostate cancer. We were in the big leagues now! Long story short (sort of), the primary care physician referred me to the urologist who referred me to the vascular surgeon who referred me to a gastroenterologist. He determined that he was going to do an endoscopic ultrasound of my pancreas. So yet another round of propofol sedation (I can see why Michael Jackson was so fond of that stuff. My brother Ren says that it's known as Milk Of Amnesia.). Thankfully, the gastroenterologist does not think that it is cancer, and he, too, has put me on a six-month follow up.

I'll be honest with you, the year 2022 was a daily struggle with pain and disability. Looking at my calendar (I still use the old-fashioned, paper kind.), there were two (TWO!) weeks in 2022 that I did not have a doctor's appointment. I spent a lot of time in doctors' waiting rooms. Bad as my situation was, I did not see a single other patient that I wished I could trade places with. There are some truly pitiful, pathetic souls out there. Their infirmities have forced them into inactivity and disability. They are overweight, old, stooped, and crippled. Not me – except for falling apart, I was in great shape. I was fortunate to give my surgeons excellent material to work with, and we have made the most of it. My goal is that when I turn sixty-seven this April, I physically will be where I was in 2021. I qualified for Medicare in 2022. It is something I worked for all my life. I earned it, but it was certainly wonderful to have it. I needed an unimaginable amount of exceedingly complicated medical care, and I received it. Every one of the physicians who laid a hand on me was at the top of their field, renowned throughout the state. So through it all, I have been grateful. I am sooooooo grateful.

....

Gratitude unlocks the fullness of life. It turns what we have into enough, and more. It can turn a meal into a feast, a house into a home, a stranger into a friend. Gratitude makes sense of our past, brings peace for today, and creates a vision for tomorrow.
Melody Beattie

....

I'll be brief (for once). Gender identity has become a huge issue in American society, a much bigger issue than it is in, say Haiti or Sudan or Iraq. As I understand it (although I don't, and never will), a man who wants to be a woman is a trans-female. I think that I have that right, but again, I don't understand it, and spend absolutely no time contemplating it. I am sixty-seven years old, and in my entire life, from childhood to senility, I have never once known a man who wanted to lop off his business, and grow boobs. Don't get me wrong, I empathize with these confused people. I myself am a lesbian, trapped in a man's body.

The epicenter of this dilemma seems to be sports. Men who think they are females want to compete against women in athletics. To date, I am unaware of any women who think that they are men who are attempting to play in the NFL or NBA. The top-rated professional female track runner in the mile couldn't beat the top 400 male runners in high school track. A swimmer who now calls himself/herself Lia was about the worst male swimmer in the entire NCAA. But swimming against women, he/she/it sets women's record times in every swim meet they enter. He/she/it is twice the size of the girls in the competition. I won't bother to go into body mass, wing-spread, testosterone, blah, blah, blah. The women (the ones born that way) aren't happy, but they're incompetent in redressing the injustice. I could solve this in one day. Go to the next NCAA swimming event. "Swimmers take your mark, set, GO!" Let Lia leap into the water to win. Let every other competitor refuse to compete. Step off the starting blocks, and go back to the locker room (before Lia joins them in the showers). Let every true-born female athlete in every sport refuse to compete in any event that a man/trans-female is allowed to enter. That would be the end of it. Period. I'm sorry that it took a man to point this out.

*Try to annihilate your opponent. Even if you're playing
your grandmother, try to beat her fifty to nothing.
If she already has three, try to beat her fifty to three.*

Bobby Riggs

(who lost to Billie Jean King in the Battle of the Sexes)

2003

This year I attended my first NASCAR race. My older brother
has attended many of these events. I have never understood his
interest. He lives either five minutes – or five hours – from Spaghetti Junction in Atlanta, depending on when you try to drive it
(If you drive it about ten minutes before it's time to be in church,
it's only a five-minute drive.). I am here to tell you that you
couldn't find no better racin' than what goes on at Spaghetti Junction when I-285 East bound, transferring to I-85 North, necks
down from a half-dozen lanes to one in about 100 yards (Never
accuse those DOT engineers of not having a sense of humor!). You
have frigid soccer moms in Volvo station wagons that pit at Buford
Highway just so they get the "rot tars" (NASCAR translation: "right
tires") for traction to cut you off at the exit ramp.

The race was awful. It was loud, smelly, and gave me a massive headache. Give me Spaghetti Junction any day. One of the
most popular things to do before the race starts is to talk about
how each driver is "gonna set the car up for the race." This is a
topic of infinite complexity to NASCAR fans, even more exquisitely convoluted than divining the starting five for an NBA basketball game (Ok, I want my five tallest black guys at center court,

now!!). I would've thought preparation for a stock-car race would have consisted of topping off the gas tank and hitting the men's room. Not so, and no single subject looms larger than tars (tires). I would have thought you'd want round ones, maybe radials, avoid re-caps, and be sure to check the air pressure. When you start picking your tires based on relative humidity and the adiabatic lapse rate at race time, your average redneck's math skills are not as up to snuff as his/her lower lip.

What made the NASCAR experience priceless was the opportunity to spend five hours in close proximity to a Real American Family. There is absolutely no possibility of Osama or Saddam ever terrorizing, much less annihilating, a Real American Family. For one thing, they speak in a language that would make the Indian Code Talkers in World War II jealous. The first hour or two, I just thought their kids were overly inquisitive. They kept asking "Did he" this? and "Did he" that? "Did he get me a hot dog?" It finally dawned on me that "Did he" was "Diddy" which many Americans grew up pronouncing as "Daddy." "Diddy (Daddy) get me a hot dog." It weren't an interrogatory, but a salutation they was 'a heftin!

Real American Families are acquainted with modest, responsible consumption of alcohol... or at least the kids are. They would wait until the parents set down a near-empty Bud before palming it under their Dale Earnhardt racing hat and chuggin' it behind their program. I heard one kid, who I swear couldn't have been ten years old, say "Damn, why can't they ever buy a Lite?" If you were below the age of twelve, you had to make some pretense at hiding your beer drinking, but if you were above the age of six, smoking seemed to be mandatory. Mothers would snatch cigarettes from their children's mouths just long enough to light their own and then hand them back to the kid.

The parents were knee-walking, three-sheets-to-the-wind, I-love-you-man drunk before they ever entered the stadium. They had to be. They had just walked a minimum of five miles across asphalt that would make the Arizona dessert seem like a wade in the crick (NASCAR translation: "Creek: a refreshingly cool and flowing body of water"), and they had done it completely barefoot!! Out of eleven family members, they did not own a single shoe between them, not so much as a flip-flop. As a matter of fact, only two of them owned shirts. Thankfully, the two shirts belonged to the two women, one of whom had biceps bigger than an NFL lineman, and the other of whom was so skinny that if she hadn't been wearing a shirt, you wouldn't have wanted to look. As near as I could figure, there were two brothers, their wives, six kids, and another man of no apparent relationship, but whose presence seemed to have a certain calming effect on all the other Clampetts.

The bleachers at Bristol are made of concrete. In a piercing summer sky, this helps make everything really bright, and the glare is a nice accent to the heat-wave mirages simmering off the asphalt – both the track in front of you and the five square miles of parking lot behind you. At any rate, since Bristol is a "short track," a five-hundred mile race takes 10,000 laps. The two "ladies" in front of me were big fans of a particular driver named Jeff Gordon. On each and every one of those 10,000 laps, as Jeff's car came into view, they would hug and jump and give each other high-fives while chanting, "Jeff Gordon, Jeff Gordon, Jeff Gorrrrrrrrrdon!!" They reminded me of rock star groupies, and I'm sure they would have been willing to toss their bras in the vicinity of his pit stop – if they had happened to be wearing any!

On about the 9,000th lap, the skinny woman's husband, who was as big as the fat woman (The fat woman's husband was the diameter of a broomstick, go figure, and for some reason I couldn't banish the image of either couple's coupling from my mind... it wasn't prurient interest, just engineering curiosity.)... anyway, the skinny woman's husband is standing there cheering and smoking (He was missing a tooth on the lower front, such that he could wedge a Marlboro into the gap and yell, "Youdaman, Rusty!!" without missing a beat or a puff.). The fat man liked a driver named Rusty, while his skinny wife was a fan of Jeff Gordon, Jeff

Gordon, Jeff Gorrrrrrrrrrdon. This seemed to create a certain tension in their relationship. The skinny woman dealt with this schism didactically, instructing her husband on Jeff Gordon's many fine points: his model of race car, his career wins, his large number of Cup points. The fat man responded scatologically, "Shut up, bitch."

Then all of a sudden, this very large man, in a state of extreme perspiration and intoxication, did a belly flop into the bleachers. I mean face first, two rows down, like a sack of rocks. In his descent, he inexplicably avoided contact with any of the other fans that only moments before had been packed around him as tightly as the sardines he had been consuming between beers and Marlboros for the last three hours. How he missed hitting any of them I'll never know, although the brief but violent episode of projectile vomiting that preceded his descent may have assisted in clearing a path. This man fell like a redwood. He fell without reservation, without restraint, without deflection. This man's skull made a hollow, thudding sound upon impact that made me weak in the stomach, a sound that brought into question whether an ambulance or a hearse would be summoned. I fully expected a flurry of cell phone calls to 911, but no one moved, including the fat man. Finally, when a small pool of blood collected beneath his chin, one of the kids nudged him in the side with a tar-stained toe. Nothing. Then the kid climbed down two rows to get to eye level with his Diddy. He tilted his head to one side, which immediately revealed two things. First, his fall had failed to extinguish the current Marlboro, tucked neatly into the tooth gap, and which was now smoldering angrily in the beard stubble just below his left cheek. Second, it was now apparent that in the future, should he choose to do so, he could accommodate two Marlboros simultaneously, the second to be placed in the bleeding stump of his upper-right, front tooth. I think it was the blood, rather than the smell of burnt flesh or vomit, that prompted the kid to climb back up and begin tugging at the hem of the skinny woman's blue jean shorts while pointing at the prone figure and mumbling, "Diddy, Diddy."

She didn't acknowledge this attention at first, but his tugging became more insistent, eventually revealing the fact that the skinny woman was wearing a red thong, which was pretty much more truth than I could handle. She was just about to turn and see what the kid's problem was, when the fat lady began to cry, "Jeff Gordon, Jeff Gordon..." so the fat man remained unnoticed for another half lap.

But finally, this Real American Family did note their fallen brother. It was then that I witnessed the most moving act of familial intimacy one could ever hope to see. As they clustered around the unconscious patriarch of their clan, the skinny woman took her pocketbook and emptied it across the sweaty, hairy back of her husband. She searched through its contents until she found a large, black Sharpie of indelible ink. She then drew Swastikas on her husband's biceps, inscribing the words "White Power" under each. Then, across the back of his shoulders, in bold type, "If you don't like it, file your complaint here," and she then drew a bold arrow pointing southward on his backside. "That'll teach him to cheer against Jeff Gordon!" she cackled. Her husband might awake the next day in the Bristol County Jail, but by golly, come shower time, he wasn't gonna be lonely!!!

. . . .

Carnation milk is best of all,
No tits to pull, no shit to haul,
No bucket to wash, no hay to pitch,
Just poke a hole in the son-of-a-bitch.

Unsuccessful submission in a contest for a Carnation Evaporated Milk advertising slogan [possibly apocryphal]

. . . .

Before we part company, let me share this observation with you. Late one afternoon this past summer, I was hurrying down to the lake to feed my ducks. I was hurrying because there was a huge thunderstorm heading our way. The wind was already picking up, the sky was a greenish purple, and the temperature was dropping fast. I had glanced at the radar on my phone, and I thought that if I moved fast enough, I'd beat that storm. I was wrong. Standing there flinging feed as fast as I could, the bottom fell out. The ducks seemed not to mind, but my dog Raleigh lit out for the safety of the golf cart (man's best friend!). In the split-second that it took for a bolt of lightning to make me realize that I needed to take off as well, I saw a yellow flutter of butterflies trying to make their way in from the lake to the shelter of the tree line. They were bobbing and weaving in flight, the way butterflies do, but it appeared for all the world as if they were trying to dodge the huge drops of rain that were deluging all of us.

In times to come, when you are being buffeted by the vagaries of life, and the tide seems too often to run against your course, *when sorrows like sea billows roll*, if you find yourself wondering how you will make your way through the storm, think of this:

Butterflies don't own umbrellas.
Coleman Hood

So now the time has come for us to part. For those of you who have travelled together through these many stories and years, I hope that you have enjoyed the journey half as much as I have.

With love,

Coleman

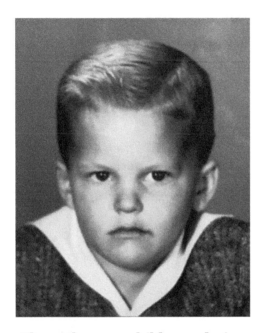

The author as a child, wondering
what he will be when he grows up.

Coleman Hood was born on Fort Jackson Army Base in Columbia, South Carolina in 1956. He was reared in Charlotte, North Carolina. He was relieved of his attendance requirements at some of the finer institutions of higher learning in the Southeast (Furman University, Wake Forest University, the University of North Carolina, and the University of Georgia). At the University of Georgia, he earned a B.S. degree in Forest Resources and a M.S. degree in Biological Engineering. In addition to being a forester and an engineer, at various times he has been a state-certified Emergency Medical Technician, a commercial driver, a private pilot, and a real estate broker. He and his wife have three daughters, three sons-in-law, and eight grandchildren. He is the perpetual steward of stray pets and a wildlife menagerie. He resides in Bishop, Georgia.

The author as an adult, wondering what he will be when he grows up.

Printed in the USA
CPSIA information can be obtained
at www.ICGtesting.com
CBHW051055241223
2911CB00011B/944